THE DEVELOPMENT OF THE SONNET

'A very useful book indeed, and one which will add to the scope of current debates about the sonnet.'

John Drakakis, University of Stirling

In this indispensable introductory study of the Renaissance sonnet, Michael R. G. Spiller takes the reader on an illuminating guided tour. He begins with the invention of the sonnet in thirteenth-century Italy and traces its progress through to the time of Milton, showing how the form has developed and acquired the capacity to express lyrically 'the nature of the desiring self'. In doing so Spiller provides a concise critical account of the major British sonnet writers in relation to the sonnet's history.

This volume is tailor-made for students' needs and will be an essential purchase for anyone studying this enduring poetic form. Poets covered include:

Petrarch
Wyatt
Sidney
Shakespeare
Spenser
Dante
Milton

Michael R. G. Spiller is Senior Lecturer in English and Cultural History at the University of Aberdeen.

THE DEVELOPMENT OF THE SONNET

An Introduction

Michael R. G. Spiller

London and New York

First published 1992
by Routledge
2 Park Square, Milton Park, Abingdon, Oxon, OX14 4RN

Simultaneously published in the USA and Canada
by Routledge
270 Madison Ave, New York NY 10016

Transferred to Digital Printing 2006

Typeset in 10/12 pt Baskerville by Florencetype Limited, Kewstoke, Avon

British Library Cataloguing in Publication Data
A catalogue record for this book is available from the British Library.

Library of Congress Cataloging in Publication Data
Spiller, Michael R. G.
The development of the sonnet : an introduction / Michael R. G. Spiller.
p. cm.
Includes bibliographical references and index.
1. English poetry – Early modern, 1500–1700 – History and criticism.
2. Sonnets, English – History and criticism. 3. Sonnets, English–
Italian influences. 4. Sonnet. I. Title.
PR539.S7S65 1993
821′.04209–dc20 92-4868

ISBN 0-415-07744-3
0-415-08741-4 pbk

Publisher's Note
The publisher has gone to great lengths to ensure the quality
of this reprint but points out that some imperfections
in the original may be apparent

to Pamela
'il soave mio fido conforto'

CONTENTS

PREFACE

The greatest sonneteer of them all, Francis Petrarch, looking back many years after the death of his beloved Laura upon what he had written with so much art and so much longing, said that

> quant'io di lei parlai né scrissi . . .
> fu breve stilla d'infiniti abissi. . . .

[Whatever I wrote of her was a small drop out of infinite depths. . . .]

He meant to praise her, not his own sonnets; but spoke perhaps better than he knew, for the sonnet is at once small, and clearly formed, and capable of holding desires from the most tremendous depths. If it were not so, it would not have been used consistently and continuously by the poets of Europe from its invention in southern Italy about 1235, a hundred years before Petrarch saw his Laura, to the present day.

My own task has been to look at the sonnet in Renaissance Britain and, by concentrating upon those sonnet-writers who seem to have done most to extend its powers, show how the self and its desires were imaged. As for what came before, considerations of length and practical use to students of the form have urged me to make choices: Petrarch, of course, is massively and justly there, but as the history of the sonnet does not often take much notice of the century before him I have discussed the sonneteers of the thirteenth century at some length, with lots of examples, all translated, both because that is when the parameters of the sonnet were formed and because the Italian material is widely scattered and difficult to get at for those with little or no knowledge of the language. I have passed over many later sonneteers of great merit, such as the Italian women poets, Lorenzo dei Medici, Michelangelo and others, who are good but of less relevance to the British sonnet; and the excellent work of Walter Monch, Sidney Lee, Janet Scott, Gary Waller and others has made it possible for me to deal lightly with the French sonnet, knowing that sources and themes are accessible to the student elsewhere.

Sonnets are all alike in form; but they can be, and were, used to talk about anything at all, and in critical discussion I have used concepts and ideas freely, as they seemed to have explanatory force. If there is a critical bias, it is against the view of the sonnet as a piece of lyrical autobiography – if that view any longer needs opposing.

Sonnets not in English are taken from available critical editions or anthologies that libraries in Britain are likely to have, and are usually in modern spelling; British sonnets are reproduced either from the original texts or in the original form from a critical edition, with the accepted alterations of *i* to *j* and *u* to *v*. All translations are my own unless assigned to someone else. For the help I have received from friends, colleagues and above all from my family, I am sincerely grateful; and my students over the years have, I hope, at least taught me what it is I ought to teach them in such a book as this.

MS

1

THE SONNET AND ITS SPACE

And if no peece of Chronicle wee prove,
We'll build in sonnets pretty roomes;
As well a well wrought urne becomes
The greatest ashes, as half-acre tombes. . . .
(John Donne, 'The Canonization')

The sonnet is Donne's original 'well wrought urne' – compact, shapely, highly finished, and able to contain, in concentrated form, almost all that is human. Donne wrote when the sonneteering vogue was at its height in England, in the years 1580–1610, and was perfectly familiar with the sonnet, singly or in groups, as the commemorator of love, when every Jack could promise his Jill that

though that *Laura* better limned bee,
Suffice, thou shalt be lov'd as well as shee.

Petrarch's achievement of a sequence of 317 sonnets and forty-nine other poems in praise of his love for one woman, his Laura, though it was imperfectly understood, was the glass of fashion and the mould of form for European sonneteers from the Renaissance to the nineteenth century. But love is not the only occupation of the sonnet, nor was it for Petrarch himself; its astonishing success and persistence has to be explained by recourse to rather wider terms.

The sonnet was invented about the year AD 1230, in southern Italy; and by the end of the thirteenth century[1] about a thousand sonnets had been written, almost all in Italian (that is, in one of the dialects of it), exploring most of the varieties of its form and most of the possibilities of its subject matter. Francis Petrarch (1304–74), writing in the middle of the century following, inherited an already very sophisticated poetic instrument. The sonnet came into the vernacular of Spain in the mid-fifteenth century, into the vernaculars of Britain and France in the early sixteenth, and into German in the early seventeenth.[2] With the exception of the Augustan poets in Britain, there have been few major poets who have not attempted sonnets; and even today, when verse is freer, formally speaking, than ever before, most contemporary poets – even such apparently wild men as e.e. cummings – have at least one or two sonnets among their lyrics. The existence of hundreds of thousands of sonnets in all the vernaculars of western Europe proves that, for 750 years at least, the sonnet has been challenging and satisfying the poetic imagination.

The sonnet is probably the longest-lived of all poetic forms, and certainly the longest-lived of all *prescribed forms*. A prescribed form, or *closed form* as it is sometimes called, is one whose duration and shape are determined before the poet begins to write: the limerick, for example, or the triolet, or the sonnet. Identity is formal, not thematic, as it is in tragedy or ode. If we suggest that an art work occurs when imaginative energy is successfully contained in a discursive structure, then in general the poet can accept varying degrees of constraint. He or she may write in free verse, whose bounds are determined only by his or her own will acting from moment to moment. Then a poet may choose a verse form such as blank verse, the heroic couplet, or *terza rima*, which compels certain kinds of recurrence – of rhyme, of rhythm – but says nothing as to whether the poem should be of ten lines or ten thousand. Next, there is strophic verse, sometimes called stanzaic verse, which defines not only rhythm and rhyme but also, in a limited way, duration – Spenser, for example, having started *The Faerie Queene* in nine-lined stanzas, must thereafter compose in units of nine lines, though he may have as many of them as he wishes. Finally, there is the prescribed form: here the duration as well as the structure of the whole poem is predetermined, as in the limerick, which must have five lines, and the sonnet, which must finish after fourteen. The poet may choose to write another one, of course, as often as he or she likes, but the poem itself ends at a point not controlled by the author's will.

If this had been felt as a frustration, poets would not have gone on writing sonnets: Alistair Fowler, in his magisterial study, *Kinds of Literature* (1982), suggests that this kind of formal or generic pre-empting of the author's decision is actually helpful:

> far from inhibiting the author, genres are a positive support. They offer room, as one might say, for him to write in – a habitation of mediated definiteness, a proportioned mental space; a literary matrix by which to order his experience during composition.[3]

The sonnet pre-emptively solves two problems: proportion and extension; and, while this is a challenge, it is also a security, a kind of metrical extension of feudalism, a definite service required and requited.

The 'proportioned mental space' which the sonneteers so consistently chose to inhabit emerges, right at the start, as the familiar fourteen-line sonnet, with eleven syllables (or ten, depending on the vernacular) to a line, dividing into eight and six, and using in the *octave* two rhymes arranged either ABAB ABAB or ABBA ABBA; and two or three rhymes rhyming CDCDCD or CDECDE or almost any possible arrangement of these, in the *sestet*. The tendency was, among the Italian poets, to have a very definite sense pause (marked, in modern editions, by a full stop, semi-colon or comma) in the octave, between lines four and five, giving thus two *quatrains* in the octave; and less clearly in the sestet, to have a sense pause between lines eleven and twelve, giving two *tercets*. Occasionally, the sestet divides four and two, a quatrain and a *distich*, but when this happens there is never any support from the rhyme: a sense couplet, in Italian sonneteering, is never marked by a rhyming couplet at the end.

Until the rhyming couplet to conclude the sonnet was reinvented by Sir Thomas Wyatt about 1525,[4] and then adopted by most British sonneteers, the pattern just described above created the space of the European sonnet for three centuries. Alternative sonnet forms did appear in profusion in the thirteenth century alongside the *sonettus consuetus* or 'normal sonnet', but none of these variants – additional lines, shorter lines inserted (indicated with a lower case letter when they occur, thus: AaBAaB), reduction of eleven syllables to seven, the three-line 'tail' of the *sonetto caudato* or 'tailed sonnet' – superseded the standard fourteen-line pattern; and only one, the tailed sonnet, achieved anything like independent status among Italian comic sonneteers. The fourteen-line sonnet is the norm, and departures from it are brief and not in any continuing sense satisfactory.

But, though this book cannot for reasons of space deal with sonnet variants, it is worthwhile here answering the question, when is a sonnet not a sonnet? May one have a sonnet of sixteen lines, or twelve? or a sonnet without rhymes? or a sonnet in trimeters, instead of the standard ten- or eleven-syllable line? When Guittone d'Arezzo, in the mid-thirteenth century, presents his readers with a twenty-two-line poem rhyming AaBAaB AaBAaB CcDdC DdCcD, why should we call it a sonnet at all?

The short answer is that there is by custom a basic or simple sonnet, of which the others are variations: it has proportion, being in eight and six, and extension, being in ten- or eleven-syllable lines, and duration, having fourteen of them. Any poem which infringes one of these parameters will remind us of a sonnet quite closely; a poem which infringes two will be more difficult to accommodate, but we will probably try to establish some procedure to account for the deformation; and a poem which infringes all three will not be recognisable as a sonnet at all, and we will regard it as something else unless there is contextual pressure – if, for example, we found it in the middle of a group of normal sonnets. So a poem which contained twenty-one lines might establish itself as a sonnet if we noticed that it was blocked out – by sense or rhyme or both – in twelve and nine, inferring the rule: eight plus half of eight/six plus half of six. And the rhymescheme of Guittone's poem above shows clearly a normal sonnet extended by shorter lines, leaving its basic structure intact. If, then, the poem is structurally a variant of the basic sonnet, we can rest happy in calling it a sonnet, too.

But once the 'pretty room' has been built, how does one live in it? Are there constraints upon the sorts of thing one can think, or say, or be in it? As we look at the practice of the early sonneteers in the chapters that follow, it seems clear that both proportion and extension affect the kind of discursive life that can be lived. The sonnet extends to fourteen lines, providing 140–54 syllables in all. This seems to be rather more, in most modern European vernaculars, than one requires for the simple expression of a feeling or state of mind, but rather less than one would like for a full discussion of that feeling or state of mind. It is certainly too short for narration: a sonnet can present a narrated event, but it must be highly compressed if anything at all is to be said about it. The proportionality of the sonnet, eight parts to six, works against any kind of simple repetition of an initial point or emotion, since the second part is structurally different from the first, and almost compels some kind of development or analysis. The voice that speaks in this room, the /I/ of the sonnet, almost has to 'make a point', to go beyond merely declaring a feeling.

Historically, the proportionality of the sonnet, which will be discussed in more detail in Chapter 2, seems to have been influenced, in the thirteenth century in Italy, by the proportions of the poetic form closest to it, the *canso* or *canzone* of the Provençal poets: this was a poem of variable length made up of a number of stanzas, each of which was divided into two (usually unequal) parts. Originally, this break seems to have been a musical requirement: a melodic unit was given out, repeated once, and then made way for a new melodic phrase. The verbal recognition of this musical alteration is first of all syntactic: a new sentence at the change, or perhaps a medial pause in a long sentence. But this in turn begets a conceptual alteration, turning proportionality of lengths into consequentiality of thought. Six is to eight as conclusion is to proposition, or as development and summing up is to statement. (This much is speculation, since none of the writers who used the sonnet in the thirteenth century left a record of their thoughts on its structure.)

To illustrate this link between proportion and thought, which is basic and crucial to the sonnet's success and distinctive voice, we may take the slightly easier example of that other prescribed form, the limerick, which consists of two similar lines, two shorter lines, and a single return to the first-line pattern:

There was a young man of Bengal,
Who went to a fancy-dress ball;
He thought he would risk it,
And go as a biscuit,
But a dog ate him up in the hall.

The pattern of statement (1–2), development (3–4) and conclusion (5) is clear. Early writers of limericks often emphasised the return of the first pattern by combining conclusion with repetition, as Edward Lear does:

There was a young lady of Bute,
Who played on a silver-gilt flute;
She played several jigs
To her uncle's white pigs,
That amusing young lady of Bute.

Later writers, however, found it much more satisfactory to treat the last line as the completion of the narrative, adding an extra item of information but sacrificing the echo, or reprise, of the opening line; and the reader of limericks now expects the returning rhythm of the last line to bring with it, like the fifth act of a play, a solution of previous incompleteness, by peripety, anagnorisis or catastrophe:

A superintelligent flea
Was having its tea on my knee:
My bloodpressure sank,
As it drank and it drank –
Then I squeezed it all back into me!

So rhythmic, metrical and conceptual patterns unite. If we think, anachronistically of course, of the sonnet as an expanded limerick, in which the octave takes the first two lines, the first part of the sestet the next two, and the last part (three lines or two, depending on the particular sestet used) the last line of the limerick, we can sense the kind of developmental pressure which the structure of fourteen lines in eight and six exerts. The extra length of the sonnet gives the writer more choice where to begin the ending than has the limerick writer: poets using the Italian form (4 + 4 + 3 + 3) show no particular preference among the last three lines for a point at which to begin to end; and, though those of a witty cast of mind will often put a clinch or *sententia* in the last line, the sense that the last tercet should be a complete unit remains strong. When the final couplet became popular in English sonnet-writing, the alternative 4 + 4 + 4 + 2 grouping emerges, to drive British poets into a rhyming couplet ending, with strong pressure towards epigram or witticism.

The sonnet, because of its brevity, always gives an impression of immediacy, as if it proceeded directly and confessionally or conversationally from the speaker, and therefore from the creator of that speaker. Since it has for so long appeared to offer a stage or arena on which the /I/ of the writer speaks to his or her audience, it is important to insist that the modes of presentation of the sonnet are not simple. With the decay of 'naïve realism' in recent literary study and teaching (that is, the assumption that a poem or a literary work is simply the words of the author in his or her own person), modern criticism has become very concerned with the *fictionality* of works of art, with understanding the ways in which the text creates in its space a self, an /I/, who interposes between writer, or speaker, and reader. It is Aristotle, in the *Poetics*, who begins the investigation of this kind of modality of presentation, when he distinguishes between dramatic works, in which the voices are persons different from the author, and narrative works, in which the speaker offers us some kind of /I/ as the source of the words ('Arms and the man *I* sing . . .'). The *Poetics* has nothing to say about the lyric voice, but the Aristotelian modal tradition has been powerfully influential among modern readers of poetry in stimulating an interest in mimesis, in the creation of fictional selves to represent our own. A recent critic of Shakespeare's sonnets, for example, instead of accepting with Wordsworth that 'with this key/Shakespeare unlocked his heart', argues that the speaker of the *Sonnets* is a victim of the rhetorical devices Shakespeare has used to create him, very much as might be said of any character in the plays.[5] Similarly, without discounting the possibility that Petrarch's sonnets contain autobiographical details (many of them are specifically dated), we would now be inclined to regard as lost labour the enormous ingenuity of the glosses in many Renaissance editions of Petrarch's poems, which laboured to detect the exact spot in the Avignon countryside where the lovers met, or where Laura waded in a stream. 'The autobiographer always writes . . . a fiction, about a third person.'[6]

The sonnet's lyric voice is a dramatic construct: authors refract their /I/ in different ways. The sonneteer may have his or her speaker narrate, to tell in effect a short story about a character distanced from /I-who-speaks/ at least as far as /I-that-was/ (a gap peculiarly important to and for Petrarch, who was obsessed with his own past); he or she may dramatise, by inventing dialogue or creating the illusion of a hearer or interlocutor, as Sir Philip Sidney loved to do; he or she may indeed make the /I/ speak of itself in an unlocated present – the archetypal lyric position – but this last is only one of the possibilities open, and is thus a constructed choice, like any other stance the poesis creates.

It is simply a matter of record that the sonnet, from the very beginning of its long career in the early thirteenth century, has offered its readers a variety of fictional positions. It has been used to mimic not just 'the sound of the sighs that nourished my heart', as Petrarch said, but every other kind of fictional persona as well. Though its shortness makes it uncongenial for objective narration, it was once used (in a sequence) for an adaptation of the French *Roman de la Rose*, called *Il Fiore*, written in Italian sonnets in the late thirteenth century, and sometimes attributed to Dante; semi-narrative sequences, such as Sir Philip Sidney's *Astrophel and Stella* (1592), and descriptive sequences, such as Folgore di San Gemignano's catalogue of the months,[7] are common; devotional and moralising sequences, in which the /I/ represents some sort of public voice giving guidance to the community, are frequent. At the level of the single sonnet, the lyric/narrative/dramatic mix is very varied, from dramatic slanging matches in the street by Cecco Angiolieri, a marvellously inventive Sienese of the late thirteenth century, through political speeches by Milton to the introspective analyses of Keats, Hopkins or Shakespeare, which have tended to stand as the quintessence of sonnet-writing. But even within Shakespeare's sonnets, a collection much less anecdotal and circumstantial than many, one notices how the voice shifts: in narrative stance,

> Alas, 'tis true I have gone here and there . . . (110)

in a dramatic situation,

> So, now I have confessed that he is thine . . . (134)

as well as in 'pure lyric':

> When I consider everything that grows . . . (15)

But what seems a very modern concern with the way in which voice comes to us in poetry, and with the kinds of persona that are constructed by texts, is really a reworking, or perhaps a recovery, of the dominant late-medieval and Renaissance habit of looking at texts as rhetorical performances; we in the twentieth century are looking from the reader's side at what these earlier poets would have approached from the writer's or speaker's side, namely, what sort of a person the text creates by its rhetorical signs.

Classical rhetoric, as taught through the schools of the centuries before the invention of the sonnet, was adept at assigning different kinds of text to different social occasions and different social levels, so that the /I/ created in, for example, an ode would be defined by the function of praising a social superior at a high level of learning. What seems to have happened, however, is that the Italian vernacular in the thirteenth century developed very fast in its creation of forms, leaning heavily upon the practice of Provençal poets, and made quite sophisticated use of the sonnet, the *canzone* and the *ballata* (a short poem with a refrain) before it occurred to any theoretician that texts composed in the vernacular were literature at all – indeed, the very word 'literature' meant 'that which was written', and thus that which was in Latin, as distinguished from that which was spoken, and thus in the vernacular. The first writer to notice the sonnet theoretically is Dante, and by the time he wrote his treatise *De vulgari eloquentia* (a title that must have sounded paradoxical at the time – 'Pop Eloquence' is perhaps the nearest we can get to it) the sonnet had been up and running for seventy years, from 1235 to about 1305.[8]

Dante's spirited defence of the Italian vernacular – or, more accurately, of the dialect of Italian which he himself spoke, the Tuscan form – in that treatise was an attempt to show that what could be done in Latin could be done in the vernacular: in the course of arguing that vernacular poetry could be as serious as Latin, he produced the first theoretical comment on the sonnet – briefly, because he intended a fuller analysis in a later part of the work which he did not complete:

> Those who have composed vernacular poetry have issued their poems in many different forms, some in *canzoni*, some in *ballate*, some in sonnets, and others in irregular and inadmissible forms. . . . *Canzoni* by themselves do all that they have to do, unlike *ballate*, which need dancers to keep time and accentuate their form; and therefore *canzoni* should be reckoned nobler than *ballate*, and hence their form should be reckoned noblest of all, since no one can doubt that the *ballata* is of higher quality than the sonnet. Whatever features of [poetic] art are found in other forms are included in the *canzone*, but not the other way around.[9]

He then describes the *canzone* as 'the only form appropriate to the highest vernacular', and promises to deal with the *ballata* and the sonnet 'in the fourth book of this work, where I deal with the middle vernacular'.

The *canzone* is superior because of completeness and comprehensiveness. Since the sonnet did demonstrably deal in Dante's time with those subjects which he thought appropriate to the highest verse – 'prowess in arms, the flames of love, and the guiding of the will' (as we might say, heroism, love and virtue) – its downgrading, which Dante assumes to be everyone's opinion, must be due to its brevity. This would prevent its employing the most elaborate kinds of rhetoric, the figures of speech that marked the highest style in classical poetics, such as epic similes, extended personifications and conceits. The sonnet can deal with high subjects, but can only do so in a simpler and therefore lower style. The writer of the sonnet cannot elevate his /I/ to epic, elegiac or tragic proportions, since these require, according to the rules of classical eloquence, rhetorical elaborations that are simply too extended for fourteen lines. Dante's brief remarks remind us that the sonnet appeared at the beginning of the fourteenth century to be a straightforward form, in which the /I/, or any other subject, appeared at a level below that of the highest art. (The quotation from Donne with which this chapter begins is clearly acknowledging the same assumption.)

To say that the sonnet is a kind of workhorse in the Renaissance lyric stable is not to devalue its role as the poem of love – even noble ladies, after all, customarily rode smaller and lighter horses. There were not wanting those who claimed that a great sonnet could reach the sublimity of the highest style,[10] but the physical limitations of its size, which have the peculiar property of constituting its identity, always made grandeur something extraneous to it, that it might reach on occasion despite its nature. It was only after the Renaissance that an aesthetic theory developed in which sublimity could be a quality of condensation, rather than expansion, of material.

However, it is interesting that a special 'resistive' theory of art did develop around the sonnet, as we can see from a number of self-reflexive sonnets written at various times from the fourteenth century to the present day. High Renaissance poetry tends to work within an expansive theory of art: that is, the poet typically asks to be given sufficient words, support, sustenance, inspiration to enlarge his efforts to enable him to stay the course of his poem. The resistive theory which appears when sonneteers talk of their form supposes on the contrary that the poet is subdued or caught, and must work or struggle against confines; or, to change the metaphor, must learn delicacy, as if handling small and fragile things. Such, again, is the theory implicit in the quotation from Donne already referred to: Pieraccio Tedaldi, writing a sonnet to instruct people how to write sonnets, warns that every line must 'dir bene a proposta il suo dovere'[11] – say what it has to say exactly to the point; Francesco Bracciolini, writing at the end of the sixteenth century, uses the figure of disadvantage turned to advantage:

> Come più ferve in chiusa parte il foco
>   dove le sue rovine ardon più strette,
> calor di Febo in circoscritto loco
>   fulmina più da sette carme e sette. . . .

[As the fire burns hotter in an enclosed space, from which its violence blazes more directly, so the heat of Phoebus (*i.e. poetic inspiration*) in a restricted place flashes out more from seven plus seven lines. . . .]

The Romantic writer Gabriele d'Annunzio most splendidly compares the sonneteer, Yeats-like, to a goldsmith:

> Otto e sei verghe d'oro, o Musa, io batto
>   su l'incude con fervido martello,
>   e ognuna di lor piego ed anello
> e pongo su 'l cuscino di scarlatto.

Poi, con più grave pazienza, in atto
d'un maestro orafo antico su un gioiello
regale, ognuna a punta di cesello
(m'è Benvenuto nel pensiero!) io tratto. . . .

[Eight and six rods of gold, O Muse, I beat out on the anvil with a busy hammer, and each of them I bend into a ring, and place on a scarlet cushion. Then, with the greatest patience, like a master goldsmith of olden time working upon a royal jewel (Cellini comes to my mind!) I work each one with the chisel's point. . . .]

This 'forma avara' ('unsparing form') that leaves no space for error, this well-wrought urn that is, in Iain Crichton-Smith's words,

a vase in bloom
gathering light about it clearly clearly
. . . its bare constant self, its paradigm
of straining forces harmonised sincerely,[12]

has always seemed both immensely challenging and immensely adaptable. No other lyric form has so consistently offered to accommodate the normal speaking voice, and at the same time so successfully challenged it to come to the point. 'Apollo himself', said an Italian critic, inaccurately but suggestively, 'invented this short poem as a touchstone for great genius.'[13]

2

SICILIANS AND CITIZENS: THE EARLY SONNET

Qualunque vuol saper far un sonetto
e non fusse di ciò bene avvisato,
s' e' vuol esser di questo ammaestrato,
apra gli orecchi e lo intelletto!
(Pieraccio Tedaldi, *c.*1330)

[Whoever wants to learn to write a sonnet,
and hasn't had the method given correct,
if he would like some sound instruction on it,
must open up his ears and intellect!]

It might fairly be said that the notion of 'coming to the point' dominates the sonnet throughout its seven centuries in Europe. Since its foreclosure is the essence of its being – or, rather, foreclosures, since the sonnet closes at eight lines and again at six, that last line being at once the close of a sestet and of an entire poem – any writer, no matter whether a modernist, a Romantic or a thirteenth-century rhetorician, must 'come to the point' if he or she is to create a sonnet at all. Interesting things happen when writers, such as Petrarch or Milton, try to devise ways of resisting closure while formally retaining it; but the sonnet is always, inescapably, a 'pointed' form, even before it becomes explicitly associated with the epigram.

Pieraccio Tedaldi, who so amiably offered to instruct novices in sonnet-writing,[1] remarks later on in the quoted sonnet that 'Undici silbe ciascun vuole punto' – 'each line should have eleven syllables'. The term 'punto' ('point') meant, as it did for Shakespeare, a full stop or a major punctuation mark; but by metonymy it comes to mean, as here, the unit of writing or thought at the end of which a stop is inserted. So, for Tedaldi, the place where a unit of thought would be marked should occur every eleven syllables, confirming the line, rather than the couplet or the quatrain, as the basic unit of the sonnet. Before Tedaldi wrote in the early fourteenth century, we find in the major manuscripts of the late thirteenth in northern Italy, which have preserved for us the first sonnets of all,[2] a layout that emphasises graphically how for writers and readers the sonnet 'made its points': sonnets are often written by the scribes with the octave in four lines, two sonnet lines per manuscript line, but with a stop, or 'punto', after each sonnet line; then the sestet is written in two lines and one, two lines and one, again with a stop after each sonnet line. The scribes also mark each couplet or tercet with a capital or a symbol such as C (='cominciamento', 'beginning'), so that the sonnet is laid out thus:

C xxxxxxxxxx . xxxxxxxxxxxxx .
C xxxxxxxxxx . xxxxxxxxxxxxx .
C xxxxxxxxxx . xxxxxxxxxxxxx .
C xxxxxxxxxx . xxxxxxxxxxxxx .
C xxxxxxxxxx . xxxxxxxxxxxxx .
xxxxxxxxxx .
C xxxxxxxxxx . xxxxxxxxxxxxx .
xxxxxxxxxx .

This is, in a conceptual as well as a graphic sense, the shape of the sonnet at least until Petrarch begins to modify it: even he, however subtle his internal structures, thinks of the sonnet as an accumulation of points, as does Shakespeare. The sense of the sonnet as a collection of briefly made 'points', with closures throughout its fourteen lines, from eleven syllable units upwards to the whole utterance of 140–54 syllables, links the sonnet to the proverb or maxim and also to the catalogue, and thus to an /I/ with wisdom and the authority to give counsel.

A very early sonnet, written by Re Enzo (Enzo, King of Sardinia, 1224–72), shows how this sense works into the pattern shown above:

Tempo vene chi sale e chi discende
tempo è da parlare e da taciere
tempo è d'ascoltare e da imprendere
tempo è da minaccie non temere;
tempo è d'ubbidir chi ti riprende
tempo è di molte cose provedere;
tempo è di vegghiare chi t'offende,
tempo d'infignere di non vedere.
Però lo tegno saggio e canoscente
che fa i fati con ragione,
e col tempo si sa comportare,
e mettesi in piacere de la gente,
che non si trovi nessuna cagione
che lo su' fatto possa biasimare.

[There comes a time for rising, and for falling,
a time to speak, and a time to keep silence,

a time to listen, and a time to act,
a time not to fear threats;
a time to obey those who check you,
a time to anticipate many things,
a time to rise against an injury,
a time to seem not to notice it.
  Still, I reckon him wise and experienced
who acts with reasonableness,
who knows how to comply with the time,
to make himself agreeable to people,
so that no cause can be found
to reprove his actions.]

A bland reflection, but with an extra irony for Enzo, who languished for twenty years in prison. The echo of *Ecclesiastes* 3 gives this poetic voice biblical wisdom and universal applicability; nevertheless this remains a fairly primitive composition, for the octave is just an assembly of single lines, though the sestet manages a more complicated syntax which unifies its six-line block, and the thought begins to develop. The pattern is there, but had not been taken full advantage of – this was something which the early sonneteers had to learn to do.

The shape and size of the sonnet, and the beginnings of the ways in which the voice might move and proclaim its identity within those limits, were established by a small group of poets working and writing at the court of the Hohenstaufen Emperor Frederick II of Sicily, who reigned from 1208 to 1250 over the southern half of Italy. Thirty-five sonnets, out of about 125 poems which survive from this period, are regarded by scholars as constituting the first European sonnets;[3] and, of these thirty-five, twenty-five are usually attributed to one man, a notary and legal deputy of the Emperor named Giacomo da Lentino. He is a mere shadow: three legal documents, one bearing his autograph, and a number of circumstantial remarks in 'his' poems attest to his existence, and it is conjectured that he was born about 1210 and died some time after 1240. When literary works are attributed to emperors and princes, one has suspicions; but the attributions to da Lentino cannot come from flattery or the magnetism of the great, and there is no reason to deny this thin shade the credit of writing the first sonnets in the world. Which among *his* sonnets were or was his first, cannot be even suggested from the traces; there are no signs of experiment, for all his sonnets have fourteen lines, and all are in the eleven-syllable line that became in Italian verse what the ten-syllable iambic line is in English.[4]

The sonnets divide into an octave and a sestet, the octave rhyming in all cases ABAB ABAB, and the sestet varying: CDE CDE (15), CDCDCD (9) and CCD CCD (actually AAB AAB) (l). All the sonnets except one deal with the theme of Love, and all are spoken by an /I/ who occasionally identifies himself as coming from the town of Lentino (now Lentini), which was and is in Sicily, twenty miles north of Syracuse. This all seems very familiar; but it is also startling, in that da Lentino appears to have invented the sonnet perfectly immediately: only one of his sonnets, 'Lo viso, e son diviso da lo viso' ('I see the face, and yet I am parted from it'), seems in any way primitive, in having the sestet repeat the rhymes of the octave, ABAB ABAB AAB AAB – a trick which blurs the fundamental difference between octave and sestet.[5]

Da Lentino has left us no critical comments, not even a sonnet about the sonnet: in trying to see the space of the sonnet as he saw it, we are forced back on the poems themselves and the ambience of Frederick's court.

The first sonnets in Italian, and thus the first in the world, emerged from an environment strikingly similar to that of the first sonnets in English, those written by Sir Thomas Wyatt (1503?–1542) and the Earl of Surrey (1517?–1547) at the court of Henry VIII. The Holy Roman Emperor Frederick II, who ruled from 1208 to 1250 over the Kingdom of the Two Sicilies, that is, the southern half of Italy and the island of Sicily itself, was an absolute ruler, but an enlightened and (for those days) tolerant one, who inherited from his forebears, the Norman kings of Sicily, a culturally very diverse realm, stretching from Naples in the north to Calabria in the south; the philosophy and literature of the Arabs, of the Sicilian and Byzantine Greeks, of classical and neo-Latin Italy, and of southern France and Spain, all flowed into Frederick's realm, and even faraway Scotland contributed Frederick's personal soothsayer, the reputed wizard Michael Scot. Due allowance made for flattery, the Emperor is said to have spoken Italian (that is, a dialect of it, since there was no single Italian language at this time), German, French (with the same qualification), Latin and Arabic, and to have been able to write Greek. Like Henry VIII, he was a patron of scholars, translators, poets and musicians, an activity which always tends to sharpen the interest of courtiers in the arts. It is perhaps anachronistic to think of Frederick as maintaining a court in the later Renaissance sense, but as he moved about among his various cities and castles, principally on the mainland, he required the centralised control of the *imperium* to be administered by a highly loyal staff of professional legal administrators, the executive arm of his own inner council or chancellery. It was to this secular corps that the inventor of the sonnet belonged.

Power and command of language go together; and central to the command that such administration required was the notion and practice of *eloquentia*, the 'speaking out' of the self in texts that were designed to persuade, control, stabilise power and enhance authority. Whether trained in Naples or further north in one of the university centres outside Frederick's dominions, such as Bologna, da Lentino and his fellows learnt *eloquentia*, that elaborated speech and writing distinctive of the educated man, by help of the *artes eloquentiae*, the textbooks of rhetoric which, with elevated vocabulary, complex syntax, figures of speech and whole anthologies of *fiori di rettorica* (striking maxims or epigrammatic turns from approved authors), assisted the budding official to signal to the world his membership of a class above the common herd – a function still served, though without the same reverence paid, by civil-service jargon today.

Such training and the writing that it produced were of course in Latin, and members of Frederick's court wrote poetry in Latin, as did educated men all over Europe. To write in the vernacular might seem to contradict the very purpose of *eloquentia*, and to write in the vernacular while simultaneously inventing a new form, the sonnet, seems to accomplish a great deal very fast. However, an extensive courtly poetry already existed, known to da Lentino and his circle, that was not in Latin: that is, the poetry of the troubadours, the courtly poets of southern France, who flourished from about AD 1100 to about 1300, and wrote in Provençal.[6] In the atmosphere of the noble households of southern France, rhetorical skill and a high degree of artifice were marks of the courtly persona; and the troubadours, who were either themselves of noble rank or were clients of nobility, developed numerous difficult verse forms, often containing language of a high degree of allusiveness and conceit – though, as befitted a vernacular art, with no great display of scholarly learning. They composed poems and music of sensual love between high-born and nobly disposed lovers, often but not always unrequited, often but not always from the male viewpoint, and often with the woman placed in the higher social position. (Worth noting here in passing is that they also sang of political and moral matters, themes which the poets of the Emperor Frederick avoided.)[7]

Provençal poets validated the practice of *eloquentia* in a language that was not Latin; they knew nothing of the sonnet (the word *sonet* exists in Provençal, but means simply 'a poem'), but they did establish and pass over to da Lentino and his circle a closely related poem, the *canso* or *canzone*, already mentioned in connection with Dante.[8] This was a long poem, but it was made up of a number of identical stanzas, and the practice of constructing these seems to bear on the sonnet. The stanzas might have from seven to nineteen lines, but because they were designed to be sung in Provençal they developed a musical structure as follows. The stanza fell into two not necessarily equal parts, called *fronte* and *sirma*, each with its own musical phrase. Each of these might again break into two, but then the second half repeated the first: the *fronte* had two *pedes* (*pes* means 'a foot') and the *sirma* had two *versus*. The major break between *fronte* and *sirma* was called the *diesis* or *volta* ('turn') in Italian.

The possible patterns, which would in Provençal be musically articulated, were thus:

Ia + Ib : II	–	pes + pes + sirma
I : IIa + IIb	–	fronte + versus + versus
Ia + Ib : IIa + IIb	–	pes + pes + versus + versus

and the simplest, not much used,

I : II	–	fronte + sirma

The fourteen-line sonnet, as da Lentino invented it, breaks the same way:

Ia + Ib : II	–	4 lines + 4 + 6
I : IIa + IIb	–	8 lines + 3 + 3
Ia + Ib : IIa + IIb	–	4 lines + 4 + 3 + 3
I : II	–	8 lines + 6.

What was a musical framework in Provençal becomes a syntactical structure in Italian, and has determined the parameters of the sonnet from the thirteenth century to the present day.

We cannot prove this debt; but no contemporary poetic form exists which is closer to the sonnet than the *canzone* stanza. Da Lentino wrote several *canzoni*, and it is interesting that none of them uses a fourteen-line sonnet scheme as a stanza; in particular, no *fronte* has eight lines rhyming ABAB ABAB. If da Lentino's choice was deliberate, what better way to signal that the sonnet was not a wandering *canzone*-stanza than by giving it a *fronte* that actually appears in no *canzone*, but which recalls a very common one – twenty-two extant *canzoni* begin with a four-line *fronte* rhyming AB AB.

Scholars have pointed out that there existed in the Sicilian area a popular verse form called the *strambotto*,[9] allegedly sung by peasants, which consisted of eight eleven-syllable lines rhyming ABAB ABAB. Again, there is no proof of indebtedness, but it is certainly not impossible that an educated circle desirous of affirming a southern Italian culture in competition with that of the north should have written distinctive poems not only in their local dialect but also deriving from local song. (The *strambotto*-form was known to Sir Thomas Wyatt from the poetry of a later sonneteer, Serafino dell'Aquila.)

No obliging peasants, however, provided da Lentino with what must be the masterstroke of the sonnet's invention: the decision to use a *sirma* of six lines. The six-line *sirma* was common in *canzoni*, and it was his genius to see that six added to eight preserves in words the principle of difference between the two parts of binary structure which was originally the *melodic* requirement of the Provençal *canso*. His contemporaries took it up, and out of 123 poems which survive from the court of Frederick II thirty-five are sonnets.

The frame was prepared: fourteen lines of eleven syllables, breaking eight and six. The speakers who advanced into that space had to learn how to use it. One requirement they inherited: that there should be a change of some kind at the end of the octave (*fronte*). The other main requirement, that of closure, was forced on them by da Lentino's decision that fourteen lines made a complete poem. To announce a theme, to change it, and to close it: these features are essentially part of the structure of the sonnet and, though they can be rearranged, they cannot be eluded. So a tripartite structure of discourse – statement, development and conclusion – belonging to a speaker whose *eloquentia* is the outgrowth of wisdom begins to appear on top of the binary structure of octave and sestet; and this is an /I/ congenial to writers for whom eloquence signalled power.

The sonnet is shaped at its beginning as a *forensic* instrument, so to speak: for pleading, arguing, asserting in a voice that is in control of worldly experience. Even in the more restricted sphere of *fin amor*, the courtly devotion made fashionable by the poets of Provence, the speaker asserts some kind of knowledge of experience, however bitter or frustrated. Da Lentino's sonnet 'Lo basilisco a lo speclo lucente' is representative of this kind of argumentative control:

> Lo basilisco a lo speclo lucente
> traggi a morire con isbaldimento;
> lo cesne canta plu gioiosamente
> quand' è plu presso a lo suo finimento;
> lo paon turba, istando plu gaudente,
> poi c'a suoi piedi fa riguardimento;
> l'augel fenise s'arde veramente
> per ritornare i' novo nascimento.
> In ta' nature eo sentom' abenuto,
> ch'allegro vado a morte, a le belleze,
> e 'nforzo il canto presso a lo finire;
> estando gaio torno dismaruto,
> ardendo in foco inovo in allegreze,
> per voi, plu gente, a cui spero redire.[10]

[The basilisk is drawn rejoicing to its death in the polished mirror, the swan sings most joyfully when nearest to its end;
the peacock is perturbed, just at its most joyful, when it beholds its feet, the phoenix really burns in order to return in a new birth.
These natures I feel I have adopted, for I joyfully go to my death, towards beauty, and I urge my song when near my end;
being joyful, I change to dismay; burning in fire, I am reborn in joy, because of you, noble lady, to whom I hope to return.]

The sonnet begins with a voice from the world of scientific learning: if the speaker emerges later as a lover, he is first of all an /I/ with the impersonal authority of the learned man. Natural science occupies the octave; the development then applies this to 'eo' (/I/) until the last line, which makes the point, the conclusion that the lady is the cause of this natural/unnatural behaviour. Because the octave has eight lines, da Lentino has used four creatures from medieval lore, fitting one to each distich; this then causes a proportional problem: each animal in turn supplies him with a point of comparison to himself, and he must deal with all four and come to a conclusion in six lines. The sestet accordingly divides 1 + 4 + 1: the first line asserts generally that he has all four natures in him, the next four distinguish the points of comparison of each, and the last concludes by referring all this to its cause, the lady, the *plu gente* of Provençal poetry.

Here, then, the statement is simply expanded by multiple examples until the octave is filled; the ingenuity we admire, as we move from knowledge displayed to argument conducted, comes in the sestet, where each apparently unrelated animal must be made relevant to the lover's condition. The conclusion, too, is neatly worked: as the phoenix 'returns' at the 'turn' (*volta*) of the sonnet, so the lover hopes to return at its conclusion – she is his 'new birth', though he does not say so. And the rather impersonal cataloguing voice of the start is nicely altered by the sudden 'per voi' ('by you') that dramatises a moment of appeal.

Da Lentino is not always so successful, but what he establishes in his better sonnets is that the form is not simply declamatory, or expressive of mood, but dialectic, a space marked out by lexical connectives indicating and joining the stages of an argument. It is a theatre for intense small arguments, or persuasions, involving a progression of ideas. Eloquence is the result of using successfully the potentialities of this form; the power of the /I/ that comes into existence in this space results from the filling of it with maximum economy, connectedness and precision. If this seems simple, even primitive, it is still a remarkable beginning, and it will lead eventually to the great sonnets of Petrarch's *Rime*, where the lyrical, self-expressive /I/ is in perfect equipoise with the argumentative, dialectical, more philosophic /I/; where vision and reason circle each other like a double sun.

If the Emperor Frederick II had been able to gain control over the centre and north of Italy as he controlled the Kingdom of the Two Sicilies, the history of the sonnet might have been different. His notaries and civil servants, who wrote so cleverly of the nature of *fin amors*, carefully avoiding all matters political or religious, might have become the intellectual elite of a centralised government in the north, and made the sonnet the lyric of a precious and restricted circle. But death intervened, and Frederick died at his castle of Ferentino on 13 December

1250, with his power still unconfirmed over half the lands south of the Alps. With him faded and disappeared the generation of cultured and rhetorically trained notaries whose invention the sonnet was; and power and influence, and literary activity passed to the cities of the north.

From the second half of the thirteenth century onwards, the major cities of the northern half of Italy – Venice, Florence, Pisa, Lucca, Arezzo, Siena, Milan, Verona, Ferrara and many others – formed communities reaching sometimes as many as 100,000 people, who tried to foster their own independence and commercial prosperity in a country not as yet unified by any central government or even a common language.[11] Municipal government demanded both political awareness and a high degree of literacy: and where there is literacy there is likely to be poetry:

> A voi che ve ne andaste per paura
> sicuramente potete tornare,
> da che ci è dirizzata la ventura;
> ormai potete guerra incominciare.
> E più non vi bisogna stare a dura,
> da che non è chi vi scomunicare,
> ma ben lo vi tenete 'n isciagura
> che non avete più cagion che dare.
> Ma so bene, se Carlo fosse morto,
> che voi ci trovereste ancor cagione:
> però del Papa non ho gran conforto.
> Ma i'non voglio con voi star a tenzone,
> ca lungo temp' è ch'io ben fui accorto
> che'l ghibellino aveste per garzone.
> (Rustico di Filippo, 1230?–1290?)[12]

[To you who fled away for fear: safely may you now return, since fortune has gone against us; you can start the war again.

No longer need you hold out, since there's no one for you to excommunicate; but, indeed, you think it a misfortune that you have now no reason to strike back.

But this I know, if Charles had died, you would find reason enough for it: yet I have little hope of the Holy Father.

But I don't want to get into dispute with you, as for a long time now I have known that you treat the Ghibellines as your servants.]

If the reader does not understand what all this is about, it is because this sonnet is now spoken by a persona from the world of contemporary politics and contemporary idiom, and is intelligible only as a highly topical gesture of defiance[13] to an audience also politically involved. This is a sonnet which has now entered political space, and its frame is occupied by a public persona who is making a statement to, or at, other public figures in front of what might be called the newsreading populace. Before the invention of printing, such poems could have been communicated only by multiple copies or by recitation by the *giullari*, the wandering players of the time; but the appearance of many similar sonnets in the middle of the thirteenth century and after suggests that a gap existed in public life into which writers could fit an utterance of political interest, localised and topical and yet available to all informed hearers, through the way in which the /I/ of the sonnet is readable as the hearer's own self, or at least a representative of the hearer's social group. The *canzone* continued to be used for longer statements: this kind of sonnet is a wall-poster, a cartoon, a gesture to catch the eye or ear.

The poet who was more than any other responsible for taking the courtly Sicilian sonnet and adapting its space to the voices of the swarming cities of the Italian plains was Guittone d'Arezzo, born in that town (also the birthplace of Petrarch) about 1230. This remarkable poet is the John Donne of early Italian poetry: like Donne he began with conventional love-poetry and developed increasingly intricate wordplay with a strong intellectual bias; like Donne he underwent a religious conversion, and turned his back upon 'all his profane mistresses'; like Donne he became preacher to his age, and used verse to reprove and instruct his fellow citizens. He died in 1294 in Bologna, his distinctive style already *passé* to the poets of the new school of the *dolce stil nuovo*.[14]

Everyone who notices Guittone, from Dante onwards, finds something rough about him: like it or loathe it, his style is extremely vigorous, in both his secular and religious phases. His output was large, and its bulk and inventiveness make him the first master of the sonnet: we have 296 of his poems, of which 246 are sonnets, an achievement rivalling Petrarch's in size. Guittone seems to have used the sonnet throughout his life as Bernard Shaw used postcards, for firing off his feelings or ideas of any kind at all for immediate impact. He learnt how to use the sonnet to hold in the incoherence of excitement, as well as to deliver the solemnity of moral pronouncements; and from the large range of his sonnets it is clear what a huge variety of expressive stances the sonnet will accommodate. Its very high degree of patterning and predictability makes it able to absorb a great deal of disturbance inside – something which Sidney and Shakespeare, in their own ways, also exploited – and Guittone noticed that he could mimic the incoherence of overmastering emotion by stunning the ear with repetitions:

> Tuttor ch'eo dirò gioi, gioiva cosa,
> intenderete che di voi favello,
> che gioia sete di beltà gioiosa,
> e gioia di piacer gioioso e bello:

e gioia in cui gioioso avenir posa
gioi d'adornezze e gioi di cor asnello,
gioia in cui viso è gioi tant' amorosa,
ched è gioiosa gioi mirare in ello.
Gioi di volere e gioi di pensamento
e gioi di dire e gioi di far gioioso,
e gioi d'onni gioioso movimento.
Perch'eo, gioiosa gioi, sì disioso
di voi mi trovo, che mai gioi non sento,
se'n vostra gioi il meo cor non riposo. (31)[15]

[Whenever I say 'joy', you thing of joy, you will understand that I speak of you, for you are a joy of joyful beauty and a joy of joyful and fair pleasure;

and joy in which a joyful future is, joy from your beauties, joy from your slim body, joy in which so much loving joy is seen that it is a joyful joy to wonder at it.

Joy of will and joy of thought, and joy of speech and joy of making joy, and joy of every movement full of joy.

So I, my joyful joy, am so unsettled by you that I never feel joy unless my heart is quieted in your joy.]

The sentiment, which emerges articulately only in the last tercet, is a common and constant one – Mozart's Don Ottavio lets it soar through 'Dalla sua pace' some five and a half centuries later – but at first it is simply rebounded, like the echo of a shout, through the lines, a great list of joys that climaxes in 'gioi d'onni gioioso movimento'. Just as the syntax begins to break down, the structure of the sonnet calls this cry of joy back into order with 'perché', and the poem ends with something like an argued position. The technique of rebounding a sound within and between the lines of the poem is something Guittone learnt from his Sicilian predecessors: here, the energy of that bounce of sound threatens a breakdown of speech itself, which only the presence up ahead, as it were, of the conclusion of the sonnet averts. The capacity to display and contain energy is a valuable resource of the sonnet ever after.

After his religious conversion, which occurred with dramatic suddenness when he left his wife and children to enter a lay order, he used the sonnet with a new deliberateness, though still with great energy. In his profane days, he had written a kind of Art of Love entirely in sonnets (which must be the first sonnet sequence in European literature); after his conversion, he wrote a countervailing sequence on the virtues and vices, twenty-eight sonnets long.[16] In this sequence he developed with force one of the other great voices of the European sonnet: the voice of moral authority and experience, an /I/ generalised and universalised to speak for the whole human condition. Here is his attack on the vice of sloth, *accidia*:

Tu vizio, accidia, a cui ben fastidioso,
operar è nemico; ètte valore
pigrizia, negrigenzia e miser poso;
lentezza e tarditate hai 'n amore.
O poltron vizio vil, miser, noioso,
e fastidioso a bon tutti tuttore,
tu ne lo stato d'ogn' om se' odioso,
peccato e danni porgi e disnore.
Corpo 'nfermi, occidi, podere strai;
onor, amor scacci, vizi accolli;
giac' e mangi' om, unde besti' una'l fai.
Vivi in te son soppellit' i folli;
periglioso e ontoso a tutti stai,
ma pur a' cherchi e a' signor più tolli. (181)[17]

[Thou vice, Sloth, to whom good is distasteful, work an enemy: your strength is laziness, negligence and wretched ease; slowness and tardiness you love.

O base cowardly vice, wretched, repulsive, objectionable to all good men always, you are hateful to the being of all men. You offer sin, eternal loss and disgrace.

You weaken the body, you kill it, you drag down our strength; you drive out honour and love and welcome vice. Man sleeps and eats, whereby you make him one with the beasts.

You are the living tomb of fools; you are dangerous and shameful to all, but yet your grip is strongest on clerics and on lords.]

Basically, this sonnet is a collection of points, an expanded *adnominatio* of Sloth; but Guittone's skill shows in his use of enjambment (l. 2) and abrupt breaks (ll. 9–10) to maintain energy and unsettle the rhythms; he has also keyed his rhymes into the 'snoring' sounds '-oso' and '-ore' and '-ai' appropriate to sloth, and has concluded with a satirical snap at the leisured classes. With its stabbing, contemptuous apostrophe, 'Tu vizio', this is the voice of the preacher: the fictional space is one in which the /I/ speaks, if not with the voice of God, then certainly with a kind of generalised authority, representing human experience with a superior and corrected knowledge of it.

If the anguish of the preacher's own personal life or struggle is available to the speaker, as it is in the sonnets of Donne, it is understood to be exemplary, representative, at least as long as the community in which the speech act takes place can be assumed to share the preacher's values even if they do not practise them with any success. (The case of Gerard Manley Hopkins, whose 'Terrible Sonnets' are the most passionate display of private anguish in sonnet literature, is somewhat different: his intellectual Catholicism sets him apart in nineteenth-century England, and his decision to speak of his loneliness and apartness cannot but make the reader aware that this /I/ sees himself not as other men.) Guittone is never in doubt that the problems he speaks of to his fellow citizens are in *their* experiential space:

> O tu, om de Bologna, sguarda e sente:
> ciò c'eo te dico a grande prode t'èe . . . (213, ll. 1–2)[18]

[O man of Bologna, attend and listen: what I say to you is of great advantage . . .]

> O carissimi miei, qual è cagione
> per che sì forte Dio disubidimo? (202, ll. 1–2)[19]

[Dearly beloved brethren, what is the reason we so resolutely disobey God?]

Many of his moral sonnets keep the form of the letter, or address one single named person, but set their terms in the space of the proverb or the maxim, where things exist unlocated, unparticularised and thus available to all. So in particular his sequence of sonnets on the virtues and vices comes from an unlocated /I/ to an unlocated audience; and thenceforward the sonnet may speak with this general moral voice to all of humanity – a potential which, in English literature, was most fully exploited by Wordsworth.

Guittone d'Arezzo is the poet of what Italian critics agreeably call 'municipalismo' – the civic spirit. One of the most bourgeois things about him is his respect for power and rank; that, and his undeviating moral earnestness (after his conversion), make him the first major poet of the new Italian cities. In his exhortatory style the sonnet becomes an instrument in the moral ordering of the commonwealth, as it was to be for Milton and Wordsworth, displaying not so much the internal life of the speaker, real or feigned, as the better selves of the captains of commerce, councils and cities as the moral voice of experience exhorts them to live.

But, if the sonnet could frame the better self of the Duecento bourgeois, it could also display his worse moments, of hate, lust, scurrility and buffoonery. The great master of the comic sonnet, as Guittone is of the moral sonnet, is Cecco Angiolieri (*c.* 1260–1312?), an engaging scapegrace who came from one of the rich families of Siena but, if we believe his sonnets, fell out with his parents, and careered through a life of wine, women and sonnets permanently short of money and full of the most scarifying abuse of anyone who crossed him. He took the sonnet to new depths of vulgarity and raucousness, but he is a skilled parodist, well acquainted with the literary fashions of the late thirteenth century, and a ferocious sender-up of their rhetoric.

Where the space of the traditional Sicilian love-sonnet creates an /I/ who worships beauty and pleads for grace, Cecco produces a speaker who worships money and pleads for sex:

L'altrier sì mi feriò un tal ticca
ch'andar mi fece a madonna di corsa:
andava e ritornava com' un' orsa
che va arrabiando e'n luogo non si ficca.
Quando mi vide, credett' esser ricca:
disse – Non avrestù cavelle in borsa? –
Rispuosi – No . . . – quella mi disse – Attorsa,
e levala pur tosto, o tu t'impicca!
  Mostravas' aspra come cuoio di riccio;
e le feci una mostra di moneta;
quella mi disse – Avesti caporiccio?
  Quasi beffava e stava mansueta,
che l'avari tenuta in fil di liccio;
ma pur ne venni con la borsa queta!   (cxx)[20]

[The other day I got up such an itch,
that I shot off to see my lady's face:
she's pacing up and down, like a bear which
is frothing mad, and can't fix in one place.
When she saw me, she saw some cash appear,
and said, 'Have you got money in your purse?'
Said I, 'Well, no. . . .' Said she, 'Get out of here!
Just spin around, or you'll get hurt, or worse!'
  – as prickly as a hedgehog on the attack.
So then I showed the colour of my cash,
and she said, 'Well now, haven't you the knack!'
  and went so sweet and jokey in a flash,
I could have led her with a strand of hemp.
I still went home with my resources limp!]

The resemblance of a purse to a codpiece probably gives the last line an extra twist!

It is sonnets in this vein that led Rosalie Colie to accuse Cecco of 'some secret instinct for slumming . . . a *nostalgie de la boue* on the part of the usually airy sonnet';[21] but there is nothing secret about this very polished piece of vulgarity. Cecco discovered, and mastered, the dramatic sonnet, the sonnet which brings to life an encounter; as has been said, the sonnet is really too short for narrative, but Cecco noticed what no one before him seems to have remarked on: that if a single sonnet line will contain a 'point', half a sonnet line is adequate for a colloquial remark or racy expression from common speech. To put it crudely, he showed that by using half lines dexterously it is possible to set up a slanging match in a sonnet, and compress a comic encounter into a single poem. The following *tour de force* is a conversation between 'Cecco' and his girlfriend Becky ('Becchina'), in which the hapless Cecco (one of whose endearing traits was that he never minded representing himself as henpecked or foolish) talks on the left-hand side in the language of the devoted lover, while Becky on the other hurls back the idiom of the streets:

> Becchin' amor! – Che vuo', falso tradito?
> Che mi perdoni. – Tu non ne se' degno.
> Merzé, per Dio! – Tu vien' molto gecchito.
> E verrò sempre... – Che sarammi pegno?
> La buona fé. – Tu ne se' mal fornito!
> N'o inver di te. – Non calmar, ch'i' vegno.
> In che fallai? – Tu sa' ch' i' abbo udito!
> Dimmel', amor. – Va', che ti vegn' un segno!
> Vuo' pur ch'i'muoia? – Anzi mi par mill' anni!
> Tu non di' ben. – Tu m'insegnerai.
> Ed i'morrò . . . – Omè, che tu m'inganni!
> Die tel' perdoni! – E che, non te ne vai?
> Or potess'io! – Tegnoti per li panni?
> Tu tieni 'l cuore. – E terrò, co' tuoi guai![22]

> [Becky, my love! – What now, you rotten knave?
> Forgiveness, if you please! – You don't deserve it.
> Mercy, I pray! – Now who's the humble slave?
> I swear, for ever . . . – Prove that you'll observe it!
> Trust my good faith! – You haven't much of that.
> I have, for you. – Don't soft-soap me that way!
> What have I done? – I've heard . . . well, you know what. . . .
> Tell me, my love! – Confound you, get away!
> D'you want my death? – Yeah, I should live so long.
> That isn't kind. – You taught me what to say.
> And I am dying . . . – Oh boy, you're just so wrong!
> God forgive you! – Why don't you run away?
> I wish I could! – Have I got you on a thong?
> You've got my heart! – I'll keep that – and you'll pay!]

Cecco wrote seven of these highly dramatic 'dialogue sonnets', an extremely difficult form popular with later Italian comic sonneteers, but which in English only Sir Philip Sidney tackled with any success. With what one might call these anti-sonnets we are at the furthest remove from the courtly pleading of Giacomo da Lentino, where the voice of a learned and polite /I/ has been replaced by 'wild and whirling words'.

By a process of inversion, then, carried out by many sonnet-writers in the Duecento, of whom Guittone d'Arezzo and Cecco Angiolieri are the most inventive, a structure designed to accommodate an /I/ defined by a courtly, abstract and rationally presented eloquence becomes a lodging-house for all the voices of the piazza. The process by which this happened is shown in the sonnets of Guittone, with their gradual opening out of the sonnet to receive voices more and more distant from the court, and the sonnets of Cecco, deliberately inverting the categories of the courtly sonnet in parody. Starting as a variant of the Provençal love-lyric in the 1230s and 1240s, the sonnet came to the next generation almost as pure form, without any classical theory prescribing tone and content. As they altered their objectives in the city-states of mid-Duecento Italy, as they spoke out on everyday matters as well as *fin' amors*, as they sent letters and news to their friends as well as pleas to their ladies, they were able to give coherence and dignity to what they said by using an *eloquent form*, small enough to control the gestures and impulses of the mind, to give a semblance of argument to a briefly entertained emotion. Conversely, the sonnet is long enough not absolutely to demand wit, like the four-line epigram: it will receive it if supplied, but its balance of eight and six will not expose the deficiency of wit (the English sonnet with its final couplet is much less tolerant of an absence of wit or clinching). Finally, as the form of the sonnet is what it is, no matter what the lexis or the theme, the sonnet is an ideal parodic device: its eloquent form, signifying order and reason, is present even when the content is exactly opposed to those things. So the form disciplines the content, creating a poetic space, even if occupied by squatters; but at the same time the content mocks the form, inverting all its values except the value of structure.

If 'to be a sonnet' meant anything more than 'to have such and such a form' – if it involved, as many early Renaissance verse types do, ideas of decorum of subject or lexis, then the sonnet might never have been extended to the world of the piazza and the market; existing, however, simply as a form ($A_{11}B_{11}AB$ ABAB $C_{11}D_{11}CDCD$), it received a wider and wider range of material, until to every 'high' element there was a corresponding 'low' one somewhere in the sonnet repertoire. When at the beginning of the thirteenth century the sonnet received some attention from theorists, it had already acquired its range, and Dante placed it in the 'middle vernacular' as a more everyday kind of poem. And when, a little later, we find a hack poet complaining that he doesn't get paid enough for his sonnets it seems that the sonnet has become one of the most versatile poetic rooms, what with an etymological pun we might call the parlour of Renaissance poesis:

> 'Deh, fammi un canzon, fammi un sonnetto!'
> mi dice alcun c'ha la memoria scema,
> e parli pur che, datomi la tema,
> io ne debba cavare un gran diletto.
> Ma e' non sa ben bene il mio difetto,
> né quanto il mio dormir per lui si scema,
> chè prima che le rime del cor prema,
> do cento e cento volte per lo letto.

Poi lo scrivo tre volte alle mie spese,
però che prima correger lo voglio
che'l mandi fuora tra gente palese.
Ma d'una cosa tra l'altre me doglio:
ch'i'non trovai ancora un sì cortese
chi mi dicesse: 'Te' il denai' del foglio.'
Alcuna volta soglio
essere a bere un quartuccio menato,
e parc ancora a lor soprappagato!
(Antonio Pucci, *c.*1350)[23]

['Come on, write me a poem or a sonnet!'
some chap requests, who isn't all that bright;[24]
gives me the theme, and thinks, once I get on it,
I ought to find the whole thing pure delight.
He doesn't know my problem in the least:
before I manage to squeeze out my rhymes,
how much my daily dose of sleep's decreased!
– I'm back and forth to bed a hundred times.
Three times the draft at my own cost I write:
I feel I must correct the thing in stages,
before I send it out to see the light;
and there's one thing that above all enrages:
I never find a customer polite
enough to say, 'Here's money for your pages!'
Sometimes my wages
are just a pint of bitter on the bar –
and then, they think I'm overpaid by far!]

3

'MAKING THE AIR TREMBLE WITH CLARITY': THE *STILNOVISTI*

In watching the sonnet acquire its voices and its space, we have arrived at the last quarter of the thirteenth century, a hundred years before Chaucer and fifty years before Petrarch began his collection of poems to his Laura. Petrarch the sonneteer had a fame so colossal and so influential that it is easy to forget that the sonnet form was a century old when, in the 1330s, he began to bend it to his purposes. In genealogical terms, he is the fourth generation of sonneteers: Giacomo da Lentino and his fellows invent the form about 1235, and establish its structure and principles, giving it a courtly and rather abstracted voice of learned pleading; they are followed by Guittone d'Arezzo and his disciples, writing in the troubled emergence of the central and northern Italian city-states in the mid-century, who bring the sonnet closer to the daily life of the piazza, and speak of all the multifarious concerns of the citizens, from the bawdy of backstreet girls to the drums of war, with a particular emphasis, because of Guittone's own powerful voice, upon practical morality and virtue. Then, when Guittone had still many years left of his long life (he died in 1294), another group of poets arose, self-consciously aiming in a different direction from the Guittonians, and proclaiming themselves writers in 'a sweet new style'. It is these writers of the *dolce stil nuovo* who gave the sonnet its musicality, a generation before Petrarch: they made it sing.

The leading *stilnovisti* (the singular is *stilnovista*) were Dante Alighieri (1265–1321) during his early years, Guido Cavalcanti (1255–1300), Cino da Pistoia (1270–1336) and the minor poets Lapo Gianni (1250?–1330?) and Gianni Alfani (b.1275). With the exception of Cino da Pistoia, all were Florentines, and they knew and corresponded with one another, often using sonnets as letters and replies in the short sequences known as *tenzoni*.[1] The Bolognese poet Guido Guinizelli (1220–76), of the previous generation, wrote a number of stilnovist poems which make him the 'founding father' of the movement.

The group made more use of the sonnet than of any other form and, because of a distinctive philosophy of love, gave the sonnet not only a new musicality, but also a new kind of /I/, a persona that was to pass on to Petrarch and his successors. The /I/ in previous sonneteering had been, as I have suggested, in a *forensic* mode, implicitly or explicitly creating an adversary (in the Lady) or at least a hearer who required to be persuaded, by a lover or by a preacher. If the speaker described or elaborated on his[2] own miseries, it was to bring about some action on the part of his hearer – granting of favour, or a recommended moral or political course of conduct. But in the sonnets of the *stilnovisti* (apart from their comic or occasional sonnets, which are much in the mode of their predecessors) the Lady, and hence her lover, appears very differently:

> The Lady of the *stilnovisti* is attenuated, and disappears into the mist of a symbol, into the undefined sweetness of a yearning towards the ideal; and wholly in the light of her eyes, in the sweetness of her smile, in the fair graces of her hair, her coming is like the gleams of sun upon a fresh dawning; her presence begets a springtime of goodness. One might say that in her shimmering, airy lightness, almost she does not possess physical attributes; and these few (eyes, smile, gold of hair, her bearing) are spiritualised and reduced, till they become mere signs of a state of mind intoxicated by the ecstasy of contemplation. She does not, I say again, make up the Other in a dialogue of love: she is the figure into which flows and is reflected the interior life of the poet – almost the symbol of self-contemplation.[3]

Mario Marti's rhapsodic account begins in what is almost a paraphrase of what we find in sonnet after sonnet:

> Vedut' ho la lucente stella diana
> ch'apare anzi che 'l giorno rend' albore,
> c'ha preso forma di figura umana;
> sovr'ogn'altra me par che dea splendore:
> viso de neve colorato in grana,
> occhi lucenti, gai e pien d'amore;
> non credo che nel mondo sia cristiana
> si piena di biltate e di valore.
> Ed io dal suo valor son assalito,
> con sì fera battaglia di sospiri
> ch'avanti a lei de dir non seri' ardito.
> Così conoscess'ella i miei disiri,
> ché, senza dir, de lei seria servito,
> per la pietà ch'avrebbe de' martiri.
> (Guido Guinizelli)[4]

[I have seen the shining star of morning, that comes as soon as day whitens, which has taken a human shape, with a splendour, it seems to me, beyond all others.

A countenance of snow, flushed with red; shining eyes, joyful and full of love – I do not believe there is a woman in the world so full of beauty and truth.

And I am so struck by her power, with such a conflict of sighs, that in her presence I dare not speak.

Would she might so learn of my longings that, without words from me, I might be her servant, through the pity she would have upon her martyrs.]

This view of the Lady, the *donna angelicata* ('angelic lady'), appears at this moment in the latter half of the thirteenth century out of philosophical and religious traditions that it is far beyond the scope of this study to discuss: here it can only be said that the Lady who in Provençal verse and in Sicilian poetry stood as the human recipient of the lover's pleas has become a symbol of an almost religious ideal of human perfection, a kind of messenger of grace and wisdom sent from God to the human spirit to raise it up to him. 'Tenne d'angel sembianza/Che fosse del Tuo regno' – 'She had the semblance of an angel, as if she came from Thy realm,' said Guinizelli in the great philosophical *canzone*, 'Al gentil cor rempaira sempre Amore' ('To the noble heart doth Love betake himself'), which was respected by the *stilnovisti* as if it were a kind of manifesto of their movement; and in that same poem Guinizelli explains that the Lady is to her lover as God is to the world – in Dante's phrase, 'l'amor che muove 'l sol e l'altre stelle'.[5]

Now, the sonnet is too short to be a philosophical instrument – for that the *canzone* was reserved – but its smaller space proved ideal for one kind of experience that, for the *stilnovisti*, was emotionally and spiritually crucial: the *salute*, the Lady's greeting. The word *salute*, the ordinary term for a greeting, carries etymologically the sense of 'salvation'. Now, if the Lady mediates the radiance of God to her admirer, then when she acknowledges him, with a word or even with a glance, she gives *salute* in two senses: she greets and saves in one moment. The Lady is of this world, indeed, and comes and goes in the city streets; but her beauty mediates the radiance of God, and when it strikes the beholder he is changed 'in a moment, in the twinkling of an eye'. It is the *appearance* of the Lady to her admirer that is the crucial event, not the communication between lover and lady. Indeed, for the *stilnovisti* the *salute* is an event which quite extinguishes subsequent conversation: their ladies hardly speak to them after greeting, and pass on their way like heavenly visitants.

The stilnovistic sonnet is not, then, a communication from lover to lady, though it may well address her directly; it is a record of a single moment whose value is in its singularity, and whose impact is entirely upon the speaker – the Lady is unchanged and unchangeable. The sonnet still functions among the *stilnovisti* as letter, as protest, as general poem of praise, but when it registers the crucial moment of the *salute* it offers an epiphany, a single event of a spiritually revealing nature, in which the reality of the /I/ is transformed, both internally and in the world around:

> Ché 'l vostro viso dà si gran lumera,
> che non è donna ch'aggia in se beltate,
> ch'a voi davanti non s'ascuri in cera;
> per voi tutte bellezze so' afinate,
> e ciascun fior fiorisce in sua manera
> lo giorno quando vo' vi dimostrate.
> (Guido Guinizelli, 'Gentil donna di pregio nomata', ll. 9–14)

> [For your face gives such light
> that there is no lady, though beautiful in herself,
> who does not seem dimmed in your presence;
> All beauties grow purer through you,
> and every flower blooms in its fashion
> on the day when you appear.]

Indeed, the moment of vision can be so striking that the /I/ of the sonnet cannot speak, producing a sonnet (or part of one) which consists of assertions that it cannot be written. The relationship of the /I/ to language alters: since the Lady is not to be persuaded, or even talked to, the function of language is not to persuade the Other, but to express the self in its new, purified and as yet stammering awareness:

> Chi è questa che ven, ch'ogn'om la mira,
> che fa tremar di chiaritate l'âre,
> e mena seco Amor, sì che parlare
> null'omo pote, ma ciascun sospira?
> O Deo, che sembra quando li occhi gira,
> dical Amor, ch'i'nol savria contare:
> cotanto d'umiltà mi pare,
> ch'ogna'altra ver di lei i' la chiam'ira.
> Non si poria contar la sua piagenza,
> ch'a lei s'inchin'ogni gentil vertute
> e la beltate per la sua dea la mostra.
> Non fu sì alta già la mente nostra,
> e non si pose 'n noi tanta salute,
> che propriamente n'aviàn canoscenza.[6]

> [Who is she coming, whom all gaze upon,
> who makes the air all tremulous with light
> and at whose side is Love himself? that none
> dare speak, but each man's sighs are infinite.

Ah me! how she looks round from left to right
let Love discourse: no words will come from me.
Lady she seems of such humility
as makes all others graceless in men's sight.
The beauty which is hers cannot be said;
to whom are subject all things virtuous,
while all things beauteous own her deity.
Ne'er was the mind of man so nobly led,
nor yet was such redemption granted us,
that we should ever know her perfectly.]
(trans. D. G. Rossetti: adapted)[7]

This is, in two senses, a miraculous opening: the felicity of the second line, with its vibrating 'r's suggestive of the shimmering of the air, and the unanswered, rapturous question of the first, show that Cavalcanti had mastered starting a sonnet well – a thing only slightly less difficult than finishing it. The octave must seize the moment and hold it clearly; the sestet can then argue about it, define it, explain it. Rather than conceiving of the sonnet as an argument or plea all through, with perhaps a word or phrase of salutation at the start, the *stilnovisti* often seem to see the octave as a space in which an appearance, a phenomenon, is described so as to present it clearly to the reader, while the sestet talks about it, moving from description to argument or explanation. So Cavalcanti's octave magnificently describes the appearance of the Lady and her effect on other women (with a clumsy and overcompressed eighth line); at the ninth line, we move from direct confrontation of those present ('Chi è . . . ? O Deo . . . dical Amor') to reflection on her qualities and the predicament of the bystanders. The vocabulary is now more abstract, and the material less visual. Subtly, Cavalcanti has used his favourite *rime rovesciate* ('upside down rhyme') in the sestet, where the sequence of the first tercet, CDE, is stood on its head, EDC, to produce an echo effect: as *canoscenza* echoes *piagenza*, and *salute vertute*, and *nostra mostra*, so the spectators in the second tercet echo the Lady, reflecting or absorbing, as far as they can, her virtue. So their *knowledge* feebly tries to grasp her *grace* (*canoscenza/piagenza*); their *redemption* depends upon her *virtue* (*salute/vertute*); and what she *shows* becomes part of *them*, however inadequately (*mostra/nostra*). The rhymescheme CDEEDC produces an effect of sonic completeness and, on the page, visual finality, as if a space had been closed off, as indeed it has.

The philosophical emphasis upon purity and light has an effect upon style: since the /I/ that speaks is speaking not 'to' but 'of', his language should show the new purity of the self of which he speaks. In contrast, therefore, to the extremely complicated wordplay of Guittone and his followers, in contrast also to the elaborate forensic eloquence of Giacomo da Lentino, loading every line with similes and abstract nouns, the *stilnovisti* adopt a straightforward syntax, and a vocabulary that is not particularly extended, once the terms of the philosophy of the New Love are understood. Consciously or intuitively, they clarified the melody of the sonnet.

Straightforwardness in the sonnet is readily definable: since the sonnet falls into invariant sections, 8 + 6 = (4 + 4) + (3 + 3) = (2 + 2 + 2 + 2) + (3 + 3) and so on down to single lines or even half-lines, straightforward *syntax* is that which, in Italian or any other language, allows its clausal and phrasal units, when these are in the order of normal speech, to align with the poetic units. Thus, to take a familiar example,

> Being your slave, what should I do but tend
> upon the hours and times of your desire?
> (Shakespeare, Sonnet 151, ll. 1–2)

shows a sentence structure exactly as it would be spoken aligned with the first two lines of the sonnet. The next example shows the structure still aligned, but not as it would be spoken:

> The rose looks fair, but fairer we it deem
> for that sweet odour which doth in it live.
> (Shakespeare, Sonnet 150, ll. 3–4)

and the next, exactly as it would be spoken, but not aligned:

> At the round earth's imagined corners, blow
> your trumpets, angels, and arise, arise
> from death, you numberless infinities
> of souls, and to your scattered bodies go.
> (Donne, 'Holy Sonnets', 4, ll. 1–4)

The entire sentence coincides with the quatrain, but at the end of each line a normally unified phrasal group is broken by being separated across the lines (enjambed): 'blow/your trumpets', 'arise/from death', 'infinities/of souls'. Thirteenth-century Italian has perhaps a higher tolerance of inversions than modern English (though one is necessarily judging from written traces), but the *stilnovisti* avoid the more elaborate reversals of syntax, and take care that such inversions as do occur coincide with poetic units, as in the eleventh line of Cavalcanti's sonnet above: 'e la beltate per sua dea la mostra' instead of 'e la beltate la mostra per sua dea'.

There is also *phonic* straightforwardness, which British sonneteers had painfully to learn: the avoidance of clusters of sounds, consonantal or vocalic, which require rapid changes of position in the articulating organs. Italian naturally lacks some of the sounds, such as *w* and *th*, which move our English lips and tongue out into the awkward shifts beloved of tongue-twister contrivers, but it has its own problems, to which the *stilnovisti* were sensitive: they generally avoid harsh sounds, clusters of consonants and the kind of repetition of sounds internally that Guittone delighted in. They have a sense of the flow of their language – or so it seems from their poetry – in exactly the same way as the second generation of British sonneteers, Sir Philip Sidney and his peers, had collectively a better ear for the liquidity of English than Sir Thomas Wyatt and his circle. They avoid, too, the extreme kinds of word repetition – da Lentino's line 'Lo viso, e son diviso da lo viso', while not awkward to say, has a riddling effect from its internal rhymes and puns that the *stilnovisti* generally avoided.

Finally, there is *lexical* straightforwardness, the maintenance of an even tenor of speech, which in practice means the avoidance of wild variations of social register, and also of incongruous registers, as that of jurisprudence or theology when talking of love. The metaphorical adventurousness of Donne or of Shakespeare of course cuts across this, and it has to be admitted that the *stilnovisti* achieve their clarity with some loss of metaphorical range. It was left to Petrarch to discover how to acquire metaphorical complexity without losing music.

The straightforwardness thus defined, of syntax, of sound and of vocabulary, assures a kind of evenness and clearness to which the neat structure of the sonnet is very responsive. The *stilnovisti* made almost no use of extended forms of the sonnet, such as the *sonetto caudato*, or tailed sonnet, or the *sonetto rinterzato*, a sonnet with inserted shorter lines doubling the main rhymes; they generally used the standard form with a preference for the tighter octave, ABBA ABBA (known as *rime incrociate*, 'crossed rhymes') as against ABAB ABAB (*rime incatenate*, 'linked rhymes'). By the end of the thirteenth century, the octave in *rime incrociate* had become almost universal. There is no such agreement over the sestet. The Sicilian CDCDCD, nearly always with a break in sense after the first tercet, CDC DCD, was much used, perhaps because when combined with an octave arranged ABBA ABBA its form also appears *incrociata* – that is, with the D inside a pair of C-rhymes, and the C inside a pair of D-rhymes: we thus see a sonnet of four enclosed groups, ABBA ABBA CDC DCD. But other arrangements – in fact, almost any combination of two and three rhymes that is possible – occur so often as to make it quite uncertain what the *stilnovisti* thought of the matter. Where three rhymes are used, the simple CDE CDE and the *rime rovesciate*, CDE EDC (giving a very decided *incrociata* effect, E's within D's within C's), seem to be the common choices. Though there is no way of proving this, it may be that the greater variety of sestets is due to the greater difficulty of writing them: after the octave, one's options narrow, and one needs freedom to rearrange one's rhymes to get the sonnet to its conclusion.

Few things dim the eyes and stuff the head more effectively than lengthy statistics of rhymeschemes,[8] and it is enough to say that the conservative patternings in the sonnets of the *stilnovisti* are consistent with their restrictions on diction, sounds and syntax in the interest of a new simplicity and musicality. As has been suggested above, this is directly connected to their philosophy of love, with its insistence upon the transformation of the lover. The sonnet had always, from its invention, been a form very suitable for the single event: a plea, a protest, an item of news, a rebuke, an insult, even a row in the street. But until the love sonnets of the *stilnovisti* the /I/ who spoke in the fictional space of the sonnet was always locatable in a *social* space: for example,

> Ogn'omo ch'ama d è amar so' onore,
> e de la donna che prende ad amare. . . .
> (Giacomo da Lentino)

> [Every man who loves must love his honour,
> and that of the lady he takes as his love. . . .]

This proceeds from an /I/ offering maxims for social behaviour, and therefore locatable in a society of lovers: the sonnet is a social act, a sharing of experience of courtly conduct. Similarly, Guittone's /I/ offers advice to fellow citizens, often historically identifiable, for their benefit as members of the city community. The /I/ is socially oriented, speaking publicly, and even in anguished poems of complaint there is, as a contemporary critic pointed out,[9] an implied debate, or at least encounter, with another person, who is to be persuaded by the speaker's recital of his woes. And sonnets in the form of letters are *ipso facto* social acts.

This dimension of the sonnet has never vanished, nor is it absent from the writings of the *stilnovisti*; but the cultivation of their philosophy of love in verse did alter the directionality of the /I/'s utterance. Since the Lady is no longer the real object of desire, but a medium to be transcended, a messenger rather than a goal, there is little point in addressing her in the old courtly fashion; what matters now is the internal transformation of the subject, and it is hard to resist the feeling, as one reads the poetry of this group, that the discourse is becoming increasingly internally directed. The /I/ speaks to himself, of himself and for himself. It is true that there are many sonnets which continue to record social moments, which make an appeal to the fellow citizen or the companions of the Lady or the bystander to witness the power of her passing or the brightness of her glance, or the misery of the unregarded lover; but it is the way of the *stilnovista* so to suspend the sonnet, unlocated in time and space, that almost no social orientation is possible, and what is left is the record of an epiphany, a moment whose meaning is entirely for the psyche of the speaker:

Di donne io vidi una gentile schiera
quest' Ognissanti prossimo passato,
e una ne venia quasi imprimiera,
veggendosi l'Amor dal destro lato.
De gli occhi suoi gittava una lumera,
la qual parea un spirto infiammato;
e i'ebbi tanto ardir, ch'in la sua cera
guarda', e vidi un angiol figurato.
A chi era degno donava salute
co gli atti suoi quella benigna e piana,
e 'mpiva 'l core a ciascun di vertute.
Credo che de lo ciel fosse soprana,
e venne in terra per nostra salute:
là 'nd'è beata chi l'è prossimana.
(Dante Alighieri)[10]

[Last All Saints' holy day, as did betide,
I met a gathering of damozels:
she that came first, as one doth who excels,
had Love with her, upon her right-hand side.
A light shone forward, through her steadfast eye,
as when in living fire a spirit dwells:
so, gazing with the boldness which prevails
o'er doubt, I knew an angel visibly.
As she passed on, she bowed her mild approof
and salutation to all men of worth,
lifting the soul to solemn thoughts aloof.
In Heaven itself that lady had her birth,
I think, and is with us for our behoof:
Blessed are they who meet her on the earth.]
(trans. D. G. Rossetti: adapted)

What appears to be a quite specific human event – a crowd of ladies meet upon All Saints' Day – dissolves into fantasy with the appearance of Love on the right, and the fiery spirit in her eyes. The objectivity of the event recedes, and we are left with the intense emotion of the speaker, transformed by what he thinks he saw.

Charting the transformation of the inner self is one of the most difficult problems of western European lyric poetry: the sonnets of the *stilnovisti*, simply because of the advent of a theory of love which directed attention away from the social world towards the mental or spiritual, represent one of the earliest vernacular attempts to do so, and begin the long European progress towards a fictional space in which the internal /I/ can be dramatised, not as a record of the thoughts of a historically located figure, but as a voice that can speak for every reader about every reader. The *stilnovisti* learnt to suspend the speaker, as Dante does above, in a kind of space of mental excitement out of time and away from real place, of which the sonnet is the verbal form.

The redirection of the sonnet's glance inwards made the *stilnovisti* adapt, and perhaps give new life to, the medieval and late classical tradition of the *psychomachia*,[11] which proved surprisingly durable as a means of mapping the life of the mind and the heart. The *psychomachia*, or 'battle of the faculties', imagines the body of man as a literal battle-ground over which the mental faculties, the emotions and the energies of the human being fight for control of the whole person; such is John Bunyan's *The Holy War*. In versions of a less anatomical cast, the body or personality may be imaged as a house (the House of Alma in Spenser's *Faerie Queene*, Book 1), a garden (*Le Roman de la Rose*), a kingdom (*Ane Satire of the Thrie Estaitis*, *Piers Plowman*) or an island (*Lord of the Flies*), with the complication that, once away from the physical body, figures representative of almost any aspect of man's social or political behaviour may enter alongside those representing the faculties of the mind. These personified qualities act as characters in dramatised conflicts.

In the brief space of the sonnet, however, only the simpler movements and attributes of the body and personality can be introduced, just as only very limited activity can be described. Since the intention of the *stilnovisti* is rarely didactic, it is perhaps misleading to call such sonnets *psychomachias*: not moral combat for the triumph of good, but a display of a state of mind, seems to be what Cino da Pistoia, for example, is trying to achieve here; his model is not a battle, but a family funeral:

Se mercé non m'aiuta, il cor si more,
e l'anima trarrà guai dolorosi,
e i sospiri usciran for dogliosi
de la mia mente adorna di dolore.
Poi che sentir li mie' spiriti amore,
di lei chiamar son stati vergognosi;
or che si senton di doglia angosciosi,
cheron piangendo il su' dolce valore.
   Io dico in verità che se mercede
non m'aiuta lo cor, che l'alma trista
girà traendo dolorosi guai.
   Ell' è una vertù che la conquista
ogn'om quando di cor gentil procede:
com'io aspetto che mi vegna omai![12]

[If mercy does not aid me, the heart dies, and the soul will utter doleful lamentations, and sighs will go forth from my mind, heavy with grief. After my spirits felt love, they were bashful in asking for mercy; now that they feel themselves racked with grief, they ask with tears for its sweet effects.

I say truly that, if mercy does not help my heart, the wretched soul will go lamenting woefully.

She (*i.e. mercy*) is a blessing that every man acquires when he acts from a noble heart: how keenly I await her coming now!]

This looks like a brief social narrative, recording the movement of a group of friends: it is in fact a way of using the structure of the sonnet to distribute parts of the self – soul, spirits, sighs and so on – in a miniature drama representing the inner mind. It is a powerful method of psychological description, and it allows the sonnet to analyse a feeling or a moment with economy and narrative vigour. Like so much else that the *stilnovisti* did, it passes to Petrarch as another mode of self-display, and persists in the European tradition – not of course only in sonnets – at least as late as Shakespeare, whose Sonnet 46, for example, should now seem to the reader to have Sicilian and stilnovistic overtones, both in its wordplay and its material.

Mine eye and heart are at a mortal war
How to divide the conquest of thy sight:
Mine eye my heart thy picture's sight would bar,
Mine heart mine eye the freedom of that right.
  My heart doth plead that thou in him dost lie
(A closet never pierced with crystal eyes)
But the defendant doth that plea deny,
And says in him thy fair appearance lies.
  To 'cide this title is impannelled
A quest of thoughts, all tenants to the heart,
And by their verdict is determined
The clear eye's moiety, and the dear heart's part;
  As thus: mine eye's due is thine outward part
And my heart's right thine inward love of heart.

But we are getting ahead of ourselves: all that has been touched on in this chapter comes together in the greatest sonnet sequence of the Duecento, Dante's *Vita Nuova* ('The New Life').[13] This short sequence, containing twenty-five sonnets, one *ballata*, three *canzoni* and two incomplete *canzoni* of one stanza and two stanzas in length, has a prose commentary from Dante himself, in which he explains the structure of each poem, and integrates it into the narrative of his love for Beatrice. It is the first sequence to join sonnets with a critical and autobiographical commentary, and that alone would make it of importance here; but, coming as it does also from the most powerful Italian genius of poetry, it offers one of the subtlest and most appealing treatments of Love and the Self in the literature of Europe.

Yet it was not a particularly influential one in the history of the sonnet:

manuscripts of the *Vita Nuova* are not numerous, and the first printed text appeared late in the Renaissance, in 1576 – a previous printing, in 1527, contained only the poems.[14] Petrarch seems not to have paid it any special attention. The achievement of the *Divine Comedy* eclipsed that of the *Vita Nuova*: like Milton's sonnets alongside his *Paradise Lost*, the poems of the *Vita Nuova* seem youthful and even occasional, and their quality is uneven. Within the complete text, however, they form part of a very complex narrative which has fascinated students not only of Dante's life and thought but also of autobiography, of medieval philosophy and theology, of narratology and of literary criticism:[15] here we can be concerned only with Dante's handling of the sonnet within the parameters of the stilnovistic lyric.

Dante has placed the thirty-one poems inside a double frame: each poem records or arises out of a moment in 'Dante's' life (that is, the person that the author of the *Vita Nuova* says he was) from 1274 to 1291, when he was in love with the girl whom he calls Beatrice. Each poetic moment is embedded in a prose narrative which links them in time and also in psychological development, producing a kind of narrative known, from previous medieval examples, as a *prosimetrum*, a mixed prose and verse narrative. The poems are then also subjected to a gloss or criticism according to the scholastic practice of 'division', that is, dividing a text up into lexical units or lexemes, and commenting on the meaning of each.

Each poem (the majority are sonnets) is introduced in the prose narrative as a text produced under the pressure of specific feelings or circumstances by the young Dante. The poem usually appears as the restatement in verse of something that has already been described in the prose text: for example, the sonnet in *VN* 37,[16] which begins 'L'amaro lagrimar che voi faceste' ('The bitter tears that you used to shed'), is introduced thus:

> After I had spoken thus to myself, addressing my own eyes, the most huge and wrenching sighs assailed me. And so that this struggle that I was having should not remain known only to the wretch that felt it, I decided to compose a sonnet, and to express in it this terrible condition. So I wrote this sonnet, which begins, 'The bitter tears. . . .'[17]

This is the first instance in European literature in which a sonnet is related to something outside itself (apart from other sonnets, that is) by another text, and it remains very rare to find sonnets accounted for, as it were, by a text that travels with them. Dante's comment brings into plain view – for him as well as for us, the readers – the two /I/s that are always present in a lyric performance, but which have not so far been remarked on in connection with the sonnet. These are the uttering or narrating /I/ (*sujet de l'énonciation*) and the uttered or narrated /I/, the /I/ described by the uttering voice (*sujet de l'énoncé*).[18] The /I/ who speaks in a sonnet, who need not be marked by the first-person pronoun, is always aware of another /I/ at a little distance, a past self or another aspect of the self; but it is unusual to find the two as clearly distinguished as they are here. Dante even objectifies the 'uttered /I/' by another name: the other /I/ is 'the wretch that felt this struggle', and the uttering /I/, though very close to the 'wretch', is the more collected, rational /I/ who decided to compose a sonnet. (The prose commentary then provides a third /I/, the author/editor who is arranging these poems and commenting on them.)

In this poetic duality, the uttering /I/ is the constructor of the uttered /I/, and any pretence that the utterance is spontaneous is merely that, since what is being said, however immediate it seems to the reader, is always in the past with respect to the /I/ that is writing the poem. This is a feature of all lyric verse, not just of sonnets; but since the sonnet by its length and structure nearly always involves a change of stance, from narrative to explanation, from description to evaluation, from present to past, it is very common, particularly in sequences, to find the uttering /I/ actually entering the text to comment on the creation of the text itself – a textual shift known as 'metanarrative'. The following sonnet from the *Vita Nuova* shows this clearly: describing one of his chance encounters with his lady, Monna Bice (i.e. Madonna Beatrice), Dante says,

> io vidi monna Vanna e monna Bice
> venir inver lo loco là 'v' io era,
> l'una appresso de l'altra meraviglia;
> e sì come la mente mi ridice,
> Amor mi disse, 'Quell'è Primavera,
> e quell'ha nome Amor, sì mi somiglia.'[19]

[I saw Lady Joan and Lady Beatrice coming towards where I was, one miracle with another. And, as my mind recalls it to me, Love said to me, 'The one is called Spring, and the other's name is Love, so much does she resemble me.']

The entry of the metanarrative voice occurs at 'sì come la mente mi ridice' ('as my minds recalls it to me'), where the /I/ writing the poem is reminded of something by his own memory, resaying ('ridice') what was said by Love to /I-that-was/ when the event happened. We often find, both in verse and in prose, the uttering or narrating /I/ representing himself or herself as a person looking up an account, or reading a book, or, as here, listening to a voice, in order to discover something about the /I-that-was/: it is with this *topos* of the 'book of memory', indeed, that Dante begins the *Vita Nuova*,[20] and Shakespeare, for example, in his Sonnet 30 ('When to the sessions of sweet silent thought') represents the narrating /I/ as recovering information by subpoenaing memory – a neat adaptation of the *psychomachia* to the problems of past and present.

By putting his sonnets inside a commentary, Dante makes himself and his readers continuously aware that the sonnet is in two ways an occasional piece. First, it relates something about a past self, a significant moment, a feeling, a piece of wisdom. Second, it is an event for the author writing it, which demands to be put into proper relation with the past event: now, many lyrics do not bother to notice this, and assume, tacitly, an easy continuity between the person writing and the person he or she was at the moment being described; but, given the particular focus of the *stilnovisti* upon *transformation* of the self, writers in a position such as Dante's can become quite obsessed with sorting out the relationship between the self that writes, now, and the self that suffered, then. If this is, generally, a morbid preoccupation of western European writers, it has at least been substantially fed by sonnet-writing since Dante's time.

As the stilnovistic lyric shifts the focus of attention of the sonnet from an external, public space to an interior space (although sonnets with an external, social focus will continue to be written), it is essential to notice, as Dante did, that the apparent grammatical unity of self which is wished on European language speakers by the monadic pronoun 'I' does not reflect a temporal or psychological unity; and when the sonnet, in Dante's hands and in Petrarch's, acquires its capacity to deal with *ontogenesis*, that is, the problem of the growth and continuity or discontinuity of self which has been one of the major topics of our literature since Augustine's *Confessions*, the sonnet *sequence* acquires a new importance: it is one of the very few literary forms that can represent both the fragmentary, immediate nature of real experience (each poem is separate) and also the continuous nature of selfhood (the poems form a sequence). Most major sonneteers show awareness that the signifier 'I' is in tension with its signified, a signified that is always multiple and always sliding under an apparently single signifier. As Petrarch puts it at the outset of his own sequence, 'era in parte altr'uom da quel ch'i'sono' – 'I was, in part, another man from what I am now'; Sidney puts it the other way round: 'I am not I; pity the tale of me.'[21]

But, however private the feelings of the narrated /I/, the narrating /I/, who is having all the bother of composing sonnets, has some desire to communicate with others, and even stilnovistic sonnets are social acts. Dante's comments in his prose text in the *Vita Nuova* upon his reasons for writing are invariably brief, but they point to a narrating self anxious to make known to the outside world – perhaps a single person, a friend, a group of ladies acquainted with Beatrice, or anyone who might read the poem by chance – what was felt by the other self, the suffering /I/ whose experiences are in each sonnet. Four times only does Dante present his writing as a kind of therapy, 'to relieve my sadness with some sorrowful words';[22] on all other occasions when he assigns a motive, it is to tell someone else. Why these people should be interested, Dante does not say, though in the somewhat cryptic narrative of the *Vita Nuova* he sometimes suggests that he was anxious to clear up a misunderstanding, and he sometimes writes verses on request, or to praise his Lady. But the sonnet is a public text, both before and after the invention of printing, written by a rhetorically skilled /I/, to demonstrate, argue or explain the effects of an internal change. If this begins to look very much like Romantic 'emotion recollected in tranquillity', it is because it is to that kind of poetry that this lyric development leads. But in the last years of the thirteenth century it also looks back towards the medieval spiritual pilgrimage, in which art has two chief functions: to praise the good and condemn the bad, and to narrate with dramatic power the stages of the spiritual ascent.

The stress laid upon the suffering of the lover, inherited from Provençal and Sicilian poetry, moves closer, in this scheme of things, to penitential writing. The soul, or the heart in stilnovistic writing, is the site of a struggle; and this struggle may be represented by *psychomachia*, as has been said, or it may be imaged in the effects of struggle, that is, weeping and sighing. The suffering self, the object of the narration, is inarticulate, since neither tears nor sighs are verbal: the narrating self then takes these sighs and gives them a textual presence: the poem is 'the sound of a sigh' or 'is written in tears'. The heart is the essential site of change, but all the heart can do is sigh:

Tanto gentile e tanto onesta pare
la donna mia quand'ella altrui saluta,
ch'ogne lingua deven tremando muta,
e li occhi no l'ardiscon di guardare.
Ella si va, sentendosi laudare,
benignamente d'umiltà vestuta;
e par che sia una cosa venuta
da cielo in terra a miracol mostrare.
Mostrasi sì piacente a chi la mira,
che dà per li occhi una dolcezza al core,
che 'ntender no la può chi no la prova:
e par che de la sua labbia si mova
un spirito soave pien d'amore
che va dicendo a l'anima, 'Sospira!'
(*VN* 26)[23]

[So noble and so pure seems my lady when she greets anyone that every tongue falls silent out of awe, and the eye dare not gaze upon her.

She goes on her way, knowing herself praised, clad graciously in humility, and seems a thing come down from heaven to show a miracle here.

She shows herself so gracious to those who admire her that she sends a sweetness into the heart through the eyes, that none can understand who has not felt it; and it seems that from her lips there comes a sweet spirit of love that says to the soul, 'Sigh!']

The whole stilnovistic process of regeneration through the *donna angelicata* is described here, in language that is as 'straightforward' as it is melodious, showing by its 'dolcezza' the effect it describes. Simplicity, if not silence, is requisite, since ordinary language falls silent before this miracle; and this sonnet is the result of the advice given in its own last line, that is, it is the articulation of a sigh, the 'sospiro', the 'under-breath' turned into the breath of speech. The final sonnet of the *Vita Nuova* performs the paradox of turning what cannot be said, because it is too subtle for human wit, into what can be read, as the narrating /I/ reconstructs the experience of the /I-that-was/: the self, imaged as a sigh, is allowed a transcendent experience, which is beyond the understanding of the narrating /I/ ('when it relates it to me, I do not understand it'), who nevertheless composes the sonnet describing it:

> Oltre la spera che più larga gira,
> passa 'l sospiro ch'esce del mio core:
> intelligenza nova, che l'Amore
> piangendo mette in lui, pur su lo tira.
> Quand'elli è giunto là dove disira,
> vede una donna, che riceve onore,
> e luce sì che per lo suo splendore
> lo peregrino spirito la mira.
> Vedela tal che, quando 'l mi ridice,
> io no lo intendo, sì parla sottile
> al cor dolente, che lo fa parlare.
> So io che parla di quella gentile,
> però che spesso ricorda Beatrice,
> sì ch'io lo 'ntendo ben, donne mie care.
> (*VN* 41)[24]

[Beyond the sphere that has the widest revolution passes the sigh that issues from my heart: a new intelligence, which Love tearfully instilled into it, draws it ever upwards.

When it arrives where it desires to be, it beholds a Lady, who is honoured there, and shines so brightly, that through her splendour the pilgrim spirit admires her.

It beholds her in such fashion that, when it speaks again to me of her, I do not understand, so subtle is its speech to the grieving heart, that makes it speak.

I do know that it speaks of that noble Lady, because it often recalls Beatrice: so that indeed I do know, noble ladies.]

In the hands of the *stilnovisti*, and particularly the young Dante, the fourteen-line Sicilian sonnet, without in the least losing its capacity to argue, instruct, plead and also mock, acquires the further capacity to mirror the epiphanic moments of the inner self, the moments at which an inner transformation occurs through contact with the ideal. Though the skills of rhetoric are still needed to articulate these moments, their visionary beauty demands, and gets, a new clarity of diction and syntax: any great ostentation of learning would destroy the sense that it is upon the ordinary life of man that the transcendental light gleams. Thenceforward the sonnet is the place where the sighs of desire can break through into speech; and by extension, a sonnet sequence is the place where we hear, as Petrarch says, 'in rime sparse il suono/di quei sospiri ond'io nudriva il core' – 'in scattered verses the sound of those sighs with which I used to feed my heart'.

4

PETRARCH: 'THE GOOD WEAVER OF LOVE VERSES'

The Italian poet and critic Giosué Carducci, writing, as poets have often done, sonnets upon the sonnet, said that Dante gave the sonnet 'the movement of cherubim, and surrounded it with gold and azure air'; Petrarch 'plucked sonnets with flowers along a running brook', and 'poured into them the sighs of his heart, a divine stream murmuring through his verses'.[1] A kind of theological ceremoniousness set against a pastoral hedonism – if the easy identification of Dante with sacred and Petrarch with profane love is unfair to the complicated souls of both men, it is still true that Petrarch's *Canzoniere*, or *Rime* as I shall call them,[2] his collection of 317 sonnets, 29 *canzoni*, 7 *ballate* and 4 madrigals, became the greatest single inspiration for the love-poetry of Renaissance Europe until well into the seventeenth century. The sonnet was not his creation, but it became his creature, and the self which its frame displayed, a rich and varied and complex one, became a mode of being in a form of discourse that few could escape if they tried to speak of love, whether they chose the sonnet itself or quite another form. The *Rime* of Petrarch is not only one of the most influential, but also one of the most complicated of European lyric achievements – more than eight hundred critical works on it have been published in the twentieth century alone[3] – and this chapter will be limited to considering his handling of the sonnet form, involving the larger issues of his life and the construction and meaning of the *Rime* only as far as these are relevant to the sonnet.

Francis Petrarch (1304–74)[4] was possessed of a very high degree of self-consciousness, and a driving ambition to distinguish himself as poet, scholar and man of letters (which he did). His personality, which he sold with considerable success to men of influence, is parcelled out among many different kinds of writing, and his output was prodigious in the three main branches of the *ars dictaminis* (rhetoric): *prosaicum* (Latin prose), *metricum* (Latin verse) and *rithimicum* (vernacular verse). If we now value him most as he appears in the last of these, he himself (though his opinions changed during his long life) set as much store at least by his achievements in Latin verse and prose. (His native tongue was northern

Italian; he spoke and read Provençal, but habitually wrote for all purposes except rhymed verse in Latin.) The play of selves extended into the events of his own life: the man who deliberately sought the remoteness of the valley of the Sorgue, north of Avignon, to be happy growing vegetables by the stream, at the same time intrigued and manoeuvred, with complete success, to have himself crowned poet laureate, with the approval of King Robert of Sicily, at a lavish ceremony on the Capitoline Hill in Rome in 1341; the man who several times described his Italian poetry as 'ineptiae' ('follies') and 'nugellae' ('trifles')[5] spent years of work in revising and transcribing these same poems for circulation. The selves of Petrarch are many and varied, shaped partly by the parameters of the genres in which he chose to narrate them, and we should no more seek the 'true' Petrarch among them than we should ask a man which of the suits of clothes he wears is his most sincere.

We are fortunate in possessing the *Rime* in a manuscript prepared by Petrarch himself, MS. Vatican 3195, the first autograph manuscript of a major European author to survive. Working with an amanuensis, Petrarch began this fine copy in 1366, and worked on it intermittently until his death.[6] The selection of poems (not all his Italian poems were included) and their order are therefore his, at least according to his wishes in the last decade of his life. Discovering why he wished it thus has occupied scholars and critics ever since, but we can at least be sure that the order we have had a meaning for the author – something which cannot be said of the English collection most nearly comparable, Shakespeare's. He provided a prefatory sonnet, a division into two parts, and a conclusion; but he also provided a title which cuts across this ordering: he called his poems 'fragmenta' – 'rime sparse' ('scattered verses') in Italian.

The collection appears highly unified (despite a small number of occasional and political poems) because almost all the poems deal with the central event of his personal life, his love for Laura. He tells us that he saw her first on a spring morning, 6 April 1327, in Avignon, and loved her for the rest of his life. She died twenty-one years later, in the morning of the same day, 6 April 1348, of the plague which was raging in the south of France; Petrarch himself was in Verona when he received the news on 19 May. The death of Beatrice, which was likewise pivotal in Dante's *Vita Nuova*, turned Dante to a higher kind of writing; the death of Laura, however, did not deflect Petrarch from writing love sonnets, though it changed their tenor, so that his *Rime* falls into two main parts, the sonnets *in vita* and the sonnets *in morte*, as later editors often subtitled the two sections of MS. Vatican 3195.

We do not know for sure who she was, but it is generally accepted that she was a certain Laura de Sade, wife of a merchant of Avignon, born about 1309 in a nearby village. She may or may not have done the things which the speaker of the *Rime* ascribes to her, but her real existence, and the dates Petrarch gives, seem to be confirmed by a note written on the flyleaf of his own copy of Virgil,[7] a note that cannot have been intended for any eye other than his own, unlike almost everything else that he said about her. And in the great *canzone* to the Virgin which closes the *Rime* there is a moving reference to Laura which in this context it is almost impossible to think false, implying that he had to keep his love secret from her (something contradicted by what is said of her in many of the other poems) because of the social consequences of professing love for a married woman:

> Vergine, tale è terra et posto à in doglia
> lo mio cor, che vivendo in pianto il tenne,
> e de mille miei mali un non sapea;
> e per saperlo pur quel che n'avenne
> fora avvenuto, ch'ogni altra sua voglia
> era a me morte et a lei fama rea.
> (366, ll. 92–7)[8]

> [Virgin, a woman is now dust, and has sunk my soul in grief,
> who while she lived kept it in tears,
> and knew not one of my sufferings;
> and had she known, yet what happened
> would still have happened, for any other desire in her
> would have been death to me, and a stained name to her.][9]

But, whatever the relationship, Petrarch took no care to reveal it except in the extended fictionalising of his literary works; and it is a measure of the gap between art and life that he was the father of two illegitimate children – one of them, his daughter Francesca, a dearly loved and lifelong companion – and we do not even know the names of the women who bore them.[10]

He began writing sonnets in the 1330s, but the great sonnet which opens the *Rime* was written much later, around 1350, so that its judgement that these poems are 'rime sparse' or 'fragmenta' is that of the mature poet after Laura's death. It is a comment on his sense of both his experiences and his presentation of them that needs explanation. Here is his prefatory sonnet, *Rime* 1:

> Voi ch'ascoltate in rime sparse il suono
> di quei sospiri ond'io nudriva 'l core
> in sul mio primo giovenile errore,
> quand' era in parte altr'uom da quel ch'i'sono:
> del vario stile in ch'io piango e ragiono
> fra le vane speranze e 'l van dolore,
> ove sia chi per prova intenda amore,
> spero trovar pietà, non che perdono.

Ma ben vegg'io or sì come al popol tutto
favola fui gran tempo, onde sovente
di me medesmo meco mi vergogno:
e del mio vaneggiar vergogna è 'l frutto,
e 'l pentersi, e 'l consoscer chiarmente
che quanto piace al mondo è breve sogno.

[You who hear in scattered poems the sound of those sighs on which I used to feed my heart, during my first youthful error, when I was in part a different man from what I am now:

for the varying style in which I weep and discourse, between vain hope and vain grief, where there is someone who by experience understands love, I hope to find pity, not forgiveness.

But well do I see now how to all the crowd I was a byword for a long time, for which often I in myself am ashamed of my own self:

and of my delirium, shame is the fruit, and repentance, and the clear understanding that whatever pleases on earth is a brief dream.]

This very assured sonnet, whose detailed construction we shall examine in a moment, begins with the traditional 'voi che . . .' apostrophe often used by Duecento sonneteers, creating a speaker who pleads before a jury: at its centre is an appeal for pity (1. 8), and it closes with a profession of repentance and wisdom gained – a wholly traditional forensic construction. The 'crime', however, is something not in the sonnet itself: it is the collection of poems following it, for which the speaker asks for pity, if not forgiveness; or, more exactly, for the swinging that occurs in them between two kinds of utterance, lamenting ('piango') and rational discourse ('ragiono'). This alternation has arisen from an alternation in the speaker's state in his past, a swinging between grief (which causes lamenting) and vain hope (which causes false rationalising). What offends, apparently, is that the /I/ whom this speaker presents as his own past self was incoherent: his personality did not stabilise, but swung between opposed states, and therefore his speech did not stabilise either. What we will read (we are to understand) will be accounts of these moments of feeling and thinking at odds with one another, accounts described in short utterances also at odds with one another, not cohering narratively or thematically – 'rime sparse', in fact.

Further, this instability of the psyche and of the tongue which is the subject of the octave leads to further incoherence in the sestet: 'di me medesmo meco mi vergogno', a line in which the present self is ashamed of and thus at odds with the past self; the repeated 'me/mi' accentuates this fragmentation of the /I/. The present self, the /I-that-is/, may now have clear knowledge, but it is still linked to the past self, the one which was guilty of 'vaneggiar' ('raving, delirium') by repentance, and so repeats in the present the duality of lamenting and reasoning: 'pentersi' ('repenting') and 'conoscer' ('knowing') parallel in the present the alternation of the self in the past. The poem, despite its fluency and its epigrammatic and confident ending, is dominated by the figure of antithesis, alternation of opposed states.

This is what Italian critics call Petrarch's *dissidio* ('variance', 'contradiction'), and it is the first time in European literature that such instability, both psychic and rhetorical, is announced as the principle of a work of poesis. Dante's *Vita Nuova*, Augustine's *Confessions* and Boethius' *Consolation of Philosophy* may deal with unstable states of mind, but the texts themselves do not proclaim it as a principle of style and construction. It is the brevity of the sonnet which makes this possible here. Petrarch has grasped that the sonnet (which dominates the *Rime*), whether operating as discursive or epiphanic, is momentary, enclosing the narrated experience in a box that is discontinuous with other boxes. Even the longer poems, the great *canzoni*, which in themselves often show marvellously subtle development and coherence, are still subsumed into a larger structure of 'fragmenta' and are only moments of resolution in an unstable inner cosmos. The sonnet, the perfection of momentary equilibrium, is the dominant form here.

Equilibrium in earlier sonnets is usually the result of argumentative coherence, working through statement to development and conclusion, or of what I have previously called 'straightforwardness', the musical and verbal clarity favoured by the *stilnovisti*. Petrarch can have either of these things if he chooses, and many of his sonnets are not in those ways a sophistication of his predecessors'. But the sonnet just quoted shows a feature distinctively his own: what the metrist Mario Fubini has called his 'architectonic' sense.[11] Controlling all the rocking antitheses in the octave is a long smooth movement of one sentence, eight lines long: every time a line appears to be making a single point, the syntax carries the reader across to the next one, sometimes with an actual enjambment, sometimes just with a continuation of the thought:

> . . . il suono
> di quei sospiri . . .
> . . . 'l core
> in sul mio primo giovenile errore
> quand' era. . . .

Even the break between the first and second quatrains is countered by the syntax, for the first four lines are, formally, just an expanded noun phrase, developing the pronoun 'Voi': the completion comes only in the second quatrain, with the sense that it is '[from] you who hear . . . [that] I hope to find pity . . .'. The sestet is broken more definitely into two tercets, but each of these runs through in a single sentence. This is a fluid movement, not the point-by-point discursive development of, say, Guittone. Petrarch's syntax winds through his sonnets, straightforward in that he makes little use of inversion to disturb normal word order, but continually crossing the line, quatrain and tercet boundaries. (He almost always respects the major break between octave and sestet.)

Into this smooth and generous movement enters, from time to time, his *dissidio*. Often when he seems to be presenting simply a moment of intense feeling, with that clear musicality which he learnt from the *stilnovisti*, something more is done, and the sonnet flexes a little under a new pressure:

> Erano i capei d'oro a l'aura sparsi,
> che'n mille dolci nodi gli avolgea,
> e 'l vago lume oltra misura ardea
> di quei begli occhi, ch'or ne son sì scarsi;
> e'l viso di pietosi color farsi
> (non so se vero o falso) mi parea:
> i' che l'esca amorosa al letto avea,
> qual meraviglia se di subito arsi?
> Non era l'andar suo cosa mortale,
> ma d'angelica forma, et le parole
> sonavan altro che pur voce umana:
> uno spirto celeste, un vivo sole
> fu quel ch'i'vidi; e se non fosse or tale,
> piaga per allentar d'arco non sana. (90)

[Her golden hair was spread to the breeze, which twisted it in a thousand sweet curls, and the lovely light glowed unstintingly in those fair eyes, which now are so reluctant to give it;

and her face seemed to me (truly or falsely, I know not) to take on the colours of pity; I who had love's tinder in my breast – what wonder if I suddenly took fire?

She walked not like a mortal being, but like one in angel's guise, and her words sounded not like a mere human voice:

a heavenly spirit, a living sun was what I beheld; and should she not be such now, the wound is not healed by unstringing the bow.]

The effortless music of the first quatrain, with its lexis of light and colour; the recognition of the angelic experience, and the effect of love blazing up within the lover – all these are familiar; the structure of the sonnet, too, seems to control the experience as we should expect, moving from the hair and the eyes to the moment when the eyes see the lover, and the face alters colour; then the first tercet records the effect of her passing, and the last sums up the meaning of the vision. But into this epiphany, so musical and controlled, there has been inserted a counter-movement: almost as an afterthought in the first quatrain comes 'ch'or ne son sì scarsi' ('that now are so reluctant to give it'), and this is echoed, just as the sonnet seems about to end on a note of highest praise ('un vivo sole', 'a living sun'), by what again is almost an afterthought: 'e se non fosse or tale' ('and should she not be such now'). The tiny word 'or' ('now'), twice almost unheard, brings in another time and another state of being: that which was may not be now – and may not even have been then, as the parenthesis, the third syntactic extra in the poem, points out. The experience is rendered in its full beauty, but it is simultaneously undercut: the structure is ordered, and simultaneously disordered (note how the last 'afterthought' actually cuts off the vision in the midst of a line: l. 13). The thought is achieved, the sonnet ends on a generalising note with a semi-proverb, but even there the proverb comes from the semantic field of violence, alien to the whole field of the rest of the poem. It is not, perhaps, until a really skilled sonneteer begins to disturb the structure of the sonnet that one realises – as in reading the comic sonnets of Cecco Angiolieri[12] – how very powerful the sonnet frame is. It will continue to bestow a sense of order achieved even while all sorts of disturbances are taking place within it – perhaps because it is, however written, always short enough to be seen at once by the eye, the reader registers a sense of completeness *before* tackling the complications inside it. It is superbly fitted to be a point of momentary lucidity for the self in turmoil; and so Petrarch often used it.

With so much ability to vary movement within the standard sonnet, Petrarch seems to have felt no need to use any of its variants: when he wanted a change, he used a *ballata* or a madrigal. All of his sonnets are of fourteen standard lines, and all make a distinction between octave and sestet – some very few excepted where the first tercet belongs to the octave. In rhymeschemes, overwhelmingly he favoured what was by his time the normal octave, ABBA ABBA, which he uses in 303 out of 317 sonnets. Twelve have the more primitive ABAB ABAB, and two ABAB BAAB. In the sestet, as there was less agreement generally, Petrarch appears to favour almost equally CDE CDE (115) and CDCDCD (108), with 66 arranged CDEDCE. He showed no special liking for *rime rovesciate* ('upside-down rhymes', CDEEDC); perhaps, with his natural tendency to flow over the internal boundaries of the sonnet, he found it too rigid.

This, then, is the 'Petrarchan' sonnet, invented about 1235 and passed to Petrarch through a series of developments in the thirteenth century: two quatrains and two tercets, marked always by a change of rhyme and nearly always by a break in syntax and thought at the 'turn' ('*volta*') between octave and sestet. The Petrarchan sonnet *sequence*, anticipated by Dante in the *Vita Nuova* but not clearly established, is a collection consisting mainly of sonnets, but punctuated by *canzoni* and with a small number of *ballate* and madrigals at irregular intervals. This is the frame which Petrarch put round the expressive self, and passed on to the admiring gaze of his successors.

But his control of movement and discourse within that frame, remarkable though it is, would not make him great without his accompanying mastery of metaphor. Metaphor is of course basic to all poesis, in prose or verse, and is certainly not peculiar to the sonnet: if it is illustrated here constantly with reference to sonnets, remember that the great *canzoni* also display it, just as Shakespeare's sonnets are remarkable for a metaphorical density and complexity that is also found in his plays. But the brevity of the sonnet does have effect upon the kind of metaphorising that can happen in it. Large wardrobes will not fit small rooms, and epic similes, allegories or extended conceits are very difficult to abridge to sonnet length; conversely the sonnet favours compact forms of metaphorical activity, such as symbolism and rapid allusion, rather than detailed mythical narration.

Metaphor is a kind of magic which transforms the world, by enabling objects to be other than they are; it is a-logical, and synthetic rather than analytic. Thus it naturally belongs, in the history of the sonnet, to the epiphanic side of self-presentation rather than to the discursive, public side. Of course metaphor is one of the resources of the good discursive speaker, and many metaphors are used in discursive sonnets, but the full power of metaphor works against the world of empirical observation and analysis. Simile, which is a kind of relaxed metaphor, denotes one of the elements of the metaphor by a comparative word:

> *Like as* the waves make toward the pebbled shore,
> *so* do our minutes hasten toward their end . . .
> (Shakespeare, Sonnet 60)

thus making it clear which element is the 'real' subject of our attention ('minutes'); and the binary nature of the simile fits easily into the sonnet, for example by having the octave given to 'like' and the sestet to 'so'. The firm placing of whatever words are used to mark the comparison ('just as', 'even as', 'so', 'thus', 'in like fashion', etc.) asserts discursive control. Metaphor, on the other hand, offers equivalences or identities – A *is* X, not just *like* X – and so slips out of the control of partition and comparison, and offers transformation or metamorphosis of a much more fluid kind. This leads into the world of myth, in which transformations of persons and physical objects are constantly offered to explain natural or psychological processes. Thus by simile love can be compared to an arrow in the heart: once it is said to *be* an arrow in the heart, we look for an archer, and Cupid appears in a mythical relation to Psyche, the soul – whence, of course, Petrarch's oblique metaphor in *Rime* 90, quoted above, of his lady, now perhaps indifferent to him, as an unstrung bow.

Petrarch accepted the stilnovistic premiss that love transforms one's vision of things, but because of the circumstances of his own life he was able to metaphorise an entire landscape to express himself, or his selves, in a way that had not been done before.[13] In 1337 he bought a small house in a deep and quite secluded valley north of Avignon, by the waters of the River Sorgue, at Vaucluse ('vallis clausa', the 'closed valley'), where he lived intermittently till 1351. (His final home, Arquà in the Eugenaean Hills of northern Italy, also gave him isolation and natural beauty.) His Vaucluse retreat gave him another side of his personality to develop, that of the scholarly recluse, turning his back on fruitless love and the corruption of the world to live close to nature; and of most relevance to the *Rime*, it gave him, with its fertile meadows, sunlit woods, steep cliffs and running waters, a real landscape to act both as backcloth and source of metaphor. For this he could have found precedent in the poems of Horace, Catullus, Propertius and other Latin poets, including his beloved Virgil; but no Italian poet before him had attempted to project a self into a natural landscape.

A single sonnet has no room for backgrounds, or elaborate circumstances or classical parallels: whatever features of landscape it takes must be rapidly connected with the life of the self that speaks it, as here, in *Rime* 219: what appears to be a Provençal *alba*, a song of awakening at dawn ('l'alba', 'l'aube'), becomes a complicated Ovidian metamorphosis, as the /I/ is drawn into a landscape at once natural and mythical:

Il cantar novo e 'l pianger delli augelli
in sul dì fanno retentir le valli,
e 'l mormorar de' liquidi cristalli
giù per lucidi freschi rivi et snelli.
  Quella ch'à neve il volto, oro i capelli,
nel cui amor non fur mai inganni né falli,
destami al suon delli amorosi balli,
pettinando al suo vecchio i bianchi velli.
  Così mi sveglio a salutar l'aurora
e 'l sol ch'è seco, e più l'altro ond'io fui
ne' primi anni sbagliato, e son ancora.
  I' gli ò veduti alcun giorno ambedui
levarsi insieme, e 'n un punto e 'n un ora
quel far le stelle, e questo sparir lui. (219)

[The new singing and lamenting of the birds at daybreak makes the valleys echo, as does the murmuring of liquid crystal down in bright, fresh and rapid streams.

She whose face is of snow, whose hair is of gold, she in whom love was never yet deceitful nor false, wakes me with the melody of her amorous dance, combing the white hairs of her aged husband.

Thus I wake and greet the dawn, and the sun that comes with it, and more so that other sun by which I was dazzled in my early years, and am still.

Some days I have seen them both rise together, and in one hour, in one moment, have seen him make the stars, the other make him, disappear.]

The apparently conventional opening of the first quatrain is disturbed by the single word 'pianger' ('weeping') – why should the birds *weep* at dawn? – to which we shall come back; with the second quatrain, we move into the world of Ovid's *Metamorphoses*.[14] The Lady of the snowy face and golden hair is Aurora, immortal goddess of the dawn (because first the sky whitens and then behind come the golden streamers of the sun, but the sonnet has no space to explain all this . . .). She is also the lover of the aged Tithonus, whose fate it was, for love of his dawn goddess, to grow ever older without dying (Petrarch lived thirty years after his Laura died), and to whom, every evening, she faithfully returned. With Aurora comes the sun: and she has not just one adorer in him, but two, as the speaker also rises to greet her, in response to her 'amorous dances'. The beautifully liquid phrase 'a*l* suon de*ll*i amorosi ba*ll*i' shows what happens when there is a shift from the natural to the mythical: what does it describe? It can only refer to the birdsong and water murmurs, since the dawn as such has no sound, and there is a complicated suggestion in 'balli' ('dances') that the birds are courtly musicians playing Aurora on to the floor of day – had this been elaborated, it would have been tedious, but left at the level of suggestion it is magical. But already the apparently natural scene with which the sonnet opens has moved into a mythical and fantastic world.

The sestet opens with the discursive marker 'così' ('thus', 'so'), the correlative of 'siccome' or 'come' ('like', 'as'), used to mark the two halves of a simile. Here there is no correlative for 'così' – to what or whom is the awakening lover comparing himself? The octave/sestet pairing suggests that the lover is like the birds (and this sonnet would then be *his* 'cantar novo' ('new song'); but there is also the suggestion that 'così' follows 'suo vecchio' ('her aged husband'), who sees Aurora depart in the morning; this is reinforced by 'et son ancora' ('and I still am [dazzled by her]') which marks the speaker as one who, like Tithonus, has loved for a long time. This instance may serve to mark a general habit of Petrarch's mind: while he can be pedantically strict, his normal employment of connectives, like 'così', relaxed their strict logicality, to allow in multiple meanings, as here. He is particularly fond of the loose Italian conjunction 'ché', which can be used like the English 'for' to mean anything between 'because' and 'and'. The pressure of metaphor, we might say, slackens the pressure of dialectic, like a root cracking a paving slab.

To return to the sonnet: in this now wholly magical world, transformed by light, this dawn has a second sun, more glorious than the one that Aurora heralds. Long use by the *stilnovisti* of the sun makes it needless for Petrarch to explain that it means his lady's eyes ('My mistress' eyes', said Shakespeare in an anti-Petrarchan moment, 'are nothing like the sun . . .'); and this sun is bright enough to make the Auroran sun disappear, as it previously had made the stars vanish with the coming of day. There is probably a delicate pun here: 'Laura/ l'aurora'. When, finally, the involved parallel between Aurora/the sun/ Tithonus/the birds and Laura/her eyes/the lover/the speaker has been disentangled from what mimics the sleepy slurred words of a man getting out of bed to look at the sky, then, and only then, can we understand why the birds *weep* – they are types of the speaker, whose sonnet is like their 'novo cantar . . . in sul dì' ('new song to the day'), and the liquid crystal of the streams represents his tears/his words, emphasised by the extreme liquidity of the rhymes in the octave (-elli/-alli). What, then, appeared to be in the first quatrain a simple description of a daybreak in Vaucluse has become by the end an extended metaphor for the poetry of the enunciating speaker, who has made 'retentir le valli' ('the vales echo') with his poetry for years. Compact, allusive, difficult, casually learned, melodious, suggestive of the speaking voice and powerfully plangent, this is lyric poetry of a density that looks forward to Yeats.

It is a feature of the landscape of a sonnet sequence that it is discontinuous: objects appear and vanish, as in dreams, though they may as in dreams recur. Petrarch, in one of the longer *canzoni* which punctuate the *Rime*, bore witness to the way in which his desires kept transforming the landscape, now here, now there, making it (in his verse) metaphorical of Laura:

> I' l'ò più volte (or chi fia che mi creda?)
> ne l'acqua chiara et sopra l'erba verde
> veduto viva, et nel troncon d'un faggio
> e 'n bianca nube, sì fatta che Leda
> avria ben detto che sua figlia perde
> come stella che 'l sol copre col raggio;
> e quanto in più selvaggio
> loco mi trovo e 'n più deserto lido
> tanto più bella il mio pensier l'adombra.
> Poi quando il vero sgombra
> quel dolce error, pur lì medesmo assido
> me freddo, pietra morta in pietra viva,
> in guisa d'un uom che pensi et pianga et scriva.
> (129, ll. 40–52)

[Many times I have (will anyone believe me?)
seen her alive in the clear water, on the green grass,
in the trunk of a beech tree,
in a white cloud, so formed that Leda
would surely have said that her daughter* paled *Helen of Troy*
like a star which the sun's beams eclipse;
and the wilder the place I am in, the more deserted,
the more lovely does my thought shadow her forth.
Then when truth banishes
that sweet illusion, there I sit down, even there,
a cold, dead stone upon a living stone,
in the guise of a man who thinks, and weeps, and writes.]

But the appearance in earlier parts of the collection of motifs and themes that occur later (like the paling of the stars here and in *Rime* 219) and the persistence of early motifs into the later verse are ways in which Petrarch, continuously revising and rearranging, presents the self as a continuum, without resorting to anything that might be called a chronology or an autobiography of his love. Certainly, the collection is punctuated by poems bearing dates (30, 50, 62, 79, 101, 107, 118, 122, 145, 221, 266, 271, 278, 364) ranging from 1334 to 1358, and only two of these (145, 266) are out of sequence; but the placing and dating are too irregular to mark any kind of phasing of his long devotion. He also decided to include poems not connected with Laura at all – poems of politics and friendship – and the effect of these diversions directed to other ends is to break any narrative sense of self-development over more than very small groups of sonnets, and leave only the continuum of a self imaged through metaphors of loss and desire.

As the sequence advances, and after the death of Laura (267), the self that speaks becomes increasingly penitent: Laura, whom Petrarch imagines in the second part of the *Rime* as returning from Heaven to speak consolingly to him, as she never could in life, becomes the *donna angelicata*, pointing him towards his final rest, in the sight of her in Heaven. The self is imaged as a point of anguish, of *dissidio* in between a past now gone and a future desired but not yet come. The present self is simply a restless consciousness caught between regret and anticipation. When this is enunciated with Petrarch's rhetorical control and musical cadence,[15] the result is the kind of plangent eloquence that later writers so much admired, but could very seldom equal:

Da' più belli occhi, et dal più chiaro viso
che mai splendesse, et da' più bei capelli
che facean l'oro e'l sol parer men belli,
dal più dolce parlare et dolce riso,

da le man, da le braccia che conquiso
senza moversi avrian quai più rebelli
fur d'Amor mai, da' più bei piedi snelli,
da la persona fatta in paradiso,
  prendean vita i miei spirti; or n'à diletto
il Re celeste, i suoi alati corrieri,
ed io son qui rimaso ignudo et cieco.
  Sol un conforto al le mie pene aspetto:
ch'ella che vede tutt' i miei pensieri
m'impetre grazia ch'i'possa esser seco. (348)

[From those fairest eyes, and from the brightest face that ever shone, and from the most lovely hair, that made gold and the sun seem less fair, from the sweetest speech and the sweetest smile, from the hands, from the arms that without stirring would have conquered those most rebellious against Love, from the fair light feet, from the form fashioned in Paradise,

my spirits once took life: now in them delights the King of Heaven, and his winged messengers, and I am left here, naked and blind.

Only one comfort do I look for in my suffering: that she who sees all my thoughts will win grace for me, that I may be with her.]

Using one of the simplest forms of organisation – the list – and a vocabulary that, with the exception of a few technical religious words, would hardly tax the understanding of a child, Petrarch moves his speaker along a chain of praise, describing, in the octave, all the parts of the body that would be visible in a normally dressed woman; with a casual skill that one will look for in vain among many later sonneteers, he senses the moment when the list might become monotonous, and changes from working with half lines to a flowing three-line clause:

da le braccia che conquiso
senza moversi avrian quai più rebelli
fur d'Amor mai. . . .

It is as if someone walking hesitantly along broke into a canter; and the momentum of praise that builds up is so great that the octave actually overflows into the sestet by half a line ('prendean vita i miei spirti'), as if the speaker cannot stop in time. But the two halves of l. 9 contain the pause that is crucial, and halts the outburst of admiration – the pause between two *times*, the past in 'prendean' ('once took, used to take') and the present, marked by the tiny but often significant word 'or' ('now'). The distance between past and present is the distance between octave and sestet, but also between earth ('qui', 'here') and heaven ('celeste'), and between sight ('più belli occhi', l. 1) and blindness ('cieco', l. 11). The long sentence peaks, as it were, in a glory of praise at 'spirti', and then reverses down into loneliness and blindness.

From the past to the present: what remains can only be the future. Just as, in the opening sonnet of the *Rime*, Petrarch's speaker, addressing his readers, contrasted past and present –

quand'era in parte altr'uom da quel ch'i'sono (1, l. 4)

[when I was, in part, another man from what I am now]

– and then looked to the future:

spero trovar pietà, non che perdono

[I hope to find pity, not pardon]

– so here, after a statement that displays the past, and halts in the present of the speaker, comes a conclusion that takes us and him into the future:

aspetto
ch'ella che vede tutt' i miei pensieri
m'impetre grazia ch'i'possa esser seco.

[I look for [the comfort]
that she, who sees all my thoughts,
will obtain grace for me, that I may be with her.]

The present /I/ is reduced to a single 'punto' of transience between past and future, a negative space that was once filled and may be again: 'ed io son qui rimaso ignudo et cieco'.

In its small fourteen lines, this sonnet distributes a lifetime and eternity: the octave for what was, the first tercet for what is, and the second tercet for what will be. After the last line, after 'esser seco' ('to be with her') there is no more, either of words or of time.

This highly controlled, systematically developed yet seemingly very simple and musical sonnet is, one feels, what the sonneteers of the Duecento might have done if they had had Petrarch's architectonic skill. Another kind of skill is shown in those sonnets which foreground the movement of the mind itself. Here the enunciating self is the subject of its own enunciation: instead of looking from a vantage-point of knowledge (even if that knowledge is nakedness and blindness) at an /I/ who is or was troubled, the speaking self finds its subject matter in the disturbance or difficulty of its own consciousness – something essential to the lyric as the poetry of the inner self, and something which Donne, Hopkins, Herbert and Shakespeare all tried to do, with varying degrees of success. The sonnet of course can never be spontaneous, because the contrivance of the rhymes is too intricate, and the closure at the fourteenth is preordained; but because it is short it can *seem* to be spontaneous, if it looks like a moment's pause for reflection, the self arrested in self-contemplation:

> Io son già stanco di pensar sì come
> i miei pensier in voi stanchi non sono,
> e come vita ancor non abbandono
> per fuggir de' sospir sì grave some;
> e come a dir del viso et del le chiome
> e de' begli occhi ond'io sempre ragiono
> non è mancata mai la lingua e'l suono
> dì e notte chiamando il vostro nome;
> e che' pie' miei non son fiaccati et lassi
> a seguir l'orme vostre in ogni parte,
> perdendo inutilmente tanti passi;
> et onde ven l'inchiostro, onde le carte
> ch'i'vo empiendo di voi (se 'n ciò fallassi,
> colpa d'amor, non già defetto d'arte). (74)

[I am already tired thinking of how my thinking is not tired of you, and how I do not yet give up life to escape so heavy a weight of sighs; and how, in speaking of your face, your hair, your fair eyes, of which I always speak, as yet my tongue and voice have not failed, night and day, calling your name;
and that my feet are not feeble and tired of following your traces everywhere, taking so many steps in vain;
and of the source of the ink, of the paper that I fill with you (if I am wrong in that, the fault is with Love, not with any lack of art).]

From its very colloquial first line through its long rambling chain of dependent clauses, down to the parenthetical afterthought tacked on at the end, this sonnet mimics the weariness it proposes as its first subject. Instead of starting with the phenomena and moving to a conclusion, it starts with the conclusion (I am tired) and moves to the evidence (which is both its own matter and its own manner); it is almost devoid of imagery and metaphors; it has some astonishing lapses of skill ('che [i] piei miei' must be one of the worst sounds it is possible to get out of four words in Italian); and its syntax trails off weakly and apparently inconsequentially (why should he be tired thinking of the source of his *ink*?) into infinitive or participial phrases, and even begins with loose connectives. The entire poem is a mimesis of a self too tired to think straight. But of course the poem actually asserts that the speaker is *not* weary: his thoughts, his tongue, his feet, his very ink and paper are ceaseless in their praise of Laura, and just at the moment when it occurs to him, apparently spontaneously, that writing poetry may be a mistake, the sonnet ends, with immaculate and precise technique, on the word 'arte'. There is no lack of art: even the rambling and riddling first sentence is a very elaborately constructed chiasmus, ABC CBA: son[o]/stanco/pensar: pensier/stanchi/sono.

It should be noted how definitely, even in the above sonnet's mimesis of the rambling mind, Petrarch conceives of his sonnets as *written*. Anyone using the epistolary form in the sonnet, or even compiling a sequence of sonnets, must to some extent have the model of writing present (Cavalcanti once wrote a sonnet 'spoken' by his pen, scissors and penknife),[16] but it remains common practice to locate the /I/ as a speaker, not a writer, even in letters, and as the European sonnet developed its fascination with intense and immediate experience it tended not to activate, except in deliberate and witty metafiction, the reader's knowledge that this voice speaking now was really written long ago. Petrarch, who spent a great deal of his own and of his amanuenses' time copying out sonnets for sending to friends and patrons, and who certainly conceived of the *Rime* as being read by a wide audience, both during his life and after his death, is apt to insist both on the ephemeral immediacy of his speech, which is usually that of the narrated /I/, the /I-that-was/, and also the permanence of the documents that carry that speech, which are prepared by the narrating /I/:

> Benedette le voci tante ch'io
> chiamando il nome de mia donna ò sparte,
> e i sospiri e le lagrime e 'l desio;
> et benedette sian tutte le carte
> ov'io fama l'acquisto, e'l pensier mio,
> ch'è sol di lei sì ch' altra non v'à parte. (61, ll. 9–14)

[Blessed be the many words that I, calling my lady's name, have scattered, with the sighs, and the tears, and the longing; and blessed be all the pages in which I win fame for her, and my thought, which is only of her, so that no lady else has a share in it.]

This duality confirms, as it proclaims throughout the sequence, the status of the sonnet: it is an immediate experience, the sound of a sigh or a tear or an outburst of praise, and therefore fragmentary and ephemeral ('pianger', 'to weep', is a metaphor for speaking) – but it is also, in its written form in rhyme, an object, an artefact which gives pleasure and gains fame, both for the writer and for the lady:

> più volte ò riprovate indarno
> al secol che verrà l'alte bellezze
> pinger cantando . . . (308, ll. 5–8)

[I have often tried, vainly, to paint in song her high beauties for the age to come . . .]

'Pinger', 'to paint', is the graphic, the permanent form of 'pianger', 'to weep'. The eternising function of the verse is something that Petrarch's constant labours on his 'rime sparse' show him to have been well aware of, and it was indeed a recurring topic in Latin praise-poetry: this means that when the narrating self enters its own narrative about the narrated self it does so *sub specie aeternitatis*, with Horace's sense that 'exegi monumentum aere perennius' – 'I have built a monument more lasting than bronze'.[17] In this way the present self, producing the text, is the tomb of the past self, and the sonnet is the epitaph.

The tension between permanence of form ('le carte . . . ov'io fama l'acquisto', 'the pages where I have won her fame') and the immediacy of content ('le voci ch'io . . . ò sparte', 'the words I have scattered') was brilliantly and influentially carried over by Petrarch into the realm of metaphor using, as has been said, the accumulations of metaphors and images that can be built up in a long sequence. The happy accident that his lady was named Laura (if indeed that was her real name, and not a *senhal*[18] bestowed by her admirer) gave Petrarch a network of metaphorical, symbolic and mythical terms which stretches over the whole *Rime*. 'Laura', or 'Lauretta', derives from 'laurus', the laurel or baytree, the tree of Apollo, patron of poets; so that the object of the speaker's love was also the object of the writer's aspiration – the woman Laura and the laurel crown of poetry (Petrarch described himself in the title he supplied for the *Rime* as 'laureatus'). By another happy accident of Italian vocabulary, 'Laura' can be heard and read as 'l'aura', 'the breeze', and also 'l'auro', 'gold'; whereby the laurel can represent both Laura herself and the speaker/poet, since the breeze can stand for Laura and the inspiration of the speaker, and gold for Laura's hair and for Apollo, the sun god, source of poetry and patron of poets. Hence by a dense combination of pun and metaphor the opening of, say, *Rime* 196 is particularly rich in meaning:

> L'aura serena che fra verdi fronde
> mormorando a ferir nel volto viemme . . . (196, ll. 1–2)
>
> [The calm breeze that through the green leaves
> comes murmuring to strike my face . . .]

or

> [Laura, in her serenity, who comes among the green leaves
> with whispered speech to strike my attention . . .]

or

> [The exalted laurel (poetry) that speaks gently among its green
> fronds (poems) and comes to strike my attention . . .]

The translator can only select one possibility, but the pun constantly merges the self and its object, as in the next sonnet (197) which refers to

L'aura celeste che 'n quel verde lauro
spira . . . (197, ll. 1–2)

[The heavenly breeze that breathes in that green laurel . . .]

– at once Laura herself, her influence on her lover, and the poetry that records her and it. (These puns are specific to Italian, but English poets in their turn made much of 'heart/hart', 'deer/dear' and 'I/eye/aye'.)

The reader is constantly aware, as these images accumulate and reiterate through the *Rime*, of both the self that weeps and the self that writes, the self caught in the transience of human love (Laura) and the self that in some measure controls that (*lauro*), the self that cannot speak for weeping and the self from which

parole e opre
escon sì fatte allor ch'io spero
farmi immortal, perche la carne moia. (75, ll. 95–6)

[emerge words and works
so made that I now hope
to become immortal, though my flesh die.]

Here Petrarch created, not just in single sonnets but by reiteration and reinforcement through the whole *Rime*, one of the richest poetic fields for representing the self ever mapped by a single poet: if narrower than Shakespeare's, less abstract than Dante's, more accessible and less idiosyncratic than Blake's, Petrarch's lexis signifies a natural world that is also the internal world of desire – particularly the desire of beauty and the pain and fear of losing it – and gave to European poetry a powerful resource of expression. The sonnet which he inherited carried an /I/ with a definite social focus: turned towards the Lady, or a friend, to the community or even to Love himself, the speaker is eloquent in the stance of pleading or praising or lamenting; and this does not disappear when Petrarch begins to insist upon the inarticulate, upon the sigh and the tear. But by concentrating upon the irrational, the inarticulate manifestations of desire and loss and hope, rather than upon the rational, he made the sonnet, as he said himself, 'the voice of a sigh': its momentary, visionary, epiphanic quality, learnt from the *stilnovisti*, he harnessed to the expression of the inexpressible inner desire or anguish, relying upon the strictness of the sonnet's form (which he kept very conventional) to control the looseness of emotion turned to metaphor. Though many of the most intricate metaphors are laid up in the great *canzoni* and sestinas of the collection, the sonnets can and do draw upon this reservoir of imagery, mirroring in their smaller surfaces and depths the great and powerful images of self that Petrarch established for all the centuries to come as a most sensitive and clear rendering of human life in its most intense engagement with beauty – of woman, of art, of God. Out of a substratum of courtly eloquence, and out of a small form whose very versatility was, when he began to write, dissipating its energies, his steady devotion, as he very truly said, made him

> sì alto salire
> . . . che tra caldi ingegni ferve
> il suo nome, et de' suoi detti conserve
> si fanno con diletto in alcun loco,
> ch'or saria forse un roco
> mormorador dei corti, un uom del vulgo! (360, ll. 112–17)

> [rise so high
> . . . that among brilliant minds shines
> his name, and collections of his poems
> are made with pleasure here and there,
> who now, perhaps, would be a rough
> whisperer of the courts, lost in the common throng!]

5

THE FORTUNATE ISLES: THE SONNET MOVES ABROAD

For more than sixty years after the death of Petrarch, the sonnet remained the possession of the Italian language and culture, and did not become established in other European countries until the sixteenth century, almost a century and a half from Petrarch's death in 1374. The reasons why things fail to happen in literature are hard to find; but a mystery there certainly is, why a form which continued to be popular in the most prosperous and cultivated country in Europe, backed by the authority of a writer who, if he owed his reputation mainly to his Latin works, was nevertheless widely read and imitated for his vernacular ones, had to wait so long for cultivation elsewhere. From the two non-Italian writers who first made contact with the sonnet, one can suggest – no more than that – why the sonnet did not at once transplant. These are Geoffrey Chaucer (1340–99) who translated a sonnet of Petrarch into English, but not into sonnet form, and the Marqués de Santillana, Inigo Lopez de Mendoza (1398–1458), who some time between 1438 and his death wrote forty-two sonnets in Spanish, avowing in the title of the collection that they were 'sonetos fechos al italico modo' – sonnets made in the Italian style. Chaucer having declined to use the sonnet form, the Marqués has the credit of writing the first sonnet outside Italy, sixty years after Petrarch's death. Then again a lull; and not until the 1520s did the sonnet become established in Britain, France and Spain.

Chaucer's encounter with Petrarch's *Rime* is limited to the translation of one sonnet, 'S'amor non è, che dunque è quel ch'io sento?' (*Rime* 132), in the course of the first book of his *Troilus and Criseyde* (ll. 400–20). When Troilus is aware that he is affected powerfully by Criseyde, he speaks a version of one of Petrarch's self-realisations, probably written (in its final version) by Petrarch about 1366:

> If no love is, O God, what fele I so?
> And if love is, what thing and which is he?
> If love be good, from whennes cometh my woo?
> If it be wikke, a wonder thynketh me,

When every torment and adversite
That cometh of hym, may to me savory thinke,
For ay thurst I, the more that ich it drinke.

And if that at myn owen lust I brenne,
From whennes cometh my wailing and my pleynte?
If harm agree me, whereto pleyne I thenne?
I noot, ne whi unwery that I feynte.
O quike death, o swete harm so queynte,
How may of the in me swich quantite,
But if that I consente that it be?

And if that I consente, I wrongfully
Compleyne, Iwis. Thus possed to and fro,
Al stereless within a boot am I
Amydde the see, betwixen windes two,
That in contrarie stonden ever mo.
Allas! what is this wondre maladie?
For hete of cold, for cold of hete, I dye.

Chaucer's three seven-line stanzas in rhyme-royal (ABABBCC) are taken from Petrarch's single sonnet 132:

S'amor non è, che dunque è quel ch'io sento?
Ma s'egli è amor, per Dio, che cosa e quale?
Se bona, ond'è l'effetto aspro mortale?
Se ria, ond'è si dolce ogni tormento?
S'a mia voglia ardo, ond'è 'l pianto e lamento?
s'a mal mio grado, il lamentar che vale?
O viva morte, o dilettoso male,
come puoi tanto in me s'io nol consento?
  Et s'io'l consento, a gran torto mi doglio.
Fra si contrari venti in frale barca
mi trovo in alto mar senza governo,
  si lieve di saver, d'error si carca,
ch'i'medesmo non so quel ch'io mi voglio,
e tremo a mezza state, ardendo il verno.

One of Petrarch's 'sighs', the /I/ represented as a confusion of perceptions and feelings, has been transferred to a character in a narrative poem who is, dramatically, at just such a point as Petrarch might have been at the start of his adoration of Laura. Now, while it is fairly certain that Chaucer was working from an Italian manuscript of the poem, we do not know how he obtained it,[1] or what was in it – all, some or only one of Petrarch's poems, with or without other sonnets, with or without Petrarch's name attached. Since this sonnet is one of the more unusual ones in which the ninth line belongs conceptually to the octave rather than being the first line of a new development, he might not even have recognised what the form was; but he does seem to echo Petrarch's sectioning in his own 21 lines, thus: 4 to 7; 4 to 7; 4 and 2 to 5 and 2. His knowledge of Italian, which he had perhaps picked up in London during his work as a controller of Customs, and because of which he was probably selected as one of the King's envoys to Genoa in 1372–3,[2] was enough to enable him to use the works of Dante and Boccaccio, but was by no means fluent, if the misunderstandings in his 'translation' are anything to go by.[3] Hence, if we feel like blaming him for failing to invent the English sonnet, we must remember that he may not have known exactly what a sonnet was.

But, if he did know, why might he have ignored it after this one attempt? Perhaps there is a clue in his handling of Petrarch's very first line: 'S'amor non è, che dunque è quel ch'io sento?' The run of this first line is 'Se quel ch'io sento non è amor, che dunque è?' ('If what I feel is not love, then what is it?'), to which the second line replies 'ma s'egli è amor . . .' ('but if it is love . . .'). Chaucer translates the first four words much more absolutely, though in themselves quite correctly: 'S'amor non è' becomes 'If no love is' – i.e. 'If love does not exist . . .'. He then has to mistranslate the reply in the second line, and give us 'And if love is'. The whole opening becomes a metaphysical inquiry into the existence of love, instead of what it is in the original, namely, an anguished query about the nature of what the speaker is actually feeling. So it continues: when Petrarch deploys his 'if good/if bad' antithesis (ll. 3–4), he intends to specify the opposed emotional effects crisply – 'aspro mortale' ('bitter and deadly') and 'dolce' ('sweet'); Chaucer, who has the extra lines to expand at this point, introduces the phrase 'that cometh of hym', for which there is no equivalent in the Italian, and this again suggests a metaphysical dimension, in which mankind receives afflictions from on high. Again, in the last stanza of Chaucer's version, he fastens upon Petrarch's metaphor of the drifting boat, which had always had a general moral application to man's error in the world, but he again strengthens the sense of the individual's helplessness by omitting 'si lieve di saver, d'error si carca' ('so light in knowledge, so loaded with error') and changing 'ch'i'medesmo non so quel ch'io mi voglio' ('that I myself do not know what I want for myself') into the much more externally directed 'Allas! what is this wondre maladie?'

Working, then, with a sonnet which was in the original a sonnet of complaint, but a complaint of personal anguish and confusion, he strengthens its metaphysical puzzlement, and reduces or omits the introspective elements. It is worth recalling that *Troilus and Criseyde*, for all its sensitivity to the lovers' emotions and sufferings, is a medieval tragedy, not a modern one, and Chaucer's rendering of Petrarch pulls in that direction, and away from the valuation of individual experience. He seems to have engaged with a Petrarchan form whose structure he observed, but whose characteristically Petrarchan drive he chose to divert back into what he himself called 'pleynt', that is, the moral protest of man faced by the hostile forces of the universe. He could not, of course, have used a fourteen-line stanza in the middle of *Troilus and Criseyde*, but he was prepared elsewhere to experiment with verse forms, and since he did not experiment with the form of the sonnet the conclusion must be that the drive of the sonnet as he knew it – maybe only in this single example – did not suit his narrative and moralising cast of mind: when he did encounter Petrarch's lyric /I/, he read it as the /I/ of medieval *pleynt*, which belonged, for him, in a narrative and didactic structure.

Rather different was the reaction of the Marqués de Santillana, a man of a no less moralistic cast of mind, but from a court and a culture much more exposed to Italian influence. Though the royal and ducal courts of Italy and Spain were frequently at odds in the fifteenth century, there was nevertheless much cultural contact between them, as there was between them both and France: the kind of contacts that move uneasily in the wake of political and military manoeuvres, as French, Spaniards and native Italians struggled for control of various parts of the Italian peninsula. The Aragonese rulers, to whom the Marqués owed allegiance, had a power base in Naples for many decades.

Where Chaucer saw in Petrarch only a convenient instance of 'pleynt', his Troilus the victim, like Everyman, of an unstable and irregular cosmos, the Marqués seems to have found rather more to his purpose as a fifteenth-century courtier. In taking the Italian sonnet across into his own vernacular, he used its space not only for 'pleynt', but also for praise and for passion – a triad to which I shall return in discussing the sonnets of Sir Thomas Wyatt, who as a courtier rather similarly placed in the 1520s in England took the Italian sonnet into his vernacular in much the same way. Not all courtiers wrote sonnets, but from the mid-fifteenth century onwards the sonnet was very closely linked to court culture and to the presentation of a courtly voice in a way that would not have surprised the officials of the court of Frederick II, but would have startled Dante, and perhaps seemed trivial to Petrarch, who congratulated himself precisely for having risen above the level of 'un roco mormorador dei corti', a rough whisperer of the court.

The fifteenth century saw the rise and establishment of a new kind of power centre which spread its patterns throughout Europe over the next century as well: what the Italian scholar Carlo Muscetta has called 'the shift from *signories* to *principates*':

> The shift from Signories to Principates during the Quattrocento was reflected in the formation of a culture organised in major

> regional centres with well marked linguistic and literary characteristics, but yet aspiring towards a national literature through impulses that become even stronger in the following century, in proportion as, among the intellectual elite, there was reborn the feeling and the ideal of national unity in reaction to foreign invasions and to the wars between French and Spaniards, who were fighting to control the peninsula.[4]

The sonnet was invented by the courtiers of a principate, that of Frederick II, in the thirteenth century; it passed to the Italian signories, and became the voice of the articulate citizens of the city states; in Petrarch it found a master who was neither citizen nor courtier, but uneasily proud of both national eloquence and individual independence; then, as the comparative neglect of Petrarch's *Rime* in the century after his death suggests, it might have died out, had not the rise of courtly centres in Italy and elsewhere found a new, or perhaps a revived, use for its brief but decisive form.

The Marqués referred twice to Petrarch, once as poet laureate, and once as the poet who during his stay at the court of King Robert of Naples composed 'many of his works, both Latin and vernacular: among others . . . his eclogues, and many sonnets, particularly the one which refers to the death of that king, which begins, "Rotta è l'alta colonna e'l verde lauro" ' (i.e., *Rime* 269). He is wrong, both about the sonnets in general and about this sonnet in particular,[5] but the remark does show that he thought of Petrarch as a court poet like himself. Whether he speaks to his king, his mistress or to the world in general, his voice is that of the courtier, one who affirms his worth by his eloquence, but always looks up towards the sources of power:

> Calla la pluma e luze la espada
> en vuestra mano, rey muy virtuoso:
> vuestra exçellencia non es memorada
> e Caliope fuelga e a reposo.
> Yo plago e lloro non ser comendada
> vuestra eminençia e nombre famoso,
> e redarguyo la mente pesada
> de los biuientes, non poco enojoso . . . (13, ll. 1–8)[6]

> [Silent is the pen, and the sword flashes in your hand, most virtuous King: your excellence is not remembered, and the Muse is free, and rests. I lament and bewail the scanty commendation of your eminence and renown, and dismiss the stolid minds of the living, with no little anger . . .]

> ¡ O dulçe esguarde, vida et honor mia,
> segunda Helena, templo de beldad,

so cuya mano, mando e señoria
es el arbitrio mio e voluntad! . . . (8, ll. 1–4)

[O sweet wonder, my life and honour, second Helen, temple of beauty, under whose hand, command and governance is my judgement and will! . . .]

En el próspero tiempo las serenas
plañen e lloran reçelando el mal;
en el aduerso, ledas cantilenas
cantan e atienden el buen temporal.
Mas, ¿qué será de mí, que las mis penas,
cuytas, trabajos e langor mortal
jamás alternan nin son punto ajenas,
sea destino or curso fatal? (21, ll. 1–8)

[In fair weather the Sirens weep and lament, fearing ill; in foul weather, they sing glad songs, awaiting the fortunate tempest; but what shall become of me, for my pains, cares, travail and mortal weariness never vary, nor change at all, whether by fate or lethal chance?]

Though he had no immediate successors in Spain, this is a voice from a world of power relations that found an echo in every European court, and that fitted the adoration of a mistress into the matrix of competition for favour and reward.

The natural sympathy of historians and literary scholars in the last two centuries for republicanism, as exhibited in the signories of Italy, has tended to create a dark image of the despots who created principates in their place, or established new dynasties in relatively minor centres. The great cultural historian Jacob Burckhardt, who was simultaneously critical of and attracted by the figure of the despotic ruler, advanced the concept of 'the state as work of art': when we recall that these states were often towns of no more than twenty thousand to fifty thousand people, including outlying villages under the town's protection, it is possible to see that one man (or woman, since there were many formidably capable women in princely positions) could almost literally construct a state, rebuilding and decorating the town around its central palace, financing and patronising its activities, as Federigo da Montefeltro did in Urbino by a long and profitable career as a mercenary commander, and appointing its officials, who themselves would build, and bestow patronage. The Montefeltri in Urbino, the Este family of Ferrara, the Gonzagas of Mantua, the Medici dynasty in Florence, the Spanish House of Aragon, whose founder the Marqués de Santillana praised, in Naples – all these and many others all over Europe have left in architecture, painting and the decorative arts enduring witness of their power, which the tourist can still admire. The literary arts are more difficult to associate with such dramatically visible expressions of power: the rapid spread of printing throughout Italy and Europe in the last quarter of the fifteenth century, and the encouragement which this gave to the diffusion of humanist education, meant that poetry became what it is usually still thought to be – the common property of a whole nation or language, however broken up in practice both these concepts were in Italy in the Renaissance.

But, even if a poet, undertaking a major work such as Dante's *Commedia* or Antonio Pulci's *Morgante* (1460–83), thought of himself as transcending local or even national boundaries to enter a European literary tradition, the sheer necessities of life – Dante and Pulci both had independent means, but the first was an exile and the second was bankrupted – obliged the writer to lock himself into the patronage of the great, often by explicit dedication or political allusion: so Dante dedicates to Can Grande della Scala, Lord of Verona, and Pulci begins his poem at the behest of Lucrezia, mother of Lorenzo dei Medici. Even so small a poem as the sonnet could take its place in this patron–client relationship; as poem of praise, of satire, of friendship, clearly it would have its political uses, but even the love sonnet wove into that complex web of courtly relations which involved highly placed women who, if they did not have power in their own right, were the access to those who did – maids of honour, wives and mistresses whose favours might not be directly sexual, but still indispensable to the rising courtier. To say this is not to deny the possibility of love sonnets based on real human affection: if Pietro Bembo (1470–1547) wrote them to Lucrezia Borgia, who was out of his sphere, he also wrote movingly of his great love, mistress and mother of his children, la Morosina (d.1535).

But those poets who wrote sonnets out of 'sincere feeling' merely raise the question of the constructed /I/ in a more oblique way. In the Cinquecento, Italy had a group of distinguished female poets who used the Petrarchan sonnet (thereby demonstrating that its metaphors and images are not gender-specific) to proclaim their love for husbands and lovers: Veronica Gambara, Gaspara Stampa, Vittoria Colonna, Tullia d'Aragona and others found the inherited Petrarchan rhetoric meaningful to construct their emotional identities – often for subsequent publication.[7]

Dura è la stella mia, maggior durezza
è quello del mio conte: egli mi fugge,
i'seguo lui; altri per me si strugge,
i'non posso mirar altra bellezza.
  Odio chi m'ama, ed amo chi mi sprezza:
verso chi m'è umile, il mio cor rugge,

e son umil con chi mia speme adugge;
a così strano cibo ho l'alma avezza.
Egli ognor dà cagione a novo sdegno;
essi mi cercan dar conforto e pace:
i'lasso questi, ed a quell'un m'attegno.
Così ne la tua scuola, Amor, si face
sempre il contrario di quel ch'egli è degno:
l'umil si sprezza, e l'empio si compiace.
(Gaspara Stampa, 1523?–1554)[8]

[Hard is my star, harder still the star of my Count: he flies me, I follow him; others vie for me, I cannot look on any other beauty.

I hate the one who loves me, and I love one who scorns me: to my humble suitor my heart is proud, and I am humble before him who dashes my hopes; for this strange food I have a hungry soul.

He continually gives me cause of new contempt; the others try to give me solace and peace: I leave them, and to him alone I cleave.

So in thy school, Love, we find always the opposite of what should rightly be: the meek are scorned, and the proud is satisfied.]

This terse and bitter sonnet, framing the emotional distress of a woman pursuing an unworthy lover against her better judgement, develops the 'Odi et amo' of Catullus into a set of Petrarchan antitheses in which the self is dramatised as a helpless oscillation between the impersonality of pronouns. After the first mention of 'mio conte' (Count Collatino di Collalto, who left Gaspara Stampa, it seems, after a three-year relationship) the /I/ is confusingly spun among 'egli' ('he'), 'altri' ('another'), 'chi' ('someone who'), 'essi' ('they'), 'questi' ('these'), 'quello' ('that one'). The image of a child bewildered underlies the apparent assurance of the argument at the end, where the lesson of the 'school of Love' is finally learnt in a cynical epigram.

If this is real anguish, it is still anguish dramatised, ordered and argued out in the rhetoric of the Petrarchan sonnet: its binary structure enhances the paradoxes of her discontent, using the resources of both the short half-line (first quatrain) and the flowing sentence (final tercet). The courtly and conventional may mask, but does not thereby abolish, the real.

But it was not by chance that the Petrarchan sonnet, and the themes and language of love so intimately connected with it, became a favourite verse form of courtiers. Petrarch himself had been a most successful salesman of his own talents; and he found a successor in Pietro Bembo (1470–1547),[9] later Cardinal Bembo, who acted as a kind of posthumous literary agent for Petrarch just at the point where the Petrarchan sonnet appeared to have run its course. Effectively Bembo constructed a new courtly eloquence in Petrarch's name that became the standard of poetic beauty all over Europe, even for those who reacted against it. In trying to do again in the sixteenth century what Dante had attempted in his *De Vulgari Eloquentia* at the end of the thirteenth – that is, to establish standards of diction and style in composition that could serve for a national literary language – Bembo may have been trying most immediately to solve the problem of regionalism; but by his choice of Petrarch as the model for poetic composition he also founded a revival of one particular genre of poetry, the lyric, and one particular form, the sonnet, in which Petrarch had excelled. As John Houston has said:

> He [Bembo] argued in his *Prose della Volgar Lingua* [*Italian Prose*] (1524) for the use of Boccaccio as a model for Italian prose and in poetry insisted that diction should be based on Petrarch. Bembo was a learned man, well acquainted with the troubadours and Duecento Italian poets, so that his choice of Petrarch as the prototype for modern Italian poetry was informed by an acute historical sense of the development of European poetry. The place which he accorded Petrarch and which he imposed by his authority solved a great problem for Italian poets. Many of them grew up speaking a northern or southern dialect; once the possibility of writing in dialect was rejected as seemed only wise to those who wished a large audience, the poet had the choice of using a kind of neutral Italian, lacking in any particular savour, or of cultivating Tuscan as it was spoken in his time, a difficult task for one who did not reside in Tuscany. Bembo's solution, the adoption of Petrarch's essentially artificial version of fourteenth century Tuscan, provided a model easily accessible to all poets.[10]

Bembo's choice of Petrarch as a master of *style* had the effect of making Petrarch also the source of themes and images. Had Petrarch written his 366 poems of the *Rime* about gardening (he was a keen gardener), then perhaps courtiers would not have followed him there; but he had written about love, and about the self in pursuit of it; and that coincided, at the beginning of the sixteenth century, with a courtly interest in ideal love which ensured the dominance of the Petrarchan sonnet in the lyric domain until the seventeenth century. As love is the main subject of the sonneteers who are the concern of the rest of this book, an outline of the theory is needed here.

Courtly society depends very heavily upon display, since power is manifested by wealth, and wealth needs to be seen to be acknowledged. If a society diverts much of its time and money to the production and display of beautiful objects, including beautiful human behaviour (the process by which the things which only wealth can purchase are also valued socially as beautiful is complex and irrational, but universal in court culture), it has to discover a rationale for the enjoyment of these things. As Roland Barthes has pointed out, Europe has evolved traditions which operate to censure, and also censor, the concept of pleasure, and intermittently from early Christian times to our own day, from Gnosticism to consumer capitalism, countervailing theories arise to reinstate pleasure, either explicitly or as a corollary of their ideas. In fifteenth-century Florence, it was the Neoplatonism associated with Marsilio Ficino (1433–99) that arose as a counterpoise to Christian asceticism. The immense distance between earth and heaven, which makes the love of God quite other than the love of earthly things, and produces the conventional Christian condemnation of the pleasures of this world (including human love) is bridged in Ficino's thinking by God's own diffusion of love throughout His creation, by which 'all things bright and beautiful' in the sight of man offer a means of rising to the contemplation of God. Not everything that human beings set their desire upon is good – one may choose to love money, or violence, or sloth – but those things that people 'naturally' find beautiful, with an intellectual understanding of their qualities, are a shadow of the radiance of God. Beyond the contemplation of physical beauty lies contemplation of the beauty of the soul, and beyond that the contemplation of the beauty of the Divine Idea.

Since something like this set of ideas had appeared in the *stilnovisti*, and since Petrarch inherited themes and images from them, it is not surprising that his sonnets should be congenial to a courtly society influenced by Neoplatonism. So he makes his appearance when Tullia d'Aragona, writing in her *Dialogo dell'Infinità d'Amore* (Venice, 1547), thus described 'amore onesto' ('virtuous love'):

> it is proper to noble persons (*uomini*), that is, those who have a noble (*gentile*) and virtuous soul, whatever they are, poor or rich; it is not generated by desire, like the other [sensual form of love], but by the reason; and it has for its chief end the transformation of self into the beloved object, with the desire that that should be transformed into the self, so that out of two, one alone is made. Of this transformation, Francis Petrarch and the most reverend Cardinal Bembo have written, often and with great subtlety. And this, because it cannot occur other than spiritually (*ispiritalmente*), is of such a kind that in love like this the chief place can only be taken by affections of the spirit, that is, in sight and hearing, and further, as being more spiritual, the imagination (*fantasia*). It is certainly true that the lover, who beyond this spiritual union desires also the union of the bodies, to make him one, as far as he can, with the beloved, and who cannot achieve this, since it is impossible for bodies to interpenetrate (*penetrin l'un l'altro*), cannot ever follow

through his desire, and so will never arrive at its end; and so, as I argued above, can never love to a conclusion.[11]

The revaluation of physical beauty as a means of beginning the ascent to a higher perception of beauty and harmony – the 'Ledaean body' that made Yeats feel

> it seemed that our two natures blent
> into a sphere from youthful sympathy,
> or else, to alter Plato's parable,
> into the yolk and white of the one shell . . .
> ('Among School Children', ll. 13–16)

brings back the worship of the *donna angelicata* in a rather different way. Petrarch had certainly celebrated Laura's physical beauty, but in the penitential parts of his *Rime* had seen that as a distraction, an obstacle to salvation; the Neoplatonic emphasis suggested that earthly love was certainly inferior, but valuable as the first step towards the divine. The admired body is now, in Milton's marvellous phrase, 'the unpolluted temple of the mind', and its beauty is manifested particularly to the ear and the eye – whence the preoccupation of the fifteenth and sixteenth centuries with women singing, playing and dancing, something that has remained important to the cultural valuation of women until our own day.

With the reinstatement of erotic pleasure went the beauty of the natural landscape, which Petrarch in his sonnets had been the first to use as a symbol of the impact of love on the self; and several of the so-called 'courtesy manuals', the Renaissance books that deal with the courtly arts, including the art of love, place their speakers in a pleasure garden of the kind that the princes of Europe were constructing around their palaces and houses. One such is the setting of *Gli Asolani* (*The Meeting at Asolo*), a series of dialogues on the nature of love which the 'most reverend Cardinal Bembo' composed before he reached that clerical eminence, while he was studying Neoplatonic thought at the court of Ferrara. Six young people, meeting in a pleasure garden belonging to the Queen of Cyprus (not a literary invention, but the cultivated, beautiful and competent Caterina Cornaro, whose sovereignty of the island of Cyprus the Venetians had forced her to exchange in 1498 for a villa at Asolo), debate the nature of love; and the book ends with a remarkable mythical poesis which allegorises the operation of love in court culture as it seemed to the young Bembo, writing at the end of the fourteenth century.

As often happened in courtesy manuals, different speakers offer competing views: after the courtier Perottino declares that love is bitter and transitory, his friend Gismondo argues the other side of the Petrarchan 'dolce nemico' ('sweet enemy'), namely that it is sweet and perpetually renewing, and Lavinello suggests that it may be either good or bad, depending on its origins. A philosophical hermit appears, to argue the Neoplatonic view that the highest form of love is founded on reason, which will rise superior to all desire, and bring the lover to the contemplation of the ideal. Bembo then provides a compact and mythical retroping of what has been said in the account of the Queen of the Fortunate Isles, a legend various versions of which appear in the sixteenth century and after, often reworked by poets who happened also to produce sonnet cycles or numbers of sonnets: Tasso, Ariosto, Spenser, Milton, Shakespeare and others. Here is Bembo's version of the myth:

> The holy masters of antiquity record among their most secret memorials, that there is a Queen in these Islands which I call Fortunate: most beautiful, wondrous to behold, adorned with rare and precious vestures, and ever young. She will have no husband, and keeps her virginity always, but is pleased to be loved and favoured. And to those who most love her, she gives greatest reward for their love; and so to the rest, proportioned to their affection to her. But all men she tests in the following manner: as each man comes before her, according as she summons one or another, she touches him with a rod, and sends him away. And they, so soon as they are out of the palace of the Queen, fall asleep, and so sleep on till she awake them again. So they come before her when they are once reawakened, and each man bears, written before him, the dreams he has had while sleeping, so that, even as they fell out, nothing added nor left, she reads them forthwith. Those whose dreams she sees to have been only of hunting, of angling, of horses, of beasts, of forests, she drives away from her and bids them go abide with those same beasts which they dreamed themselves to be among, for, says she, if they had loved her, they should some time at least have dreamed of her; wherefore, since they have never done so, she bids them go live with their beasts. Those others in whose dreams have been thoughts of commerce, of the rule of families, of the commonweal or of other such matters, yet but little bethinking them of their Queen, she makes them variously be such merchants, such citizens, such officers of state, loading them with charges and with cares, and giving herself little care for them. But those who have dreamed of her, she keeps by her in her court, there to remain and to discourse with her amid music and song and all manner of infinite contentments, this one more near her and that one yet further off, according as their dreams lingered on her.[12]

This powerful fantasy of female domination, both desired and feared, which runs through the *Odyssey* (Calypso, Nausicaa, Athena herself and

Penelope), has its strongest incarnation in Circe, the enchantress who punishes men for their natural appetites by transforming them into swine. Here Bembo, while retaining the sense of menace in the rod of sleep (a very complicated political and sexual symbol), turns the enchantress of the *Odyssey* into a benevolent queen/sibyl. No doubt there is an elegant compliment intended to Caterina Cornaro; but beyond that, since the fable insists on its esoteric status, there is the type of the Renaissance princess, ruling over a community of men (and women, though the devotion of women to women is not relevant here) in a palace/garden of ideal beauty, entry into which is conditional upon the possession of a noble soul, steady devotion and eloquent witness of it (the dreams are *written*). In the tradition of the Wise Woman that descends from the Wisdom literature of the Old Testament and Socrates' Diotima through Boethius' Lady Philosophy to the *donna angelicata* of the *stilnovisti*, and which was avidly developed and promoted by princes[13] such as Catherine de Medici and Elizabeth I of England, the female ruler represents the union of Truth, Power and Beauty: truth to search the hidden thoughts of men, power to judge their deeds and order their actions in accordance with truth, and beauty to compel their acceptance of her truth and power. The practical reality that a Renaissance court was a place of seeking, displaying, testing and rewarding can then be locked into a myth of truth, expressed in poetry as worship of a beloved enchantress, whose power derives from some transcendent source and is exhibited through her beauty:

> Stella, the onely Planet of my light,
> Light of my life, and life of my desire,
> Chief good, whereto my hope doth onely aspire,
> World of my wealth, and heav'n of my delight,
>   Why doest thou spend the treasures of thy sprite
> With voice more fit to wed Amphion's lyre,
> Seeking to quench in me the noble fire
> Fed by thy worth, and kindled by thy sight?
>   And all in vaine, for while thy breath most sweet,
> With choisest words, the words with reasons rare,
> Thy reasons firmly set on Vertue's feet,
> Labour to kill in me this killing care,
>   O thinke I then, what paradise of joy
>   It is, so faire a Vertue to enjoy.
>
> (Sir Philip Sidney, *Astrophel and Stella* 68)

The motif of enchantment and transformation, which is the courtly development of the sense of confusion expressed in earlier lyric *pleynts*, runs like a thread through the Renaissance sonnet and its accompanying literature – in Sidney's sonnet, Stella's voice has the power of Amphion's lyre, which could animate trees and stones. This motif provides a rich set of metaphors for the internal changes wrought by love and desire: falling asleep, as in Bembo's myth, or being deprived of movement or speech, is one such enchantment; being caught in the beloved's hair is another (apparently invented by Petrarch). In his very complicated range of natural metaphors involving various sorts of entanglement or transformation (hair, trees, branches, water, stones, fire, ice) Petrarch returned into the sensual and physical world what the *stilnovisti* had imaged as a moral transformation of the lover. For them, the powers of the beloved may be miraculous, but are never, until Dante's *Rime petrose*, physically dangerous; Petrarch was so strongly fascinated in his sonnets with the dynamics of desire, rather than with the moral state to which it might lead, that he animated the whole natural world, including the human body, to symbolise its effects. The Neoplatonic idea that the beauty of the world is responsive to natural human desire enables the fifteenth- and sixteenth-century poets to luxuriate in natural description, particularly of the body of the beloved, using Petrarchan vocabulary, and simultaneously to place the beloved at the centre of that world as its ruler, showing by her enchantments the strength of desire, and by her beauty the virtuous knowledge to be reached by ascent through desire.

The Queen of the Fortunate Isles has, then, a considerable progeny, some like their mother and some her antitype: Ariosto's Angelica, full of eastern promise; Tasso's Armida; Sidney's Stella; Spenser's Acrasia and his Faerie Queene herself; Shakespeare's Dark Lady, with her antitypes in the late comedies, Perdita, Miranda and Helena; Milton's Emilia and his Lady in *Comus*; one can even see behind the tormented sonnets of Sir Thomas Wyatt that very real and tragic dark-eyed enchantress Anne Boleyn, mother of the much worshipped Queen Elizabeth.

If the Renaissance sonnet responded to the courtier's need to proclaim an identity in a patronage system in which women were influential, and adapted Neoplatonic and Petrarchan ideas to do so, it also responded to an ideal of style, likewise promoted by Cardinal Bembo, which may have arrived in Britain too late to affect Sir Thomas Wyatt, but certainly influenced his successors in the sonnet. For this I return to the closing lines of Bembo's fable, where the Queen awards three kinds of destiny to her would-be courtiers, in a passage which has stylistic as well as social implications.

Three destinies are awarded: to live wild in the forests; to live as a citizen, in trade or public office; and to live as a courtier among 'sollazzi d'infinito contento' ('all manner of infinite contentments'). This division of men's conditions is at once hierarchical, corresponding to the peasant, bourgeois and aristocratic divisions; topographical, corresponding to country, city and court; evolutionary, because mankind was thought to have progressed from woods and caves to cities, and from cities to the refinement of benevolent monarchy; and then finally facultative, since living with the beasts is a passionate existence, like that of Swift's Yahoos; trade or administration involves the practical intellect; and remaining at court to discourse with the Queen (as the paragon of wisdom and truth) involves the contemplative intellect, reaching up to the ideal. Wisdom – the Queen – awards men their station in life according to their capacity to reach up the ladder of ascent to the ideal, which is determined by their ability to imagine the form of the ideal – hence the dream test.

However, not only the content of the mind, but also the style in which the mind displays its imaginings shows the nature of the person; and, as there are three levels of existence, so, too, in Renaissance rhetorical theory there are three levels of style, just as there had been for Dante. As George Puttenham puts it in his *Arte of English Poesie* (1589), a very readable work which is simultaneously a courtesy manual and a handbook of poetic rhetoric:

> because this continuall course and manner of writing or speech sheweth the matter and disposition of the writers minde, more than one or few words or sentences can shew, therefore there be that have called stile, the image of man . . . for man is but his minde, and as his minde is tempered and qualified, so are his speeches and language at large, and his inward conceits be the mettall of his minde, and his manner of utterance the very warp & woofe of his conceits. . . . For if the man be grave, his speech and stile is grave: if light-headed, his stile and language also light: if the minde be haughtie and hoate [hot], the speech and stile is also vehement and stirring: if it be cold and temperate, the stile is also very modest: if it be humble, or base and meeke, so is also the language and stile. . . . Therefore . . . I will as neere as I can set downe, which matters be hie and loftie, which be but meane [middling], and which be low and base, to the intent the stiles may be fashioned to the matters, and keepe their *decorum* and good proportion in every respect. . . .[14]

In Bembo's fable, the highest destiny is accompanied by rational discourse ('ragionare') along with 'music and song and all manner of infinite contentment', and the higher the social rank, the better and sweeter the eloquence. 'The Queene our soveraigne Lady', said Puttenham, 'easily surmounteth all the rest that have written before her time or since, for sense, sweetnesse and subtiltie . . . even by as much oddes as her owne excellent estate and degree exceedeth all the rest of her most humble vassals.' If few princes could in reality reach that level of excellence – Lorenzo dei Medici and James VI of Scotland are perhaps the most accomplished – they could at least have about them courtier poets who could celebrate their magnificence in magnificent style. The desirability of matching the highest power with the highest style produced, in every country where there was a national or powerful regional court, a concern for what is usually called 'the problem of the vernacular' – with which, after this Neoplatonic explanation, we come back to the role of the sonnet in Renaissance poetry.

Cardinal Bembo, like Dante before him, Joachim du Bellay in France, James VI in Scotland, George Puttenham in England and many more,[15] asked the question, 'What words in the vernacular have the greatest dignity?' For Dante, writing his inquiry *De Vulgari Eloquentia* before the rise of Renaissance humanism and with substantially no literature in vernacular Italian, give or take a few hundred sonnets, the answer was difficult: it involved considering the practice of those who had high rank, education or 'nobleness of soul', to see what they did, and then, noticing that it was possible to speak in dozens of different dialects, further to consider, by a largely subjective assessment, which region had the most pleasing and dignified speech. Dante, not surprisingly, chose his native Florence for the honour. But when Bembo wrote his inquiry, his *Prose della Volgar Lingua* (1525) (*Italian Prose)*, there was both a classical humanist tradition and a vernacular literary tradition available to him, as there was to the authors who in other nations later asked the same question. So his answer took a different form, and invoked the concept of imitation, which was responsible for the enormous diffusion of the sonnet form throughout Europe, as well as of other literary kinds.

The words that had the greatest dignity, in the humanist tradition, would be those words used by the vernacular authors who had successfully imitated the most dignified authors of Greek and Roman times; so also, if one wanted the entire range, for authors imitating middle- and low-style classical authors. There is, of course, a circularity in this procedure: one obtains a theory of high style by studying those who have successfully imitated the classics, or by successfully doing it oneself; but one cannot know what success is without having a theory of style in the first place. Whence, of course, comes a certain arbitrariness of taste, nor did poets always take great notice of what rhetoricians prescribed for them. Nevertheless, when Puttenham praises Sir Thomas Wyatt and the Earl of Surrey for their poetry, he shows the concept of imitation working for national prestige, as the English vernacular – and, by implication, the English monarch – is elevated by writers doing with their language what the best Italians (known to be the best because Italian courtly rhetoricians like Bembo had said so) had done for the language of Italy:

> In the latter end of the same kings raigne [Henry VIII] sprong up a new company of courtly makers, of whom Sir *Thomas Wyat*

> th'elder & *Henry* Earle of Surrey were the two chieftaines, who having travailed into Italie, and there tasted the sweet and stately measures and stile of the Italian poesie as novices newly crept out of the schooles of Dante, Arioste and Petrarch, they greatly polished our rude and homely maner of vulgar Poesie, from that it had bene before. . . .[16]

There is in this homage to both Petrarch and Bembo: for in his phrase 'the sweet and stately measures and stile of the Italian poesie' Puttenham is referring, perhaps at several removes, to the most influential single theory of the poetic vernacular, that according to which Bembo, obeying humanist ideals, placed Petrarch at the centre of the courtly style. For in trying to free the poetry of his own time (and the prose, but we are here considering verse) from what he considered the corruptions and extravagances of Petrarch's fifteenth-century successors he performed the familiar humanist (and Protestant) manoeuvre of *redire ad fontes* – 'returning to the sources'. What is noblest, or most virtuous, whether in style or in blood, lies in the past, in an identifiable figure who can, like an Old Testament patriarch, bequeath to his successors his qualities. What passes biologically from father to child (in the hazy state of early-Renaissance science, it was not at all clear how nobility was transmitted)[17] can be seen by analogy as passing from master to pupil, as in Puttenham's scholastic metaphor above, and thus from text to reader: any suitable author of the past can be set up as a kind of literary father, obedience to whose precepts will confer nobility of style on the son.[18] It is a pleasant irony that Petrarch, who with his devotion to Cicero, Augustine and Virgil gave this idea currency in Renaissance humanism, should himself have become the poetic father of the European love-lyric; or, to change the metaphor yet again, in Mario Equicola's words, 'that abundant spring that all come to, whence numberless streams flow down to the poets of our days'.[19]

Now, stateliness and sweetness, often called gravity and delight, for which Puttenham praises 'the Italian poesie', do, as stylistic qualities, have something of the same opposition as 'work' and 'play';[20] and, while a single person, whether prince or poet, may exhibit both, they will not normally be shown simultaneously. They belong to different occasions, and different identities – the public face and the private, perhaps. As far as Petrarch as stylistic role model was concerned, his own division of his *Rime* into *canzoni* and short forms (including the sonnet) offered his disciples an accommodation of grandeur and delight,[21] which also took in the other stylistic pairings of 'high' and 'low' and 'long' and 'brief'. These binary oppositions have their correlates in other modes: in the field of mental activity, 'length' and 'brevity' correlate with 'invention' and 'wit', since invention requires expansion of one's material, whereas wit implies concentration of it. The public and private aspects of style correlate with different activities: war and heroism are appropriate to long poems, because they are public activities; love is appropriate to short poems, because it is a private emotion. (Something like this distinction is feasible in regard to the *canzoni* of Petrarch as opposed to his sonnets.) And finally, since public affairs are the province of men, long poems are masculine and short poems feminine – which may mean, as it does frequently in the Renaissance, that long poems are dedicated to men and short poems to women.

To describe the sonnet by any one of these terms (it is, for example, inescapably a *short* form) is thus to locate it in a matrix of relations at once stylistic, social, political and personal. The critic Bernardino Daniello, in his treatise *La poetica* (1536), laments the failure of poets of his own day to make use of classical poetic theory, and asks rhetorically:

> If they read those works, and found in them, if not all these precepts, instructions and rules of composition, then at least the principal and most necessary ones, who knows if they might not yet give themselves to writing, not merely romances, sonnets and odes of love, but loftier, more serious and more glorious poems than these are?[22]

Here the sonnet, because it is a modern form, is seen as trivial, irregular and domestic, belonging to an area of life set apart from what is rational, noble and worthy of public renown. George Puttenham, speaking much less dismissively, also places the sonnet in a matrix of civil, social and personal relations in a way wholly typical of his century:

> The first founder of all good affections is honest love, as the mother of all the vicious is hatred. It was not therefore without reason that so commendable, yea honourable a thing as love well meant, were it in Princely estate or private, might in all civil common wealths be uttered in good forme and order as other laudable things are. And because love is of all other humane affections the most puissant and passionate, and most generall to all sortes and ages of men and women, so as whether it be of the yong or old or wise or holy, or high estate or low, none ever could truly bragge of any exemption in that case: it requireth a forme of Poesie variable, inconstant, affected, curious and most witty of any others, whereof the joyes were to be uttered in one sort, the sorrowes in an other, and by the many formes of Poesie, the many moodes and pangs of lovers, throughly to be discovered: the poor soules sometimes praying, beseeching, sometime honouring, avancing, praising: an other while railing, reviling, and cursing: then sorrowing, weeping, lamenting: in the ende laughing, rejoycing & solacing the beloved againe, with a thousand delicate devises,

> odes, songs, elegies, ballads, sonets and other ditties, mooving one way and another to great compassion.[23]

Puttenham is of course rather grossly confusing the love of friendship, devotion and loyalty with sexual love, so that he can simultaneously defend love as the basis of the bonds of civil society, and yet patronise lovers ('poor soules') as people in the grip of uncontrollable oscillations of violent and contrary feelings – a notion by this time thoroughly established as Petrarchan. If we pass over this confusion for the moment, notice that the sonnet (and the other forms bracketed with it) is a 'devise', a product of artifice designed to proclaim the user's nature to others, as in heraldry; witty and 'delicate', calling for mental alertness to please others; a form of social request, whereby those who are 'poor' can influence others to better their condition; passionate, so that it exposes the feelings, but at the same time an utterance 'in good forme and order', so that violent emotions can be contained within a commonwealth; and productive of 'compassion', which Puttenham probably intends in its primary sense of 'sharing of feelings' rather than 'pity'. The expressive function of the sonnet is not omitted ('sorrowing, weeping, lamenting') but it is wholly subordinate to the persuasive function of poetry, and the proclamation of oneself in a social and ordered context, for the advancing of human civil society, itself ultimately a rational, not a passionate matter ('not therefore without reason . . .'). The persistent Renaissance myth of poets as the first civilisers of humanity lies behind this very striking image of human emotions producing a Babel of sounds, which can only be brought to order by the forms of poetry – of which the sonnet is one. And perhaps in the confusion of ideas which we noted at first there is a restatement of the paradox which the Sicilians voiced in their sonnets, which the *stilnovisti* rearticulated in theirs, and to which the Neoplatonism of Bembo gave fresh impetus in the minds of sixteenth-century poets: that love is at once the most dislocating of human feelings and the one which most strongly impels the heart to 'gentilezza', that quality at the centre of ideal courtly behaviour.

6

WYATT, SURREY AND THEIR LEGACY

'The sixteenth century', says the sonnet's great French bibliographer, Hugues Vaganay,[1] 'is the century of the sonnet', and indeed the statistics are numbing. In Italy, France, Germany and Britain, it is estimated, between 1530 and 1650, some 3,000 writers produced about 200,000 sonnets, and the list of sonneteers includes almost all those who made any kind of name as poets in that period. In Britain, these two dates delimit the age of the sonnet: there are no British sonnets before about 1530, and very few after 1650, until the sonnet revives in the nineteenth century. Vaganay reminds us[2] that one of the commonest uses of the sonnet was one that escapes the attention of literary critics routinely: the sonnet of compliment at the beginning or end of a volume of theology or law or some quite unliterary subject accounts for a significant proportion of that massive 200,000.[3] After that, spiritual and moral sonnets, occasional sonnets and love-sonnets divide the field between them, with love-sonnets slightly, but only slightly, preponderating. In Britain, with a population much smaller than those of Italy and France, and with a sonnet 'vogue' that lasted for a much shorter time (roughly from 1580 to 1600), the output of sonnets was much smaller, and the proportion of those sonnets which dealt with love was higher. Sonnet sequences rarely exceed a hundred sonnets, and all the sonnet sequences of the age, even under the loosest definition of sequence,[4] offer only about 2,000 sonnets: in the absence of any census of British sonnets in miscellanies and in the prefatory and epilogue material of printed books, one might guess that about 4,000 sonnets is the British contribution. Alongside Torquato Tasso's 1,000 sonnets, the seven hundred or so sonnets of Ronsard, and the capacity of quite minor French and Italian writers to produce five or six hundred sonnets, the British contribution may even seem slender; yet it was concentrated, distinctive, and engaged the minds of the best writers of the age: Sidney, Spenser and Shakespeare, Donne, Herbert and Milton, all of whom altered slightly the capacity of that very flexible form.

Indeed, the very first British writer to use the sonnet, Sir Thomas

Wyatt (1503?–42), altered it very considerably: he made the first formal change in the structure of the sonnet since its invention in southern Italy in the early thirteenth century. In considering Wyatt's introduction of the form to Britain and his recasting of it, one has a slight sense of historical replay: for the sonnet was invented, as was said in Chapter 2, at the court of Frederick II, an enlightened, cultured and also ruthless despot, by a courtier academically trained for diplomatic service, writing for and in a group of courtiers, and seems to have offered a kind of courtierly utterance safely below the level of political action. So, too, Sir Thomas Wyatt's new sonnet at the court of Henry VIII, a cultured but ruthless sovereign, was brought in by a courtier academically trained for royal service, writing among his peers, and offering a persona locating itself just under the level of political explicitness.

It is tempting to think that if we knew as much about the private lives of Frederick's courtiers, like Giacomo da Lentino, as we do about the lives of Wyatt and Surrey[5] we could locate the very first sonnets in a matrix of power relations, and understand more clearly the positions which their speakers seek to create; so that we could make something more than coincidence out of the similarity of circumstances between the sonnet's appearance in Italy in 1235 and its appearance in Britain about 1530. Let us press the point. The sonnet enters Britain and France, and re-enters Spain, at the same time. At the court of Francis I of France, the poet Mellin de Saint-Gelais (1487–1558) and his friend Clément Marot (1492–1549) were spreading the knowledge of Petrarch and of later Italian poetry, and the first French sonnet was published in 1539, having been written in 1529. At the court of the Emperor Charles V of Spain, the poet Juan Boscán (1493?–1542)[6] reintroduced the sonnet under Italian influence some time after 1526 (it having lapsed after the première of the Marqués de Santillana). Wyatt himself, who may on his diplomatic missions abroad have met Saint-Gelais, Marot and Boscán, probably began writing sonnets after his visit to Italy in 1527. This triple and well-nigh simultaneous invasion of the great royal courts of Europe signals not only the pre-eminence of Italian poetry as the source of *gravità* and *dolcezza*, forcefully urged by Pietro Bembo's critical work, *Prose della Volgar Lingua* (1524), but also the need of the members of these courts to express themselves in a recognised form of eloquence. The forensic oratory of classical humanism, actively taught in the schools and colleges of Europe, made little practical sense in the courts of despotic princes, where decisions were not taken by popular acclaim in assemblies swayed by eloquence, but made within a system of patronage, the sovereign at its head.[7] If the courtier spoke, it was not so much to teach and to persuade, as to please: it was by no means cynical in Puttenham to put into his *Arte of English Poesie* the warning, 'See ye speake to the king your maister, either nothing at all, or else that which pleaseth him'. Before the courtier could please, he had to proclaim himself as a would-be pleaser (whence the proliferation of extremely lavish dedications); but having secured attention by dedication or apostrophe ('Voi che ascoltate . . .') he had to offer current coin in the language of discourse. Here Italy had issued indubitably acceptable funds of wit and eloquence – on the reserves of Petrarch and Serafino anyone could draw. Sir Christopher Hatton, courtier to Queen Elizabeth, has left us a record of a marvellous court moment in which pleasing, poetry and Petrarch came together: 'The Queene stoode up and bade me reache forth my arme to reste her thereon. Oh, what swete burden to my next songe. Petrarke shall eke out good matter for this businesse.'[8] An act of favour, instantly perceived as an opportunity for ingratiation; the opportunity is followed up in a poem, and Petrarchan eloquence gives the moment its 'form and pressure'.

Wyatt has left us no comment on his own poetry beyond the poetry itself, and though some of his poems can be dated plausibly, particularly those that seem to bear on his involvement with Anne Boleyn,[9] before he was warned off by his master the King, we cannot be certain when he began to write sonnets. It seems likely that he became aware of Italian poetry in 1526, when he went to the French court, and that he would have extended this acquaintance the following year, when he visited Italy, and could well have met Pietro Bembo in Padua. What he brought back was in fact not one but two new poetic forms: the sonnet, the chief form of Petrarch, and the *strambotto*, the favoured form of Serafino de' Ciminelli (1466–1500), usually known as Serafino dell'Aquila from his place of birth.

The conjunction of the two is significant in Wyatt's verse. The strambotto (the word passed into English, though the form did not become more popular than similar, home-grown stanzas) was originally a popular song form, supposed by some critics to have been adapted by Giacomo da Lentino to make the sonnet; at the end of the fifteenth century, in the hands of Serafino and his followers, it was a short, witty, pseudological poem that concluded with a couplet, typically rhyming ABABABCC. The strambotto did not survive as a fashionable form in English verse because it was already very similar to short lyric stanzas which English poets, including Wyatt, were accustomed to use in the vernacular, but it is the likeliest source for Wyatt's major contribution to the sonnet; that is, the alteration of the sestet from 3 + 3 to 4 + 2, ending with a rhymed couplet. It seems most probable that Wyatt, working with the strambotti of Serafino, was impressed by their epigrammatic neatness, and as a means of enforcing the wit and elegance of his own sonnets transferred the concluding couplet to his versions of Petrarch.

It is hard to resist the conclusion that, though Wyatt was writing his poetry just at the time of Bembo's idolising of Petrarch, he either did not know of, or had little interest in, the balance of *gravità* and *dolcezza* which was so important to later sonneteers. His Petrarch selection is hard to explain: for though he certainly translated some of the quintessentially Petrarchan antithetical sonnets, such as 'Pace non trovo' (*Rime* 134: 'I fynde no peace') and 'S'una fede amorosa' (*Rime* 224: 'Yf amours faith'), he also noticed such a difficult occasional sonnet as *Rime* 98, addressed not to Laura but to Orso Anguillara, a Roman gentleman, apparently to console him for being kept from a tournament by illness:

Orso, al vostro destrier si po ben porre
un fren che di suo corso indietro il volga,
ma 'l cor chi legherà che non si sciolga,
se brama onore e 'l suo contrario aborre?
Non sospirate: a lui non si po torre
suo pregio, perch'a voi l'andar si tolga,
ché come fama publica divolga
egli è già là che null'altro il precorre.
   Basti che si ritrove in mezzo 'l campo,
al destinato dì sotto quell'arme
che gli dà il tempo, amor, vertute e 'l sangue,
gridando: 'D'un gentil desire avampo
col signor mio, che non po seguitarme,
et del non esser qui si strugge et langue.'

[Orso, on your steed one can put a rein that will turn him back from his course, but as for your heart, who can bind it so that it will not come free, if it desires honour and detests its opposite?
No regrets: no one can take away the worth of it, though you are prevented from going; for as public knowledge relates, it is already there, where no one else can take precedence.
   Let it suffice that your heart is in the field on the appointed day, displaying those arms given to it by the age, by devotion, nobility and birth, crying out, 'With a noble longing I am inflamed, as is my lord, who cannot follow me, and suffers, and is sick that he is not here.']

We cannot know whether Wyatt simply happened to recall this sonnet on an occasion when, like Orso, he could not attend some important courtly event; but he uses the sonnet as the basis for an astonishing dramatisation of mental conflict, the more disturbing because so obliquely expressed, without any of Petrarch's clear circumstantiality:

Though I my self be bridilled of my mynde,
Retorning me backeward by force expresse,
If thou seke honor to kepe thy promes,
Who may the hold, my hert, but thou thyself unbynd?

Sigh then no more, syns no way man may fynde
Thy vertue to let, though that frowerdnes
Of ffortune me holdeth; and yet, as I may gesse,
Though othre be present, thou art not all behinde.
  Suffice it then that thou be redy there
At all howres; still under the defence
Of tyme, trouth and love, to save thee from offence;
Crying, 'I burne in a lovely desire
  With my dere maisteres, that may not follow,
  Whereby his absence torneth him to sorrowe.' (27)[10]

Anne Ferry, in her acute discussion of Wyatt's sonnets,[11] has pointed out that it is his habit to ambiguate Petrarch's thought or at least to make it more abstract: as he can translate his original word for word when he chooses (e.g., 'With my dere maisteres, that may not follow'), departures from it must be deliberate. So in the last line Petrarch's specific reference to Orso's illness has become the more general 'torneth . . . to sorrowe'; the circumstantial 'on the appointed day' has become 'at all howres'; the word 'backeward', which literally translates 'indietro', is quite clear, visually, when applied as Petrarch has it to a horse, but quite another when applied to 'me' – in what sense can one's 'mind' make one go backward? And the marvellous alexandrine at line 4 (one of three in the poem, suggesting deliberate patterning) – 'Who may the hold, my hert, but thou thyself unbynd?' – can mean, as Petrarch's line does, 'Who can hold you so that you don't immediately free yourself?' and also, because of the phrase 'to kepe thy promes', which is not in Petrarch, 'Who may force you [to keep your promise] unless you free yourself [to go forth to keep it]?' 'Who may the hold . . . ?' becomes a kind of metaphysical assertion of the freedom of human resolve.

Since Wyatt has removed the military event from the poem ('there' replaces 'in the field') it is by no means clear what kind of thing the promise involves, and hence it is unclear what the 'hert' is. It is obviously valour in Petrarch; and what guarantees that valour for Orso, namely his ancestry ('tempo'), his loyalty to his superior ('amor'), his nobility ('vertute') and his breeding ('sangue') have become in Wyatt's poem the much more problematic 'tyme, trouthe and love', the phrase 'the defence of tyme' already being complicated by 'At all howres' just above it. This /I/ is quite unlocated in space and time, and exists in a universe of abstract terms, a whirl of social coercions that have no anchor in a sensory world, and are menacing without being visible.[12] Even the self is fragmented, as the heart and mind are externalised in the tradition of the *psychomachia*, figured as shadowy officers in a world of conflicting commands. The /I/, which commands the heart but is commanded by the mind, itself commanded by fortune, is paralysed and absent at the end, where Wyatt, using with advantage what Petrarch gives him, lets loose a cry of unfocused desire – 'lovely' not because it is graceful but because it is concerned with the need to love and be loved, in the widest courtly sense – which the feminine half-rhyme both clinches and allows to fade away into space.

Wyatt was quite untouched by Italian Neoplatonism, and his desire is not for any kind of transcendent goal, for the self as it were to rise above itself, but simply for the self to be securely positioned in the matrix of tangled forces surrounding it. He gets from Petrarch the sense of the sonnet as a moment of psychic instability, to be worked through; but the instability is social, not cosmic, and the great metaphors of light and air and water are beyond him. If he happens upon a quasi-Platonic sonnet, we can see how even there he creates a sublunary /I/, locked into the coercions of courtly space:

Son animali al mondo de sì altera
vista che 'ncontra 'l sol pur si difende;
altri, però che 'l gran lume gli offende,
non escon fuor se non verso la sera;
et altri, col desio folle che spera
gioir forse nel foco, perché splende,
provan l'altra vertù, quella che 'ncende;
lasso, e 'l mio loco è 'n questa ultima schera.
Ch'i'non son forte ad aspettar la luce
di questa donna, et non so fare schermi
di luoghi tenebrosi o d'ore tarde;
però con gli occhi lagrimosi e 'nfermi
mio destino a vederla mi conduce,
et so ben ch'i'vo dietro a quel che m'arde. (*Rime* 19)

[There are animals in the world with sight so refined that it withstands even the sun; others, because the great light hurts them, come out only towards evening.
And others, with a mad longing that thinks perhaps to enjoy the fire, because it glows, discover its other power, the one that burns; alas, my place is in this last group.
For I am not strong enough to look on the light of that lady, and I do not know how to make a shield of shady places or the late hours;
yet with my weeping and weak eyes my fate leads me to look on her, and I know well that I follow behind what burns me.]

The Platonic contrast between eagles and bats, types of those that rise to divine knowledge and those that are incapable of the light of truth, extends to include moths, the type of the foolish lover; but Petrarch, following the legacy of the *stilnovisti*, suggests that the lover, too, is following a light like the sun, and though he may be burnt he is at any rate no bat of ignorance. Wyatt, picking up the metaphor of defence in Petrarch's second line, intensifies the sense of both the sun and the lady as enemies, and the lover as manoeuvring desperately to avoid attack, instead of tenaciously pursuing:

> Som fowles there be that have so perfaict sight
> Agayn the Sonne their Iyes for to defend,
> And some bicause the light doeth theim offend,
> Do never pere but in the dark or nyght.
> Others reioyse that se the fyer bright,
> And wene to play in it as they do pretend,
> And find the contrary of it that they intend.
> Alas, of that sort I may be by right,
> For to withstand her loke I ame not able;
> And yet can I not hide me in no darke place,
> Remembraunce so foloweth me of that face,
> So that with tery yen swolne and unstable,
> My destyne to behold here doeth me lede,
> Yet do I know I runne into the glede. (24)

The crucial line is the ninth, just at the turn of the sonnet, where Wyatt alters the Platonic 'I am not strong enough to look upon [her] light' into the much more humanly aggressive 'I am unable to withstand her look' (even Wyatt at his clumsiest could not have supposed that 'aspettar la luce' meant 'withstand the look'!). Thereafter the shield, which protects one's weakness while one still advances, becomes a hiding-place; the 'weak' ('infermi') eyes become 'unstable'; and the pursuit becomes a rush into something the lover would rather avoid. Again, then, the sense of the /I/ as victim of coercive energies, social rather than cosmic in nature.

What the structure of the sonnet does, as always since its invention, is to give positive form to a confession of unstable form. Wyatt, because of his aspirations as a courtier, had constantly to negotiate his position relative to those above and below him, and acquire loyalty or protection by pleasing, that is, by imaging the self according to the construction of others' wills. The poesis of this stance involves utterances which confess weakness (to secure protection and favour), profess devotion (to attract reward), and exhibit self-knowledge (to establish the presence of an /I/ to be protected and rewarded). Here the couplet comes into its own. In the sonnet above, Petrarch has given Wyatt a 'sense couplet', for his last two lines exhibit a self-awareness expressed in a conclusive paradox: that the lover goes ineluctably and willingly to what will destroy him: the accomplishment of the sonnet ratifies the words 'so ben' ('I well know'). What is well said is taken to be properly known. Building on that, Wyatt intensifies the paradox by substituting 'yet' for Petrarch's 'et' ('and'), and ratifies the secureness of the knowledge by the soundness of the rhyme. It is perhaps an exaggeration, but not much of one, to say that it was the bent of Wyatt's mind to move his speaker in his sonnets towards a definite truth of prudential experience, for which the couplet was the ideal container.

For as one formal sign of Renaissance secular sententiousness, the couplet, whether at the end of the sonnet or elsewhere, gives scope for the display of another form of courtly wit: the proverb, maxim, adage or, as the rhetoricians called it, the apophthegm.[13] Rosalie Colie defines it as

> a sub-literary small form intended to transfer culture and to communicate important values, more a literary 'device' than a genre, and workable into any kind of literature an author might choose. This is the adage, the *sententia*, a quotation from an authoritative source (biblical, classical, proverbial) which sums up a mass of experience in one charged phrase, demonstrating the community of human experience – in short, the adage is *literally* a common place, a convergence point of consensus.[14]

The proverb is still used in common speech when we wish to identify ourselves as part of a larger human group subject to general 'laws' of conduct or of fate; it stabilises or controls uncertainty by invoking a higher authority (usually left unidentified) whose voice the speaker temporarily assumes, thereby becoming wiser than himself, and also wittier, since proverbs and adages are usually memorable because they have some kind of rhetorical enhancement: alliteration, internal rhyme, a striking metaphor. Sixteenth-century rhetoric embraced not only proverbs from popular speech, but also maxims drawn from classical authors, and offered published collections of these for study, collection in personal commonplace books and incorporation in one's own writing. At the most learned level, the adage merges into literary quotation, as in Robert Burton's *Anatomy of Melancholy*; at the level of work intended for popular reading, the vulgar proverb is extensively used, as in George Herbert's poetry: in between lie works which exploit all sources and also invent their own, such as Montaigne's and Bacon's essays. Bacon's *Essays*, indeed, belong to the tradition of courtesy manuals, offering rules of conduct and worldly wisdom to men in, or aspiring to, public life, and offer their *sententiae* not simply for the pragmatic advice they contain, but also as an imitable style of speech: the courtier should not only know that (to quote Bacon) 'Revenge is a kind of wild justice', but should be able to say that, or something like it, to enhance his reputation for gravity and wit. Thomas Dekker defined the courtier, satirically, as 'he that talkes all Adage and Apothegme', and in the writings of Montaigne and the humbler Thomas Whythorne we can see how even in the explicitly proposed task of representing the private self the Renaissance speaker reached for adages to secure his /I/ by general authority.[15] Viewed in this light, even Hamlet's self-communing in his 'To be or not to be' soliloquy can be seen as amazingly *im*personal, a tissue of general *sententiae*.

It is possible to make a poem entirely out of maxims, such as the lyric by Wyatt which Richard Tottel printed in his *Miscellany* (1557) under the title, 'Of dissembling wordes':

> Throughout the world, if it wer sought,
> Fair wordes ynough a man shall find:
> They be good chepe, they cost right nought,
> Their substance is but onely winde:
> But well to say and so to mene,
> That sweet acord is seldom sene. (192)

But the length of the sonnet resists the simple stringing together of independent maxims, and encourages a discursive handling of them: at the same time the couplet, invented by Wyatt and endorsed by his successors, offers the chance of a witty conclusion. This combined gravity and wit, in a combination that had been boundlessly attractive in Italy, was to prove equally so in France, and did not lose its appeal altogether until the mid-seventeenth century in Britain, when a new kind of discursive clarity favoured the heroic couplet at the expense of the quatrain. But to return to Wyatt: in choosing Petrarch as his sonnet-master, from whom he derives seventeen of his thirty-two sonnets, he was following a poet not at all inclined to the maxim (though he did translate *Rime* 140, one of the very few Petrarch sonnets to end with a proverb: 'Bel fin fa chi ben amando more' – 'He makes a good end who dies loving faithfully'). What he learnt from Petrarch was how to dramatise inner anguish; what Serafino seems to have suggested to him is how this might be combined with wit and clarity, to produce that combination of passion and weight masked by grace and acuity that was the desirable courtierly style – what Spenser praised in Sir Philip Sidney as 'highest conceits, longest foresights, and deepest works of wit'. He could not foresee the love-sonnet craze of the 1590s, but he must have been aware of Petrarch's reputation in France and Spain, and sensed the need to English him at home. Just as the relatively small output of the Sicilian sonneteers was imitated and then developed in the northern Italian cities, so the relatively small output of Wyatt and his younger colleague, the Earl of Surrey, was imitated and then developed by later British writers – who could also, of course, go directly to Petrarch and his Italian and French followers if they wished. But a desirable and operative persona, which the sonnet structure to some extent determined, now sanctioned the sonnet form, and offered itself to other writers as a possible way to be in the world of courtly poesis.

Neither Wyatt nor his younger colleague, Henry Howard, Earl of Surrey, published their poems: Surrey was executed for treason at the age of thirty, and Wyatt, even if he intended to publish, as his poem 'Yet well ye kno' (142) seems to prove, died prematurely and suddenly of a fever. Now, since the sonnet is a very short poem, it has always had to be aggregated for transmission, or, if written as an occasional piece, inserted into its occasion, like Hugh Holland's sonnet 'Upon the Lines and Life of the Famous Scenicke Poet, Master William Shakespeare' into the First Folio of Shakespeare's plays. Some occasions are very evidently textual: epitaphs are intended to mark the place of the person now dead, so that the text as it were replaces the person; dedicatory or complimentary sonnets refer to the volume in which they occur. But most occasions – giving a present, professing love, sending a rebuke – do not assume a textual form, but vanish once they have been lived, and the sonnet remains as the only thing from which the occasion can be reconstructed. Petrarch solved this problem of intelligibility by aggregating his own sonnets into a collection whose main subject was Laura: thus those sonnets which do not refer to Laura at all, or which were originally addressed to someone else, can be understood as part of a larger narrative. The same appears to have happened, but this time without the author's overseeing of it, in Shakespeare's *Sonnets*. The Petrarchan sequence, which dominated British sonnet-writing at the end of the sixteenth century, is probably the most powerful template for organising sonnets. The next most powerful is the 'author' – a sufficiently large number of sonnets (mixed with other lyric forms, perhaps) can be transmitted simply because they are the work of one person; and finally sonnets (again mixed with other kinds of lyric, if need be) can be grouped by tone and content: 'grave and godly', or 'pleasant and conceited' or 'passionate'. All these modes of ordering can of course be used together; but unless the sonnets are formally linked, as in *corona*-form, there is always a problem of aggregation, caused by the essentially enclosed nature of the sonnet itself.

Hidden away at the back of a small volume of Calvin's sermons, and thereby probably without influence on contemporary poets, is the very first sonnet sequence in English literature, published within three years of *Tottel's Miscellany* in 1560 by a woman poet, Anne Lock, mother of Henry Lok the religious sonneteer. Presenting it as 'a meditation of a penitent sinner', she used Surrey's model to craft a sequence of twenty-one sonnets, solving the problem of aggregation by keying each one as a paraphrase to one verse of Psalm 51. Her passionate persona is thus a development of the /I/ of the Psalms, but she also prefaced the paraphrase with five preliminary sonnets of her own, written syntactically as one continuous utterance. Her verse is metaphorically simple, and much given to lexical redoubling; but her ear is faultless – better than Surrey's – and her command of enjambment in the service of the flow of passion is astonishing at so early a date, and unequalled until Sidney began to write:

> Loke on me, Lord: though trembling I beknowe
> That sight of sinne so sore offendeth thee,
> That seeing sinne, how it doth overflowe
> My whelmed soule, thou canst not loke on me
> But with disdaine, with horror and despite.
> Loke on me, Lord: but loke not on my sinne.
> Not that I hope to hyde it from thy sight,
> Which seest me all without and eke within,
> But so remove it from they wrathfull eye,
> And from the justice of thyne angry face,
> That thou impute it not. Loke not how I
> Am foule by sinne: but make me by thy grace
> Pure in thy mercies sight, and, Lord, I pray,
> That hatest sinne, wipe all my sinnes away. (11)[16]

But Anne Lock's poetry came just too late to enter Tottel's pages, and to see how the problem of putting sonnets together was tackled we go to the title-page of the first erotic lyric sequence published in Britain, Thomas Watson's *Hekatompathia* (1582), which, though made up of eighteen-line stanzas rhyming ABABCC DEDEFF GHGHJJ, set a precedent for later sonneteers. His title-page reads:

> THE/'EKATOMΠAΘIA/OR/PASSIONATE/*Centurie of,*/Love/ *Divided into two parts:where-/of, the first expresseth the Au-/thours sufferance in Loue. the/latter, his long farewell to Loue/and all his tyrannie./* Composed by *Thomas Watson*/Gentleman: and published/at the request of certaine Gentle-/men his very frendes.

The Greek title, and the very gentlemanly origins of the text, serve to guarantee the contents against triviality, and preserve the fiction that a gentleman does not publish for profit or vulgar fame. The word 'passionate' identifies the subject matter (love-poetry) – this will not be homiletic or didactic verse; and the term 'centurie' gives a numerological coherence to the contents, just as Petrarch had done by selecting 365 + 1 poems (a year and a day) for his *Rime*. Then, too, just as Petrarch had divided his *Rime* into two parts, interpreted by his commentators as sonnets before and after the death of Laura, so Watson (after Poem 79) divides his collection into two, suggesting some sort of moral revolt against Love, and the coherence of a psychodrama. The sixteenth-century reader, who would browse through a title-page as we read the blurb on a book jacket, is thus instructed how to read this lyric collection, and in what register of social, moral and rhetorical activity to place it. For the educated reader, each poem (called a 'sonnet' by Watson) is prefaced by a gloss, not unlike Dante's in his *Vita Nuova*, indicating what the poem is about, where the conceits derive from and, if there is a source text in another language, what it is – a practice *not* followed by later sonneteers.

Wyatt and Surrey, who might well have organised their lyrics in some such fashion, did not live to do so, and the first English sonnets were presented to their readers in a different way, which (because the book was extremely popular) may actually have held up the development of the sonnet which was to occur in the 1580s and 1590s. Their sonnets were published for the first time in the book I have already referred to as *Tottel's Miscellany*, though that now very common name is not its original title: in 1557, Richard Tottel published, and may himself have edited, *Songes and Sonettes, written by the ryght honorable Lorde Henry Haward late Earle of Surrey, and other.*[17] It contained at first 41 poems attributed to Surrey, 97 poems attributed to Wyatt, 40 poems attributed to Nicholas Grimald (1519?–1562?), and 94 by 'uncertain authors'. Of these, 13 are sonnets by Surrey, with two more added in the second edition; 27 are sonnets by Wyatt, though three were converted by Tottel out of rondeaux; 3 are sonnets by Grimald, and 9 are by the rest. There is a small number of irregular sonnets.

Now, although the sonnets by Surrey, who comes first in the volume, and those by Wyatt, who comes second, are clustered together, the word 'Sonettes' in the title does not, perversely, refer exclusively to fourteen-line poems in octave and sestet. And since Tottel's phrase 'Songs and Sonnets' (however spelt) was the first use in print, and since it became a catchphrase for the next century, a digression is required here on the meaning of 'sonnet' and the effect of its use. Though in Provençal and in very early Italian usage, *sonet* or *sonetto* simply meant 'a short lyric poem', the massive achievement of Petrarch and the colossal amount of true sonnet-writing in Italian quickly stabilised the meaning to denote the fourteen-line poem rhyming in octave and sestet, with variants such as the tailed sonnet permitted. In Britain, however, throughout the sixteenth century and even in the seventeenth, the word 'sonnet', particularly in the phrase 'songs and sonnets', often meant no more than 'a light poem': not always short, and not always lyric, since in some collections ballads are called 'sonnets'.[18] Since Tottel's phrase distinguishes between 'sonnets' and 'songs', it seems that poems which were repetitive and written in short lines suitable for music were regarded as 'songs', while more discursive poems, including true sonnets, were thought of as 'sonnets': a sonnet could of course be set to music, but in that case its text would by itself normally be thought of as a sonnet. In Thomas

Whythorne's autobiography of the mid-sixteenth century, written about 1576, before the sonnet sequences of the last two decades, the word 'sonnet' is used of poems ranging from two lines to eighteen lines in length. A single passage makes his terms reasonably clear: talking about publishing his music, he declares that he had 'made many songs to be sung of 3, 4 and 5 parts, or for voices, as well as that which I had made to be played on virginals or the lute. . . . And also I purposed to put with every song a sonnet of mine own invention for a ditty thereto' (spelling modernised),[19] thus making it clear that a 'sonnet', whatever its length, was a composed text which could be used as a 'ditty' (words for a song);[20] whereas a 'song' was either music waiting for words or words suitable for music. George Gascoigne, the first sixteenth-century British writer to define the sonnet as we understand it, tried in 1575 to clear the confusion up:

> Then have you Sonnets: some thinke that all Poemes (being short) may be called Sonets, as in deede it is a diminutive worde derived of *Sonare*, but yet I can beste allow to call those Sonnets whiche are of fourtene lynes, every line conteyning tenne syllables. The first twelve do rhyme in staves of foure lines by cross meetre, and the last two ryming togither do conclude the whole.[21]

And the royal poetic theorist James VI, noting that 'for compendious praysing of any bukes, or the authoris thairof, or ony argumentis of uther historeis, qhuair sundrie sentences, and changis of ppurposis are requyrit, use *Sonet* verse',[22] was quite clear that sonnet verse was 'of fourtene lynis, and ten fete in every lyne'. Yet as late as 1611 the two great Italian and French dictionaries of the age, Florio's and Cotgrave's, respectively defined *sonetto* as 'a Sonnet, a Canzonet, a Song' and *sonet* as 'a Sonnet, or canzonet, a song (most commonly) of 14 verses'.

When Thomas Watson published his *Hekatompathia* of 1582, which was composed of eighteen-line poems which he called 'sonnets', the volume contained two true sonnets, one of which hails Watson as the new Petrarch, to whom the stars have destined 'the *Thuscan's* poesie,/Who skald the skies in lofty *Quatorzain*', and the word 'quatorzain' is used in the title of that sonnet and also in the title of a sonnet by Watson himself: 'A Quatorzain of the Authour unto this his booke of Lovepassions'.[23] It is not clear from this whether Watson would have put a 'quatorzain' into the larger category of 'sonnet' along with his own eighteen-line poems, but he certainly recognised the distinctive form of the true sonnet by using the word. Similarly Thomas Campion, in his polemic against rhymed verse, *Observations in the Arte of English Poesy* (1602), declares that

> in Quatorzens, methinks, the poet handles his subject as tyrannically as *Procrustes* the thiefe his prisoners, whom, when he had taken, he used to cast upon a bed, which if they were too short to

> fill, he would stretch them longer, if too long, he would cut them shorter[24]

– thereby adding the endorsement of an expert poet to what has been said above about the peculiarity of fourteen lines: that that is too long for a simple point, and too short for a narrative or developed argument. Campion himself was not a sonneteer, which may explain why as late as 1602 he used the rather pedantic 'quatorzain'.

As we emerge from this digression, the reader might be forgiven for feeling that during the high point of sonnet production in Britain nobody really knew what a sonnet was. The situation, however, can be summed up briefly thus:

1. From the time of Wyatt until about 1575, the word 'sonnet' meant 'a lightweight poem, usually short, without explicit features adapting it for music'.
2. From 1575 onwards to the middle of the seventeenth century, the word 'sonnet' normally meant 'a fourteen-line poem in octave and sestet'. This was enforced by the nearly universal practice among writers of sonnet sequences, of putting 'Sonnet X'[25] at the head of each sonnet; if the sonnets carried only a number, the word 'sonnet' would appear on the title-page. However, the old catchphrase 'songs and sonnets' still suggested that a sonnet was any short poem, and was so used, for example by John Donne.
3. The word 'quatorzain' was very rarely used, but is applied to true sonnets.

To return now to the link between Wyatt and Surrey and the sonnet sequences of the century's end, *Tottel's Miscellany*: the fact that as early as 1575 George Gascoigne defined the sonnet as of twelve lines rhyming 'in staves of foure lines by cross meetre' and 'the last two ryming togither', testifies to the extraordinary success of Tottel's often reprinted anthology in selling the new 'English' rhymescheme (ABAB CDCD EFEF GG, invented and favoured by Surrey; or ABBA ABBA CDDC EE, Wyatt's model) to the poets of the nation.

To say that is not to claim that Tottel made the sonnet as a form immediately popular; but those writers who did attempt the sonnet after the *Miscellany*'s publication used the rhymeschemes and structures which Wyatt and Surrey had developed, rather than the Italian or French rhymeschemes also available.[26] The French were indeed ahead of the British in sonnet production in the middle of the sixteenth century, producing occasional sonnets, love-sonnets and even Petrarchan sequences in quantity from the late 1540s onwards; further, they had evolved, and quickly adopted as a regular form, a sestet containing a rhyme couplet, and no British writer who could read French at all could have been ignorant of it; yet it was almost entirely ignored in favour of the 'English' form.

The 'French sonnet', if I may now call it that, was invented by Clement Marot (1496–1544) in a sort of upside-down version of Wyatt's procedure: if Wyatt was prompted to put the couplet at the end of the sonnet by observing its witty effect in the *strambotti* of Serafino, and because of its use in already existing Engish stanza forms, Marot, it seems, rearranged the sestet of the sonnet to have a couplet at the beginning (CC DEED: more rarely, CCDEDE) because of the French *sixain*, a short form already in use, rhyming AABCBC. Now, it is clear why someone with a fondness for epigram and *sententia* would find this unsatisfactory: the couplet so used is a form of closure, and the beginning of the sestet is always the opening of its development. The result is that French sonneteers never[27] use the CC rhyme couplet as a sense couplet, and, indeed, may well produce sonnets in which the rhyme couplet does not work with the sense, and a sense couplet does not harness rhyme:

Père du ciel, si mil' et mile fois
Au gré du corps, que mon desire convie,
Or que je suis au printemps de ma vie,
J'ay asservi et la plume, et la voix:
Toy qui du coeur les abismes congnois,
Ains que l'hiver ait ma force ravie,
Fay moy brusler d'une celeste envie,
Pour mieux gouter la douceur de tes loix.
Las! si tu fais comparoitre ma faulte,
Au jugement de ta majesté haulte,
Ou mes forfaictz me viendront accuser,
Qui me pourra deffendre de ton ire?
Mon grand péché me veult condamner, Sire,
Mais ta bonté me peult bien excuser.

(Joachim du Bellay, 1522–60)

[Father of Heaven, if thousands of times to the service of the flesh, which holds my lusts, since now I am in the springtime of life, I have lent my pen and my tongue,

Thou who knowest the abysses of the heart, when winter shall bereave me of my strength, make me burn with heavenly desire, the better to relish the sweetness of thy laws.

Alas! if thou bringest my sin to account at the bar of thy high majesty, where my trespasses will bear witness against me, who can defend me from thy wrath? The greatness of my sin will damn me, Lord, but yet thy goodness may well pardon me.]

Although the rhyme does enforce the distance between God and the sinner (*faulte/haulte*), an English writer, one feels, would have dramatised the antithesis in the last two lines by clinching it with a rhyme:

> Lord, my great sin to death doth sentence me,
> But yet thy goodness comes to set me free.

There are subtler uses of this medial couplet – for example. to suggest a conclusion which turns out to be provisional or wrong[28] – but, whatever its virtues, it was ignored by the British writers who followed *Tottel's Miscellany*.

Thus, 'in spite of all temptations, To belong to other nations' British writers accepted for imitation and admiration the 4 + 4 + 4 + 2 structure of Wyatt and Surrey, with its very strong tendency to impose a neat conclusion on the sestet of the Italian sonnet. By placing Surrey's poetry first in the *Miscellany*, Tottel may also have enhanced the prestige of the divided octave, for out of Surrey's fifteen sonnets twelve change rhyme in the octave, thus: ABAB CDCD EFEF GG, producing an easier form to write, and one in which three separate blocks of thought, instead of two, are suggested. Wyatt, like the French sonneteers, preferred the unified octave, ABBA ABBA.

The problem of aggregation, referred to earlier, was solved by Tottel by giving titles to all the poems,[29] titles in which the word 'lover' occurs whenever there is the slightest excuse (and sometimes when there is not). So we have 'How the lover perisheth in his delight, as the flie in the fire' for Wyatt's 'Some fowles there be' (24); 'The lovers life compared to the Alpes' for 'Like to these unmesurable montayns' (33); and, more crisply, 'A renouncing of love' for 'Ffarewell Love'. For many of the poems, the speaker's action is characterised as the expression of dissatisfaction: the lover 'excuseth', 'renounceth', 'complaineth', 'waileth', 'describeth his restless state' and so forth. Though there are poems in the collection that refer to specific events or places – e.g., Surrey's 'When Windsor walls susteyned my wearied arme' or 'Wiat being in Prison, to Brian' – the generalised figure of 'the lover' bestrides this poetic world like a colossus, moving from poem to poem in restless jumps, and voicing feelings that, though they alter constantly from poem to poem, throughout reverberate a sense of 'unquiet'. The lover, as Archspeaker of this collection, is a person either alone or turning away from someone hostile to him (we are speaking still of the titles, which are much simpler than the texts they appear with), and since he is a creation, in the titles, not of the contributing poets but of their editor, he does not appear, as Petrarch does in the *Rime*, both as the person who suffers and the writer who, retrospectively, describes that suffering. That measure of artistic control is absent, and the lover has an element of randomness and confusion that is not present in the sequences of Petrarch or (to take a contemporaneous example from France) Joachim du Bellay, in his *L'Olive* (1549–50).

Extending the slightly fanciful notion of an Archspeaker to the poems in the collection that do not deal with love, we might suggest that the other person walking about in this collection is the courtier of 'adage and apophthegm' – many of the poems have titles which are maxims, or bits of maxims, or promise sententious advice: 'Not to trust to much but beware by others calamities'; 'They of the meane estate are happiest'; 'All worldly pleasures fade'; 'N. Vincent to G. Blackwood, agaynst wedding'; 'Marcus Catoes comparison of mans life with yron' (our courtier has had a humanist education). Though only a minority of these titled poems are sonnets, the effect of the titling is to project on to a larger scale the persona already noticed in the sonnets of Wyatt: the courtier, restless and introspective, who is also concerned to please by an elegant philosophising. The two archspeakers are really one, and the sonnet, which has a fairly concentrated presence in the early part of Tottel's volume,[30] is particularly well adapted, as Wyatt and Surrey had fashioned it, to hold both in balance. 'The Lover waxeth wiser, and will not die for affection.'

The subsequent popularity of Tottel's arrangement of texts, and the way in which it served both as a model for later miscellanies and as a reservoir of poetic materials for plagiarism and for imitation, make it important to note that in passing on this powerful courtly poetic persona, the joint production, as it were, of all his authors, Tottel did one other thing to influence the style of his century: he smoothed out the phrasing and regularised the metre of his contributors. Since we possess one Wyatt manuscript from which (perhaps at one remove) Tottel worked,[31] we can compare his printed versions with Wyatt's own, and note how far his alterations extended: comparisons cannot be made with manuscripts of the other authors, but it is safe to assume that the man who changed three rondeaux by Wyatt into sonnets[32] would not have been shy of altering anything else that did not seem appealing. Tottel's 'adaptation' of one of Wyatt's particularly gnarled and intense sonnets shows the kind of smoothness that was becoming desirable. Wyatt:

> How oft have I my dere & cruell foo
> with those your Iyes for to get peace and truyse
> profferd you myn hert but you do not use
> emong so high thinges to cast your mynde so lowe
> Yf any othre loke for it as ye trowe
> there vayn weke hope doeth greatly theim abuse
> and thus I disdain that that ye refuse
> it was ones mine it can no more be so
> Yf I then it chase nor it in you can fynde
> in this exile no manner of comfort

nor lyve allone nor where he is called resort
He may wander from his naturall kynd
so shall it be great hurt unto us twayn
and yours the loss and myn the dedly pain

With that version (reproduced from the Egerton MS.) as copy, Tottel produced this:

The lover prayeth his offred hart to be received.

How oft have I, my deare and cruell fo:
With my great pain to get some peace or truce,
Geven you my hart? but you do not use,
In so hie thinges, to cast your mind so low.
If any other loke for it, as you trow,
Their vaine weake hope doth greatly them abuse.
And that thus I disdayne, that you refuse.
It once was mine, it can no more be so.
If you it chase, that it in you can finde,
In this exile, no maner of comfort:
Nor live alone, nor where he is calde, resort,
He may wander from his naturall kinde.
So shall it be great hurt unto us twayne,
And yours the losse, and mine the deadly payne.

The title simplifies quite crudely the very complicated negotiations that Wyatt has created in this piece of heart bargaining: it may be that Tottel did not understand what the sestet meant, but he has certainly been willing to sacrifice the intricacy of this pseudo-diplomatic sonnet to regularise the metre. The 'I/eyes' pun in l. 2, which was not available to Wyatt in Petrarch's Italian (*Rime* 21),[33] and which became a favourite of Shakespeare and his contemporaries, evidently offended Tottel, and in smoothing the line by substituting 'to get some peace' (x / x /) for 'for to get peace' (/ x x /) he removed it also, reducing the sense of antagonism between lover and lady. 'Given' is certainly more mellifluous than 'profferd' with its bunched consonants, but also less precise – a proffer is *not* a gift, as any diplomat would know. 'In' in l. 4 removes the eleventh syllable from the line, but also changes the meaning: 'emong so hie thinges' means 'among such great affairs as you are properly concerned with', whereas 'in so hie thinges' means 'in such high affairs as this' – which is a low affair, as the rest of the line says. The sense of the lady as an enemy of much higher rank than her lover is muddled, if not lost. The repeated 'that' in l. 7 also annoyed Tottel, who rearranged the first 'that' further up the line: but again the meaning is changed, since in Wyatt's position it means 'the thing which you refuse' – i.e., my heart, while in Tottel's line the word 'that' appears to refer to something in the previous two lines, which is nonsensical.

In the sestet, Tottel needed only to remove the word 'then' to restore the line to ten syllables: his substitution of 'you' for 'I' in 'If you it chase' makes a conventional and clear change from 'I' in the octave to 'you' in the sestet, but quite destroys Wyatt's intricacy: the point is that if the *lover* rejects his own heart, which cannot any longer be his, since it has been formally proffered, then the heart is exiled; if the *lady* now also rejects it, it cannot as an exile find sanctuary anywhere else, and cannot live alone (since a heart needs a body). She will lose a valuable proffer and he will lose a most faithful retainer. But the whole bitterness of exile – what Mowbray in *Richard II* describes as

> to turn me from my country's light
> To dwell in solemn shades of endless night

is lost if the sestet does not start with 'If *I* . . .'. Wyatt's deft use of the half-line of the sonnet to oscillate between self and other, /I/ and /you/, has been very much attenuated, in the interests of a smoother but more conventional and slacker sonnet.

'Editorial changes of the kind mentioned', says Hyder Rollins in his edition of *Tottel's Miscellany*, 'were most unfair to Wyatt, but at the same time they no doubt enhanced his reputation.'[34] He and Surrey became the two new fathers or teachers of English poetry, and particularly of the sonnet, which writers in the 1560s, 1570s and 1580s began to imitate, sometimes using Wyatt's model, but on the whole preferring Surrey's, with its more frequent change of rhymes. There was no doubt that in their verse elegance and sententiousness combined to admiration, as George Turbervile declared in 1567, the year of the sixth edition of *Tottel's Miscellany*, praising Surrey,

> Whose pen approovde what wit he had in mue,
> Where such a skill in making Sonets grue.
> Eche worde in place with such a sleight is coucht,
> Eche thing whereof he treates so firmly toucht,
> As Pallas seemde within his noble breast
> To have sojournde, and beene a daylie guest;
> Our mother tongue by him hath got such light,
> As ruder speach thereby is banisht quight. . . .
> A mirrour he the simple sort to traine,
> That ever beate his brayne for Britans gayne.[35]

7

'I AM NOT I': THE SONNETS OF SIDNEY

Penelope Devereux, Lady Rich (1563–1607), who was certainly responsible for the erotic fascination that produced Sir Philip Sidney's *Astrophel and Stella*,[1] may also thereby have been responsible for the whole Elizabethan sonnet-sequence craze: for until she entered Sidney's life in the early months of 1581 neither he nor anyone else appears to have thought of writing a sequence of English sonnets in the Petrarchan style. This post-Tottel failure to produce, between 1557 and 1582, what the French were writing in enormous numbers and well-structured sequences, has puzzled and even irritated critics: Sidney Lee, in his energetic account of cultural transference at the time, *The French Renaissance in England* (Oxford, 1910), repeatedly speaks as if a kind of depressive melancholia, a mental blackness, had invaded Britain in these years; and even J. W. Lever accuses the young Spenser of 'some deep-rooted aversion to the sonnet as a mode of self-expression', and a 'negative approach'.[2]

Granted that it is always difficult to explain the non-appearance of works of art, we can try to suggest a reason here without resorting to notions of national psychosis or Freudian repression: sonnets were being written in those twenty-five years, usually on the model of Surrey, not in any great numbers, but almost always in collections modelled on *Tottel's Miscellany*, that is, as lyrics on the same footing as sixains, dizains, odes, song forms and couplet poems. Even Sidney, who from 1577 onwards was writing poetry very vigorously, and with a consciousness that English verse was in need of reform, seems to have continued to use the term 'sonnet' in its older, wider sense: in his prose romance, *Arcadia*, the first version of which, called the *Old Arcadia*, was composed between 1577 and 1580, he inserted sixteen true sonnets along with many other kinds of verse, but only two of the sixteen are actually described as 'sonnets' in the text – the remainder are indifferently called 'verses' or 'songs'. In the collection of poems composed at the same time, up to 1581, and published after Sidney's death as 'Certain Sonnets', there are again thirteen sonnets mixed with other lyric forms, and the term 'sonnets' in the title (which may not have been Sidney's own) seems to refer to the whole collection, not simply to the true sonnets therein. In assembling the collection himself, Sidney gave it a slight structure; but, whatever he called it in his own mind, he had no thought of it as a sonnet sequence. For all his extensive experimentation with different verse forms, and with Italian as well as English true sonnet forms, Sidney is still thinking, up to 1581, of a collection of 'sonnets' as similar to *Tottel's Miscellany*.

So, too, minor writers such as Barnabe Googe (1540–94), George Gascoigne (1542–77), George Turberville (1540–1610), Thomas Howell (a retainer of the Sidney family, whose dates are unclear), and even the Latin poet Daniel Rogers (1536–91), also acquainted with Sidney[3] – all of these thought of sonnets as simply one kind of lyric poetry to be aggregated in miscellany form, though credit must be given to Gascoigne for publishing technically the second sonnet sequences in English, in his *A Hundreth Sundrie Flowres* of 1573: a narrative sequence of three sonnets and a moralising sequence of seven in *corona*-form.

A glimpse of direct contact with French sonneteering is provided by the young Spenser (he of the 'negative approach') who at the age of seventeen, in 1569, contributed poems to a handsomely illustrated volume edited by John van der Noodt, called *A Theatre wherein be represented . . . the miseries and calamities that follow the voluptuous Worldlings*.[4] Spenser contributed translations of two poetic visions of mutability, the one a version by Clement Marot of Petrarch's *canzone* 'Standomi un giorno solo a la fenestra' ('Being one day at my window all alone') (*Rime* 323); and the other a translation of a sonnet sequence by Joachim du Bellay (1522–60), his 'Songe' or 'Vision', which was itself inspired by Marot's translation of Petrarch's 'Standomi un giorno'. For Marot, Spenser used a twelve-line stanza, as Petrarch had; for du Bellay, confronted with fifteen French sonnets in sequence, he used fifteen *blank verse* sonnets, an extremely rare form; it clearly did not occur to him in 1569 that a sequence of English rhymed sonnets would have any special value.

The next question to be asked is: What kind of coherence could a sequence of sonnets confer upon the experience contained in them? Three sequences were printed in the decade in which Sidney wrote *Astrophel and Stella*, and they, in their various ways, suggest how the business of forming a sequence looked to those who were embarking on it without predecessors. The first printed sequence (with due credit given to George Gascoigne, as mentioned above) is Thomas Watson's *Hekatompathia* of 1582: though its poems are of eighteen lines, it is a very determinedly planned and offered sequence; the second is *Pandora* of 1584, by John Soowthern, probably the worst volume of verse ever printed in English, but undeniably containing sonnets in sequence; and the third is James VI of Scotland's *Twelf Sonnets of Invocations to the Goddis* of 1585.[5] None of these poets is likely to have read Sidney's sonnets, unless in very small numbers in manuscript.

The simplest sequence is James VI's: it is what may be called a 'categorial' sequence, that is, each sonnet describes or deals with one item from a category, such as the days of the week, the planets or, as in James's sequence, the pagan gods. Here the /I/ is simply a describing voice, who 'tells', 'descrives' or 'declares', and the emotional quality of each sonnet comes from the object described, not from the speaker.

> And first, o *Phebus*, when I do descrive
> The *Springtyme* sproutar of the herbes and flowris,
> Whom with in rank none of the four do strive,
> But nearest thee do stand all tymes and houris:
> Graunt Readers may esteme, they sie the showris,
> Whose balmy drops so softlie dois distell,
> Which watrie cloudds in mesure suche down powris,
> As makis the herbis, and verie earth to smell
> With savours sweit, fra tyme that onis thy sell
> The vapouris softlie sowkis with smyling cheare,
> Whilkis syne in cloudds are keiped closs and well,
> Whill vehement *Winter* come in tyme of yeare.
> Graunt, when I lyke the *Springtyme* to displaye,
> That Readers think they sie the Spring alwaye.[6]

If this sonnet lacks argumentative crispness (it is hard to be dialectical about landscape), it has a gentle fluency appropriate to its preoccupation with rain, and James has used the favourite Scottish sonnet form, usually known from its great English exponent as the *Spenserian*[7] sonnet, in which each quatrain picks up a rhyme from the previous one but also introduces a new one, rhyming thus: ABAB BCBC CDCD EE. This form, the most intricate of all sonnet rhymeschemes, was never popular in England, but we shall meet it again in discussing Spenser's sequence, the *Amoretti*.

John Soowthern's *Pandora* is actually the first printed sequence of love-sonnets, and also the first sequence addressed to a named mistress – who, as is wholly typical of the man, is not called Pandora, but Diana. The verse is hilariously and wildly incompetent (it has been suggested that Soowthern was a native French speaker, which would explain why the three poems in French in the volume all rhyme and scan, while the English ones never come near it); but, in his desire to score a series of poetic firsts in English, Soowthern does indeed show the new intertextuality of love poetry in the early 1580s: whereas earlier writers imitated Italian or French models, but rarely acknowledged any previous poetic voice other than Petrarch's, Soowthern, using a French sonnet form, is much more inclusive:

The Greeke Poet to whome Bathill was the guide,
Made her immortall, by that which he did sing:
And (were it so I know not but) of Corine,
We faine the patrone of the Latine Ovide,
And since them (Petrarque) a wise Florentine,
Who turned his Mistres into a tree of Baye.
And he that soong the eldest daughter of Troye,
In Fraunce hath made of her, an astre Divine.
  And like these knowne men, can your Soothern write too:
  And as long as Englishe lasts, immortall you.
I the penne of Soothern will my fayre Diana,
Make thee immortall: if thou wilt give him favour:
For then hee'll sing Petrark, Tien, Ovide, Ronsar:
And make thee Cassander, Corine, Bathyll, Laura. (2)[8]

The poetic lover is now an echo not only of Petrarchan 'wisdom', but also of Ovidian and Anacreontic sensuality, and, in a spirit of national rivalry, of the immortalising voices of Ronsard ('Cassandra') and Desportes ('Diana'). The sonnet sequence is a literary rebirth in England of the great tradition of European love, creating texts that confer honour and impart wisdom – and hence are fit gifts for such as the Earl of Oxford, just as William McGonagall wished to impress Queen Victoria.

Thomas Watson, whose view of his own sequence has been discussed in Chapter 6, would have agreed with this desire for pedigree: in setting out his collection of one hundred eighteen-line poems, dedicated like Soowthern's to the Earl of Oxford, he expressed the usual courtierly deprecation of his 'idle toyes proceedinge from a youngling frenzie', but carefully indicated all his sources, and gave status to his material by dividing it, like Petrarch's *Rime*, into two parts, the chronicle of a life of love and repentance.

In adopting the very powerful Petrarchan template, which makes the second section of the sequence a moral corrective to the passionate erotic intensity of the first, Watson was in effect giving firm shape to what was implicit in all the various titles of the poems in *Tottel's Miscellany*: while any single poem may represent passions and desires, a larger poetic enterprise will progress towards some kind of wisdom, whether of a Neoplatonic, Christian or simply humanly moral kind. Even before Petrarch, Guittone d'Arezzo had shaped his own sonnets by counterbalancing his love sonnets with moral sonnets: this allows the single sonnet to function as a record of a 'patheticall' /I/, but also gives the whole poetic enterprise a moral function, according to the demands that humanist culture made of art. The courtier's eloquence can thus be admired in each poem, and yet be rounded off with praiseworthy sententiousness. Some later writers do this very perfunctorily, like Sir William Alexander at the end of his *Aurora* sequence of 1604; others, like Drummond of Hawthornden, use it with full Petrarchan seriousness; something like this shape is discernible in the two parts of Shakespeare's *Sonnets*.

In turning now to the sonnets of Philip Sidney (1554–86),[9] we have, ironically, to consider them, Petrarch-fashion, both *in vita* and *in morte*: for the sonnets were composed in one set of circumstances, and published after his death in another. Sidney was mythologised by his age: turned into a national hero and pattern of courtliness after his public funeral, he also became a pattern for poetry – so much so that entire handbooks of rhetoric were based on examples of his writing.[10] Yet this pattern of courtliness was not in his life particularly successful by his age's standards: his knighthood he only obtained because he was a stand-in at an investiture ceremony; his political service was limited to a relatively trivial embassy in 1577 and, eight years later, the governorship of Flushing, which took him to the battlefield of Zutphen, from the injuries of which he died on 17 October 1586; not one of his sonnets is written to his Queen; and his literary fame derives wholly from the works written in the vacant years when she would not employ him in her service.

But, however much Sidney would rather have engaged in politics and diplomacy, his interest in literature was serious and intelligent, and very productive. After his embassy in 1577, he began writing the romance known as the *Old Arcadia*, finished about 1580,[11] which contained a number of sonnets all spoken or sung by characters in the novel. After the *Old Arcadia* was finished, or perhaps while it neared completion, Sidney was collecting a number of miscellaneous poems that do not seem to have had anything to do with the *Old Arcadia* or with *Astrophel and Stella*: this collection, which included thirteen sonnets almost all of the Wyatt–Surrey type, was first printed in 1598, in the third edition of *The Countess of Pembrokes Arcadia*, which despite its title was a collected edition of Sidney's writings. It is this collection, called 'Certain Sonnets' in the 1598 volume, that first shows Sidney thinking sequentially: the collection begins with two sonnets yielding 'unto [the] loathed yoke' of Love, and ends with two penitential sonnets, 'Thou blind man's marke' and 'Leave me, o Love'. This is a faint echo – perhaps a pre-echo, if such a thing can exist – of Thomas Watson's pattern in *Hekatompathia*.

Then he met Penelope Devereux: and though his fascination started, as he himself pointed out, 'not at first sight, nor with a dribbed shot' (*AS* 2)[12] as the Petrarchan lover should, it none the less had an electrifying effect both on Sidney's poetry and on the course of the English sonnet. In a very few months he composed a sequence quite unlike anything written before or, despite the looming talents of Spenser, Shakespeare and Drummond of Hawthornden, anything written after.

The facts behind it are quickly summarised. Penelope, eldest daughter of the first Earl of Essex, and sister of the unlucky second Earl, executed for treason in 1601, came to court as the young ward of the Countess of Huntingdon in January 1581. Five years before, when she was 13 and Sidney was 22, her father on his deathbed had suggested that she and Sidney might marry; but there is no evidence that the two children had ever seen one another until 1581. Sidney was much at court that year, but by his own admission (*AS* 2) did not fall instantly in love with her; by September, she was betrothed to Robert, Lord Rich, and on 1 November she married him. Thereafter, for about six weeks while he was still at court, and again for three months in early 1582, Sidney was both near to her and fascinated by her: he declares in *Astrophel and Stella* that he made advances to her and tried to seduce her, but that she repulsed his advances. But in late 1581 Sidney himself seems to have considered marriage to Frances Walsingham (whom he eventually married on 21 September 1583), and there was talk of marriage between him and Penelope's younger sister Dorothy in January 1582. In late spring Sidney left the court to spend time with his father, Sir Henry Sidney, who was on the Welsh border as Lord President of Wales, and spent the summer and possibly the autumn away from court and from Lady Rich; it is in that span of time that *Astrophel and Stella* appears to have been composed.

Lady Rich bore her husband four children before 1589, and shortly after the death of her lastborn became the mistress of Sir Charles Blount, apparently with her husband's complaisance. They divorced in 1605, and in December of the same year she married Blount, now Earl of Devonshire, illegally. She died in 1607. After Sidney's death she was identified as 'Stella', and after the publication of the sequence was apparently happy to be identified in printed dedications as Astrophel's love. Though her marriage to Lord Rich was not a happy one, there is no evidence that she was coerced into it, that she would have married Sidney given the chance, or that she ever had sexual relations with him. Neither Sidney's sister, the Countess of Pembroke, nor his wife, who survived him, appears to have objected to the publication of *Astrophel and Stella*. A concern for propriety may have delayed the publication of the sequence, which contained some unflattering references to Lord Rich; when it was first published, in 1591, some of these references were omitted,[13] and also omitted were some of the more sexually aggressive verses from the Songs, and the section of Song 8 in which Stella confesses that she loves Astrophel.

What distinguishes Sidney's sequence from all others is not its relative sexual explicitness – Ronsard and Jean-Antoine de Baïf, in particular, had brought the sensuality of Greek lyric verse and of Ovidian poetry into the sonnet before Sidney wrote – but the fact that it is, lightly and pervasively, funny. It does not end with humour, certainly, and many sonnets have a plangent intensity that Petrarch might envy: but through the whole sequence runs a tone of absurdity and irony that justifies our saying that Sidney created the first deconstructive lyric persona in the sonnet's history. Petrarch, as was shown in Chapter 4, complicated the /I/ of the sonnet by making his readers aware of the gap between the /I/ that writes *now* and the /I/ that suffered *then*, but both these /I/s are equally real in the mimesis: the /I/ that writes is to be imagined by the reader as speaking directly to him/her in the text; the /I/ that suffered is a real memory of the /I/ that writes. Deconstructive[14] irony enters when through some deliberate enhancing of the artifice of the text itself (and the sonnet is so arbitrary a construction that little needs to be done to remind the reader of the fact) *both* /I/s are seen to be the invention of a sign system – in this case the Petrarchan convention – which is itself the product of an implied Writer concealed behind the text. The reader is then taken to – or even marooned on – a metafictional level, where s/he is continuously aware of the arbitrary fictionality of the text.

Something like this had been done by Cecco Angiolieri (discussed in Chapter 2) when in his comic sonnets he forced the extreme chaos of human argument or street brawls or random cries into the extreme formality of the sonnet, staging a collision between art and life that draws attention to the arbitrariness, or absurdity, of both; Thomas Watson, by admitting that his passions were invented and then revealing his borrowings of them from other writers, also deconstructs his own verses, though not with comic intentions. Sidney, with perhaps a more intellectual interest in metafiction, has a wider range of devices, and had the advantage over all other sonneteers (except Spenser and Shakespeare) of having already written, in *The Old Arcadia*, a very complicated and witty metafictional narrative, in which are already the ingredients of *Astrophel and Stella*. One cannot play this sort of game without knowing that one is doing it, and when Sidney proposed to himself to write a poetic sequence about his love for Stella he must have considered his new narrative strategy with some care. The decision to use both sonnets and songs does not seem to be taken in imitation of either Petrarch or his own *Arcadia*; since the songs are nothing like Petrarch's *canzoni*,[15] nor do they punctuate the sonnets regularly, as the shepherds' poetry does in the *Arcadia*: they do, however, provide more extended means of doing things that the sonnets attempt: narrating a seduction (Song 2); upbraiding Stella in a kind of flyting (Song 5); and conversing with her (Songs 4, 8 and 11).

The decision to use sonnets with an Italian octave (ABBA ABBA or variants) but with an English sestet (eighty-five of the 108 sonnets end with a couplet rhyme, EE) must have been taken with the notion of a sequence in mind; for in the *Arcadia* Sidney had experimented widely, not to say wildly, with the sonnet form, resurrecting some very strange rhymeschemes, such as AAAA AAAA AAAA AA ('Howe is my sun') and ABAB BABA ACAC CC ('Do not disdain'), and in 'Certain Sonnets' he had used the English sonnet many times (ABAB CDCD EFEF GG). Since not a single sonnet in *Astrophel and Stella* has an English change of rhyme in the second quatrain, and not a single sonnet fails to change rhyme at the sestet, Sidney must have planned to exclude the other kinds as a way of making his sequence cohere.

He must also have noticed that a very large number of the sonnets he was writing in that summer of 1582 were apostrophic sonnets, that is, beginning or containing an address to some person or thing:

> Reason, in faith thou art well served . . . (10)

> In truth, o Love, with what a boyish kind
> Thou doest proceed . . . (11)

> With how sad steps, o Moone, thou climb'st the skies . . . (31)

> Sweet kisse, thy sweets I faine would sweetly endite . . . (79)

Sixty-two sonnets out of 108 contain an apostrophe, calling for the attention of some person (including Stella, who is directly addressed in thirteen sonnets) or thing: a far higher proportion than in any other British sonneteer. The effect of apostrophes is usually solemn: Petrarch, who uses the apostrophe about forty times in his *Rime*, tends to use them to speak with or to the powers that rule his life, Love, Death and his Lady, as well as to friends or patrons. But if the apostrophe is used, as Sidney does, in rapid succession to invoke a wide variety of objects the effect is rather the reverse: every fourteen lines, the speaker's attention appears to swing away to another thing, and the impression is one of excited and constant movement, and a certain extravagance of gesture, which Shakespeare mocks through Bottom's apostrophe-clogged speech 'O grim-lookt night, o night with hue so black' in *A Midsummer Night's Dream* (V.i).[16]

But Sidney does not merely use apostrophes in quantity: he intensifies the very thing which the apostrophe was principally supposed to do, that is, give the dramatic illusion of the presence of a third party. The comic sonnets of Cecco Angiolieri and of the most famous Italian comic sonneteer Il Burchiello (1404–49) are often quite literally small dramas, incorporating the dialogue of various people into the sonnet, and Sidney several times reinvented this device for himself, writing the words of an imaginary interlocutor into the verse:

> Come let me write, 'And to what end?' To ease
> A burthned heart. 'How can words ease, which are
> The glasses of thy dayly vexing care?'
> Oft cruell fights well pictured forth do please.

'Art not asham'd to publish thy disease?'
  Nay, that may breed my fame, it is so rare:
  'But will not wise men think thy words fond ware?'
Then be they close, and so none shall displease.
  'What idler thing, then speake and not be hard?'
What harder thing then smart, and not to speake?
Peace, foolish wit, with wit my wit is mard.
Thus write I while I doubt to write, and wreake
  My harmes on Ink's poor losse, perhaps some find
  Stella's great powrs, that so confuse my mind. (*AS* 34)

The 'foolish wit' that Sidney dismisses in line 11 is of course his own 'better' judgement, but the reader is asked to imagine a busybody interrupting the speaker as he tries to write, and engrossing the speaker's attention until with 'Peace, foolish wit' he turns back with an apologetic shrug to his original addressee, the reader: 'Thus write I while I doubt to write . . .'.

More commonly Sidney writes the sonnet, as he could have learnt to do from Wyatt or from Ronsard, so that it appears to be one side of a conversation actually taking place, the reader, reduced to the status of eavesdropper, obligingly supplying the other:

Be your words made (good Sir) of Indian ware,
  That you allow me them by so small rate?
  Or do you cutted Spartanes imitate?
Or do you meane my tender eares to spare,
That to my questions you so totall are?
  When I demaund of *Phenix Stella's* state,
  You say forsooth, you left her well of late.
O God, thinke you that satisfies my care?
  I would know whether she did sit or walke,
How cloth'd, how waited on, sighd she or smilde,
Whereof, with whom, how often did she talke,
With what pastime, time's journey she beguilde,
  If her lips daignd to sweeten my poor name.
  Say all, and all well sayd, still say the same. (*AS* 92)

This brilliant piece of desperate conversation, which constructs some feebly protesting Lord Prodnose[17] in its interstices, is fully dramatic: that is, it creates within the text offered to the reader (*Astrophel and Stella*) a smaller text not addressed to the reader, in which imagined persons – a lover and a courtier – play out a scene. The whole sequence is a sustained dramatic illusion, almost as visibly sustained for the reader as Shakespeare's great hypotyposis in *Henry V*:

Think when we talk of Horses, that you see them
Printing their prowd Hoofes i'th'receiving Earth:
For 'tis your thoughts that now must deck our Kings. . . .
(Prologue, ll. 26–8)

Since Sidney, Shakespeare and their contemporaries were trained to think of texts as persuasive constructs, this is less daringly metafictional than it might seem to us now; but it remained at the discretion of the writer to emphasise the persuasion, or the construct. Petrarch, in the sonnet to the readers which opens the *Rime*,[18] emphasises persuasion: he asks pardon for the failure of his style to achieve coherence, and simultaneously suggests that the intensity of his incoherence will beget pity; Sidney, as we shall see, emphasises construction, and thereby draws attention to the gap between reality and the text which pretends to be that reality.

Sonnets dealing with the creation of texts – there are thirteen of them – appear throughout the sequence, and inevitably affect the reading not just of each of themselves, but of the entire sequence. Since the great opening sonnet is one of these, their recurrence cannot be accidental, and may, as was said earlier, be a byproduct of the writing of the *Old Arcadia*. It is difficult to see what, other than a highly metafictional interest, could produce this, one of the few English sonnets to deal with composing the sonnet:

My Muse may well grudge at my heav'nly joy,
If still I force her in sad rimes to creepe:
She oft hath drunke my teares, now hopes to enjoy
Nectar of Mirth, since I *Jove's* cup do keepe.
Sonets be not bound prentise to annoy:
Trebles sing high, as well as bases deepe:
Grief but Love's winter liverie is, the Boy
Hath cheekes to smile, as well as eyes to weepe.
Come then my Muse, shew thou height of delight
In well raisde notes, my pen the best it may
Shall paint out joy, though but in blacke and white.
Cease eager Muse, peace pen, for my sake stay,
I give you here my hand for truth of this,
Wise silence is best musicke unto blisse. (*AS* 70)

As a sonnet acting as prologue to a group of sonnets celebrating the winning of Stella's love (though this theme enters in the sonnet before, 69) this would make well-crafted sense: the octave deals with the problems of settling upon an appropriate style, and the sestet then summons the Muse and his pen to embark upon it; the whole is done with Sidney's usual immediacy, as his speaker turns from talking to the reader about the Muse (who is perhaps standing in the window, looking glum) in lines 1–4, raises his voice with a series of breezy and reassuring commonplaces (lines 5–8) and then appeals to her to come back to the table and join in composing (lines 9–11). The sections of the sonnet correspond to sections of the conversation, and the turns, from quatrain to quatrain, from octave to sestet, to movements 'on stage'. But the final tercet is different: it makes sense only if there is a stage direction invisibly there after line 11: '(She beginneth to sing, and it to write)'. The speaker then interrupts a song (which is not sung) and a poem (which is not written) with 'Cease, eager Muse, peace pen . . .', and offers his own piece of writing ('my hand' means both a hand extended to seal a pact or an affirmation, and 'a piece of my handwriting' – we should recall that as Sidney wrote these words he was actually using his own handwriting, and probably never thought to see the words in print): the piece of writing which he offers is the *sententia* 'Wise silence is best musicke unto blisse'. After that the poem falls silent: the white space that follows the last line then becomes the ideal 'song'.

Here, then, we have a sonnet about the intention to compose a sonnet, which is actually started after line 11 (though we cannot hear or see it) and is then aborted, and replaced by a better kind of song, which, although it is silence, can actually be seen and heard if the reader looks at the white paper after the poem finishes. But we are also faced, literally, with the materiality of a finished sonnet on the page: Sidney (who would suppose his readers to be reading from a holograph or scribal copy) *has* given us his hand, and we must ask: is this a sonnet of 'delight', and is it true? And is it, then, better music than the 'silent song' which follows it?

This is a witty deconstruction of sonnet-writing, which because it takes notice of the textual materiality of the sonnet on the page (if the reader thinks how the speaker could give his hand *to his pen*, there arises a very physical sensation of writing) goes well beyond Petrarch's attempts to write poems which say that they have failed as poems. We should notice, too, that making a sonnet into a witty account of the inadequacy of sonnet-writing does not absolve the writer from writing the sonnet well, since, indeed, to write it well intensifies the deconstructive paradox. Sidney was a formidable versifier right from the start, as the poems of the *Old Arcadia* show, and this sonnet has a clever use of enjambment: particularly in lines 9–11, one can see that Sidney had learnt to achieve the effect of agitated and urgent speech by running the sentences across the line boundaries – some ten years before the major Elizabethan dramatists began to work out how to do it in stage plays.

If we ask, before going on to consider Sidney's multiple ironies further, why he should have wanted to construct his sequence thus, we have to speculate: the fact that in the *Old Arcadia* he surrounds passionate speeches with ironies both of situation and of language might justify saying that Sidney was unable to regard anything other than ironically: as a modern critic has said,

> He creates the special effect of surprising us into going back and re-evaluating aspects of what are conventionally understood to be solemn affairs. His characteristic mode of thought in his own life as well as in his art seems to be a criticism of weakness in our conventional understandings or constructions of experience.[19]

That is well said, but does not explain why this characteristic mode of thought should have operated in an enterprise which was singular and special, that is, his tribute of love to Penelope Rich. But if, as the historical evidence seems to suggest, he wrote the sequence in a very short time *after* the event, then he must continually, as he wrote, have been faced with the irony that what each sonnet represented as the truth of his love had not happened at all, in the sense that the verses addressed to Stella had not actually been sent or shown to her: that the exasperated conversations with Lord Prodnose had not occurred; that the cries of despair and black fits of woe had not been uttered as he wrote them, and now that he was uttering them in sonnet form the object for which he wrote was no longer attainable. Consider, for example, the ironies that arise from one of the very last sonnets, 106:

> O absent presence *Stella* is not here;
> False flattering hope, that with so faire a face
> Bare me in hand, that in this Orphane place,
> *Stella*, I say my *Stella*, should appeare.
> What saist thou now, where is that dainty cheere
> Thou toldst mine eyes should helpe their famisht case?
> But thou art gone, now that selfe felt disgrace
> Doth make me most to wish thy comfort neere.
> But heer I do store of faire Ladies meete,
> Who may with charme of conversation sweete,
> Make in my heavy mould new thoughts to grow:
> Sure they prevaile as much with me, as he
> That bad his friend, but then new maim'd, to be
> Mery with him, and not thinke of his woe. (*AS* 106)

The conversation between hope and the speaker is carried on as hope ushers him into the Presence Chamber, where courtiers came to seek whatever they thought would help their case. Since Stella is not, after all, there (Penelope Devereux had been appointed one of the Queen's attendants) as promised, hope prudently fades away, leaving the speaker to face a superfluous crowd of ladies, whose conversation has about as much chance of distracting his mind as of making an amputated limb grow again – the analogy in the last tercet suggests that the speaker feels Stella's absence like a 'maim', which is of course another kind of absent presence.

But in 1582, on the borders of Wales, Sidney could not have written that first line – or edited it, supposing it written before – without realising that the whole of *Astrophel and Stella* is an 'absent presence':[20] Stella is there insofar as the text creates her as silent interlocutor in the sonnets, but is not there in the physical sense, nor could he have had any hope that she might be in his 'Orphane place'. The wholly modern-sounding phrase 'absent presence' has Derridean ironies that extend beyond this single sonnet: for in forcing the point of the illusory nature of the textual experience by the oxymoron, Sidney was resorting again to the figures of paradox and pun (there are two meanings for 'presence' and for 'case' here) that continually appear throughout the sequence. Joined to these is the figure of repetition or *traductio* (using a word in several cognate forms), which, by drawing attention like the other figures to the wordishness of words, destabilises the meaning: the word, which is properly a sign of the thing, becomes present as a word, and the meaning absents itself.

While this kind of ambiguating wordplay does not occur in every sonnet, it occurs often enough throughout the sequence to sensitise the reader to verbal repetitions, and thus uses puns and *traductio* as a kind of cue to switch attention to the metatextual level. For this speaker, and thus this author, is highly conscious of textuality:

> *Stella* oft sees the verie face of wo
> Painted in my beclowded stormie face:
> But cannot skill to pitie my disgrace,
> Not though thereof the cause her selfe she know:
> Yet hearing late a fable, which did show
> Of Lovers never knowne, a grievous case,
> Pitie thereof gate in her breast such place
> That, from that sea deriv'd, teares' springs did flow.
> Alas, if Fancy drawne by imag'd things,
> Though false, yet with free scope more grace doth breed
> Than servant's wracke, where new doubts honor brings;
> Then thinke my deare, that you in me do reed
> Of Lover's ruine some sad Tragedie:
> I am not I, pitie the tale of me. (*AS* 45)

To soften the heart of the tyrant Stella, the lover must convert himself from a real person into a text: but Sidney not only suggests that Stella should treat him as if he were a book ('Your face, my thane, is as a book, where men/May read strange matters . . .'): he declares, in one of those last-line clinches of which he was so fond, that he *is* a book, a narrative of his own love. We can hardly not notice that we ourselves are actually reading 'the tale of me' in *Astrophel and Stella*, and that this sonnet, through the very immediacy and force with which it pretends to represent the living Astrophel, is not him, but only the tale of him. Where, then, can /I/ exist, since the moment /I/ represents itself it becomes the tale of 'me' – subject changing inexorably into object? Sidney has further undermined the status of the 'real' Astrophel by indicating at the start of the sonnet that his true grief is already a text – and therefore not true:

> *Stella* oft sees the verie face of wo
> Painted in my beclowded stormie face . . .

This sense of the unreliability of the surface appearance is of course the obverse of the Renaissance courtier's obsession with pageant and show, something particularly cultivated by Queen Elizabeth. The more intense the effort expended upon rhetorical and artistic 'creation', the greater the irony of having to treat that creation as if it were real, and its language as if it really represented things: so the desperate Earl of Essex, having flattered his Queen as a goddess, found that she behaved like a goddess when he spoke real words to her: 'I sued to her Majesty to grant it out of favour,' he said of one of the disasters of his Irish command, 'but I spake a language that was not understood, or to a goddess not at leisure to hear prayers.'[21] Sidney achieved the fame after death he barely achieved in life, precisely because he was reread, and his readers *did* 'pitie the tale of me' – or, rather, the two tales, the one of his life and death, and the other of his love told in *Astrophel and Stella*.

Sidney may have designed his sequence with that in mind but, if so, he quite remarkably avoided any reference in it to the immortalising power of poetry, a topic which was quite routinely used by later sonneteers. All the sonnets invoke the mimesis of the lover actually talking of his feelings or experiences as he pursues Stella, sometimes to the readers, sometimes to fellow poets, sometimes to Lord Prodnose, sometimes to Stella, sometimes to any object in the universe that might listen, and in default even of that, as that belated Petrarchan lover, Cherubino, declares to his Countess,

> e se non ho chi m'oda,
> Parlo d'amor con me!

[and if I have no one to listen, I talk of love to myself!]

The sequence creates the persona of the lover as an /I/ in a continual state of restless excitement, always poised on the brink of some new movement, whether in hope or in frustration. The witty, ironic, narrating /I/ does not, however, suggest what *his* activities might be for: the first sonnet is the only sonnet which could be thought to reflect on the nature of the whole sequence, and thus be prefatory, like Petrarch's *Rime* 1; it should be taken with Sonnet 2, which imitates Petrarch's *Rime* 3 in giving an account of how the affair started, but ends with a comment on the purpose of the sequence:

[I] now employ the remnant of my wit,
To make my selfe beleeve, that all is well,
While with a feeling skill I paint my hell.
(*AS* 2, ll. 12–14)

Sonnet 1 is written in twelve-syllable lines (one wonders if Sidney had read and remembered the two translations of Petrarch's *Rime* 1 and 3 into fourteeners in *Tottel's Miscellany*), and thus stands out visually from what follows:

Loving in truth, and faine in verse my love to show,
That the deare She might take some pleasure of my paine:
Pleasure might cause her reade, reading might make her know,
Knowledge might pitie winne, and pitie grace obtaine,
I sought fit words to paint the blackest face of woe,
Studying inventions fine, her wits to entertaine:
Oft turning others' leaves, to see if thence would flow
Some fresh and fruitfull showers upon my sunne-burn'd braine.
But words came halting forth, wanting Invention's stay,
Invention, Nature's child, fled step-dame Studie's blowes,
And others' feete still seem'd but strangers in my way.
Thus great with child to speake, and helplesse in my throwes,
Biting my trewand pen, beating my selfe for spite,
'Foole,' said my Muse to me, 'looke in thy heart and write.'

'Not at first sight', perhaps, but 'in mine of time', as Sonnet 2 says, the reader will notice the pun in the first line: 'Loving in truth, and *feigning* verse my love to show . . .'. As the eminent critic Touchstone well knew, 'the truest poetry is the most faining', and with a dazzling display of rhetorical figures the speaker pirouettes through the octave, only to 'halt' at the sestet, which seems to disclaim all this in favour of 'writing from the heart'. But the sestet, too, is full of rhetorical flourishes – prosopopoeias, metaphors, aposiopesis, apostrophe – so that the final anti-rhetorical point, in what is surely Sidney's best-known one-liner, is reached after a virtuoso rhetorical display of the ineffability topos. This is so different from the rhetoric of Petrarch and his imitators in Italy that one is tempted in this to call Sidney, who was often hailed as the English Petrarch, an anti-Petrarchan writer. Petrarch questions the value of his love for Laura, but never its reality; Sidney questions the reality of his love for Stella, but never its value. He gives with great immediacy all the Petrarchan marks of the lover – his anguish, his oscillating feelings, his humility, his idealism, his commitment to serve, her cruelty and his devotion; but he adds to that the sensuality of Ovid and the French sonneteers, with a colloquialism of style which his contemporaries perceived as very English, and wittily deconstructs the whole enterprise by repeatedly drawing attention to the metafictional problems of 'loving in truth' while 'feigning verse'.

That his contemporaries noticed this (after his death) and enjoyed it is strongly suggested by the critical preface to the first edition of *Astrophel and Stella*, written by Thomas Nashe (1567–1601), a sort of rhetorical costermonger, prepared to throw at his audience any rhetoric that would sell, but an intelligent man and a good critic. His preface, written in the persona of a showman inviting customers into booths in the Fair of Literature, announces Sidney thus:

> Gentlemen, that have seene a thousand lines of folly drawn forth *ex uno puncto impudentiae*, and two famous Mountains to goe to the conception of one Mouse, that have had your ears defned with the eccho of Fames brasen towres when only they have been touchd with a leaden pen, that have seen Pan sitting in his bower of delights, and a number of *Midasses* to admire his miserable hornepipes: let not your surfeted sight, new come from such puppet play, think scorne to turn aside into this Theater of pleasure, for here you shal find a paper stage streud with pearle, an artificial heav'n to overshadow the fair frame, and christal wals to encounter your curious eyes; while the tragicommody of love is performed by starlight.
>
> The chiefe actor here is *Melpomene*, whose dusky robes, dipt in the ynke of teares, as yet seeme to drop when I view them neere. The argument cruell chastitie, the Prologue hope, the Epilogue dispaire; *videte, quaeso, et linguis animisque favete*.[22]

Under Nashe's hyperbolical contempt for earlier poets, there is a shrewd perception. Sidney's speaker, Astrophel, is played by Melpomene, the muse of tragedy, and the words ('dusky robes, dipt in the ynke of teares') have dramatic immediacy ('yet seeme to drop') rather than tedious didactic length, and also dramatic form and coherence (prologue/argument/epilogue) rather than the pointless movement of a miscellany ('hornepipes'). Yet, for all the tragic vividness that lets us see the lovers as though their walls were crystal, this is *acting* on a carefully constructed stage: the movements are on paper, the tears are represented by pearls, and the heaven, the stage roof, is 'artificial'; the gods of this theatre of passion are inventions of human wit. And what is played 'by starlight' (a reference to Astrophel's declaration in Sonnet 68 that Stella is the 'onely Planet of my light') is not a tragedy, but a tragicomedy, despite its ending in despair, in a theatre of Pleasure.

Sidney himself imagines Astrophel, in Sonnet l, attempting to write so that 'the deare She might take some pleasure of my paine', and although the pleasure to be obtained from the perusal of Astrophel's woes was a literary one the metaphor of playing, or 'showing', woes inside a theatre of pleasure (which is not a Petrarchan metaphor) is fundamentally representative of the positioning of the Renaissance courtier's /I/. The courtier is one who must constantly recount his dreams of the Queen of his Fortunate Isles (to recur to Pietro Bembo's myth) before her court, and if his 'woes' are sufficiently intense she may grant him the favour of being a permanent actor, as it were, which will turn his woes to comedy. As Cynthia to Sir Walter Ralegh, as Gloriana to Spenser, as Oriana to a host of poets and musicians, Queen Elizabeth demanded simultaneously respect for her chastity and constant expressions of desire, and it may well be that, in writing to, for and about Stella, Sidney was displacing his frustrated political ambitions. Certainly the performance of woe inside a theatre of pleasure is a very powerful paradigm for anyone seeking power, wealth or favour in Elizabethan England, whether from the Queen herself or from the lesser courts of great ladies such as Sidney's sister, the Countess of Pembroke, or Lady Rich herself.

To be heard at all, the courtier had to 'show' or display his woe, and this required the artifice of eloquence (not necessarily in words – a jousting shield or a New Year's gift might serve as well as an ode or a sonnet). Both to praise what he desired and represent his own failure to attain it, the courtier needed the skills of pleading, so that the Prince might be pleased, and by being pleased be pleased to give; and this involved courtly speech in the paradox of exhibiting a high degree of skill in the confession of its own inadequacy to praise sufficiently. Robert Sidney, Philip's brother, himself a more than competent sonneteer, put it precisely in one sonnet of an unfinished *corona*-sequence:

> Though the most perfect style cannot attain
> The praise to praise enough the meanest part
> Of you, the ornament of Nature's art,
> Worth of this world, of all joys the sovereign;
>   And though I know I labour shall in vain
> To paint in words the deadly wounds the dart
> Of your fair eyes doth give, since mine own heart
> Knows not the measure of my love and pain
>   Yet since your will the charge on me doth lay,
>   Your will, the law I only reverence,
>   Skill-less and praiseless I do you obey;
>   Nor merit seek, but pity, if thus I
>   Do folly show to prove obedience;
>   Who gives himself, may ill his words deny.[23]

Though Wyatt and Surrey had to a certain extent anticipated him, it was Philip Sidney's achievement to create the /I/ of the sonnet in this distinctively courtly (not pastoral) posture of anguished devotion to an unattainable beauty, controlled by a self-aware eloquence both approving and deprecating, perfectly poised between wit and seriousness, and he made what we might call the courtly Petrarchan sequence the fashion of his age, 'changing poetry in our language' as Anne Ferry says. But he altered the poesis of the /I/ not only on the level of the sequence, but also on the level of the single sonnet, as his brother's effort above shows. Though his particular fondness for the Italian octave was not copied by more than a few later sonnet-writers (Henry Constable's *Diana* of 1594 is the only sequence to make large use of this rhymescheme), his modifications of the sonnet's movement were widely copied, as were some of his mannerisms.

In the sonnet above, Robert has learnt enjambment, so that he can run a sentence through a quatrain, building up momentum; he has learnt also the use of monosyllables to give an appearance of plainness and solidity; and, possibly the most difficult thing of all, he has learnt the use of the stops and starts and inversions that give the illusion of a speaker thinking hard as he speaks – a dramatic technique that Donne saw, and copied, and that Shakespeare himself took some time to master. This sensitising of the ear and mind to dramatic movement within the sonnet and to wordplay of all kinds made it possible to foreground the problems of identity and courtly positioning in quite a new way, and even if Robert Sidney's manuscript is more interesting as a unique glimpse of a Sidneian sonneteer at work than as evidence of an original talent we can detect Philip Sidney's powerful problematics of the self in later and intenser work:

> Since I left you, mine eye is in my mind,
> And that which governs me to go about
> Doth part his function and is partly blind,
> Seems seeing, but effectually is out;
> For it no form delivers to the heart
> Of bird, of flower, or shape, which it doth latch:
> Of his quick objects hath the mind no part,
> Nor his own vision holds what it doth catch;
> For if it see the rudest or gentlest sight,
> The most sweet favour or deformed'st creature,
> The mountain or the sea, the day or night,
> The crow or dove, it shapes them to your feature:
>   Incapable of more, replete with you,
>   My most true mind thus maketh mine untrue.
>
> (Shakespeare, Sonnet 113)

What most marks Sidney off from his two great peers in the art of the sonnet, Spenser and Shakespeare, is his comparatively slack control of metaphor: the great Elizabethan sonnets after Sidney are those which can retain what he taught, the dramatic urgency and ironic interplay of words, but can also unify the sonnet by imposing a metaphorical movement (which is not the same as merely elaborating a conceit) in the sequence of sections. The decay of Petrarchan rhetoric into a flourishing of antitheses and gestures was something that Sidney rightly disliked among those who

> poore *Petrarch's* long deceasèd woes
> With new-borne sighes and denisend wit do sing (*AS* 15)

but he missed, or did not choose to imitate, the great metaphorical richness in Petrarch that unifies not only single sonnets but also sonnet with sonnet throughout the *Rime*. One of the very few sonnets in which Sidney appears to have a direct debt to Petrarch shows this difference between the two poets:

> Who will in fairest booke of Nature know,
> How Vertue may best lodg'd in beautie be,
> Let him but learne of *Love* to reade in thee,
> *Stella*, those faire lines, which true goodnesse show.
> There shall he find all vices' overthrow,
> Not by rude force, but sweetest soveraigntie
> Of reason, from whose light these night-birds flie;
> That inward sunne in thine eyes shineth so.
> And not content to be Perfection's heire
> Thy selfe, doest strive all minds that way to move,
> Who marke in thee what is in thee most faire.
> So while thy beautie draws the heart to love,
> As fast thy Vertue bends that love to good:
> 'But ah,' Desire still cries, 'give me some food.' (*AS* 71)[24]

What holds this finely constructed sonnet together is not metaphorical but argumentative coherence; Sidney is trying to demonstrate a paradox (that Virtue can lodge with Beauty – the paradox that Hamlet and Ophelia have a cruel passage of wit about in the 'nunnery scene'), and the verbs are chiefly to do with mental knowledge: 'learne', 'reade', 'find', 'marke', 'draw', appropriate to the Neoplatonic, or even stilnovistic, idea of the Lady as the heiress of the light of Supreme Reason. Petrarch, starting with the same idea, moves it rather differently:

> Chi vuol veder quantunque po Natura
> e 'l Ciel tra noi, venga a mirar costei
> ch'è sola un sol, non pur a li occhi mei
> ma al mondo cieco che vertù non cura;
> et venga tosto, perché Morte fura
> prima i migliori et lascia star i rei:
> questa aspettata al regno delli dei
> cosa bella mortal passa et non dura.
> Vedrà, s'arriva a tempo, ogni vertute,
> ogni bellezza, ogni real costume

giunti in un corpo con mirabil tempre;
allor dirà che mie rime son mute,
l'ingegno offeso dal soverchio lume.
Ma se più tarda, avrà da pianger sempre.
(*Rime* 248)

[Who will see how much Nature and Heaven can do among us, let him come to gaze upon her who alone is a sun, not only to my eyes, but to the blind world which cares not for virtue;

And let him come quickly, for Death steals first the best, and leaves the sinful; awaited in the kingdom of the blest, this lovely mortal thing passes, and does not stay.

He will see, if he comes in time, all virtue, all beauty, all princely habit, joined in one body with miraculous tempering; And then he will say that my poems are dumb, my wit damaged by excess of light. But if he comes late, he will have cause to weep for ever.]

Apart from the difference I have already noticed, that Sidney focuses on himself while Petrarch turns outwards from himself to the world, Petrarch has accepted from the start the stilnovistic metaphor of *light* for *knowledge* and *sight* for *apprehension*, which enables him to talk very immediately about movement: 'venga . . . venga . . . vedrà . . . avrà' – suggestive of the fairground caller's 'Roll up! roll up! Have a look, don't miss your chance!' Whereas Sidney mixes, or confuses, the metaphor of the book of nature with the sun of reason, so that neither metaphor works through into the sestet, Petrarch simply submerges the metaphor of the sun, which is like the Lady in that it passes quickly across the sky and does not stay, and is a union of beauty, virtue and royalty in one planetary body 'with miraculous tempering'; but it does not reappear verbally until the second-last line. The submergence of the metaphor makes it unnecessary to indulge, as Sidney does, in extra conceits, and while Sidney provides a witty and ironic last line, showing that he is actually unable to practise the lesson he has just spent thirteen lines 'proving', Petrarch concentrates the power of light sombrely, by making it pass through the sonnet from beginning to end, and disappear in a last flash before the final line. We have a very strong and grave sonnet from Petrarch, and a brilliant and ingenious one from Sidney.

Sixteenth-century rhetoric could describe metaphorical wordplay very intricately, but lacked a sense of metaphor as an alternative mode of perception. For Puttenham, metaphor like all figurative language is a kind of error and deceit, only permissible in poetry because it is employed for 'pleasant & lovely causes and nothing perillous', and because 'all his abuses tende but to dispose the hearers to mirth and sollace by pleasant conveyance and efficacy of speach, they are not in truth to be accompted vices but for vertues in the poetical science very commendable'.[25]

Even Sidney, who in his *Defence of Poesie* comes nearer to an understanding of the creativity of metaphor than any other critic of his age, still thinks of poetic figuration as a kind of legitimate 'feigning': operating with a series of descriptors of 'reality' which he opposes to poetry, such as 'true', 'regular', 'essential', 'substantial', he cannot find an intermediate category of being between 'fiction' and 'truth', and so can only justify poetry by as it were mitigating its falsehood:

> Neither let this [superiority of poetry over Nature] be jestingly conceived, because the works of the one [Nature] be essentiall, the other [poetry] in imitation or fiction: for everie understanding, knoweth the skill of each Artificer standeth in that *Idea*, or foreconceite of the worke, and not in the worke it selfe. And that the Poet hath that *Idea*, is manifest, by delivering them [the ideas] foorth in such excellencie as he had imagined them: which delivering foorth, also is not wholly imaginative, as we are wont to say by them that build Castles in the aire: but so farre substancially it worketh, not onley to make a *Cyrus*, which had bene but a particular excellency as nature might have done, but to bestow a *Cyrus* upon the world to make many *Cyrusses*, if they will learne aright, why and how that maker made him.[26]

It comes so near, that passage, to an understanding of the generalising or symbolic capacity of metaphorical vision, but finally makes 'imaginative delivering forth' only superior to 'real' existence in so far as more of a good thing (wise rulers like Cyrus) is superior to one of it. Sidney has enough of the humanist Neoplatonist in him to realise that the imagination idealises, or as he said 'delivers a golden [world]', but any attempt to give this golden world epistemological status turns back into courtly or civic instruction. However, his presentation of the passion of Astrophel, by virtue of its theatrical vigour and elegance, did have the effect of making his contemporaries concentrate, in their sonnet-writing, upon the /I/ as that part of the human spirit which tries to rise from darkness to light; and the very looseness with which in his poetry these metaphors were interpreted encouraged a whole series of reworking of the myth of Laura – or the Queen of the Fortunate Isles. If many of these were dull and repetitive, others, by Spenser, Shakespeare, Drummond and (fitfully) by lesser talents, expanded the dramatising of self and the capacity of the sonnet in new directions.

8

THE ELIZABETHAN SONNET VOGUE AND SPENSER

In 1575, the poet George Gascoigne put it on record that 'I have beene willing heretofore to spende three houres in penning of an amorous Sonnet';[1] twenty-six years later, the production rate seems to have increased, for Ben Jonson has his Matheo declare, in *Every Man in His Humour* (1601), that 'I am melancholie my selfe divers times sir, and then do I no more but take your pen and paper presently, and write you your halfe score or your dozen of sonnets, at a sitting'.[2] This spontaneous overflow of powerful feelings is a comic symptom of late-Elizabethan melancholia, but shows both how common and how easy sonnet-writing could be for the would-be gentleman. If the reader will refer at this point to the Appendix, which gives a chronological table of the sonnet sequences published after the appearance of Sidney's *Astrophel and Stella*, s/he will see that the sonnet craze was concentrated in four years, from 1593 to 1597, with the addition that at that time a number of poets who published later, like Shakespeare, in the reign of James VI and I, were writing and circulating sonnets privately. The only major sonneteer to compose wholly outside this period is Drummond of Hawthornden. One has the impression that after the publication of *Astrophel and Stella* (which also contained sonnets in Sidney's manner by Samuel Daniel) there was a hushed period of intense scribbling, after which, in 1593, the presses began to clatter, and even after 1597 continued to reprint sonnet collections of the most popular authors. The market was also favourable to late printings of juvenile verse; and while it is possible that Shakespeare's reputation as a dramatist encouraged the publication in 1609 of his sonnets, probably written ten years before, the same cannot be said for Sir William Alexander, Earl of Stirling, or Sir David Murray of Gorthie, who published their youthful sequences in 1604 and 1611. Fulke Greville, who as a close friend of Sir Philip Sidney had probably begun writing sonnets earlier than any of his living contemporaries, continued to work on his sonnet sequence, *Caelica*, till his death in 1628 (it was published in 1633); and thus the oldest poet of the Sidney generation just overlapped at that point with the young Milton, who was beginning to experiment with the sonnet at that time.

A short craze, then, with a long sedate aftermath which attracts our interest because of the occurrence of the sonnets of Shakespeare, Drummond and Milton. In trying to move over this very varied and uneven ground, I think we have to consider reading strategies and purposes, since only specialists now read more than a handful of the sonnets of the 1590s, and even specialists might ask for some solid justification for spending more than ten minutes in the company of the author of *Zepheria* or *Diella*.

If one asks why so many sonnet sequences of the same pattern should have been written at this time, the simple answer, that they saw a chance of making money or finding employment by exploiting a popular form, has a certain force; but there were many other popular forms, such as the verse romance, which the sonneteers could have tried instead (and did often try as well); and, while they may have been compelled by poverty or lack of advancement to write, they were not compelled to write *sonnets*. And if one persists in seeing the minor writers as mere fashion-followers, still the question remains: Why was this, then, a fashion? What did it offer that was congenial, whether to writers or to readers? The sequences of the end of the sixteenth century seem to offer three main kinds of discourse in which speakers can, to use Hopkins's term, 'selve themselves': the passionate, or desiring; the reflective, or stoical; and the Anacreontic, witty and lightly learned. Let us look at these briefly in turn.

The word most commonly used to describe the discourse of love-poetry, and particularly of sonnets, was 'passionate', which had a wider sense than it has today: we should say 'impassioned', meaning 'expressive of strong feelings towards some desired (or detested) object'; 'desire' in the singular conversely had a narrower meaning than today, denoting sexual appetite, and thus often being opposed to love (' "But ah," Desire still cries, "give me some food" '). In those senses, then, the sixteenth-century sonnet in Britain makes itself particularly into the discourse of the 'passionate' or (as we should say) desiring /I/. Men who are in love with real and attainable women may write love-sonnets to them with perfect sincerity, using this discourse; men who are in love in some less sexual sense with unattainable women (their patroness or sovereign) or with some goal of a non-human kind may use the love-discourse as analogy, and the sonnet as a theatrical utterance within the arena of courtly performance. And since love is constantly retroped as homage and service, often within the *topos* of pastoral, it is even possible for homosexual love to be celebrated without offence to Elizabethan standards.

It is, of course, possible to read these sonnets as simply expressive of basic human emotions, and to find their congeniality in their capacity to express love. J. W. Lever suggests, in his discussion of this period of sonneteering, that 'As the supreme and inalienable individual experience, love necessarily became the central theme of literature during this epoch'.[3] But it has to be said at once that it is because of the Elizabethan construction of 'love' in poetry that we, following the Romantic poets, make the assumption (if we do) that love *is* 'the supreme and inalienable individual experience'; Lever's echoing in that phrase of the American Declaration of Independence might remind us that love, like democracy, is a construction of social and political systems. Failure to recognise this will leave the reader of the Elizabethan sonnet open to being disconcerted at many points by local evidence. Why should a number of sonneteers have written love-poetry to women with whom they were not in love? Or to quite nonexistent women? Why should Robert Sidney have written a Petrarchan sequence of passionate complaint and melancholy while very happily and romantically married to his wife, Barbara Gamage? And why are so many sonnets translations or adaptations of other writers' work? One or two writers did indeed write their sonnets to women with whom they were fully and feasibly in love – Edmund Spenser, for example, and Drummond of Hawthornden (probably) – but to most others Lever's absolute form of Love does not apply.

Let us suggest a different approach. Within a few lines of the sentence quoted above, Lever shrewdly observes that at the period 'Desire is pre-eminently desirable, and calls forth no serious moral rejoinders'. By 'desire' he means what Sidney means, namely sensuous sexual feeling, of which there is indeed a great deal in the verse of the period; but the point may be taken in a wider sense. It has been argued in the previous chapters that one of the great continuities in the history of the sonnet is its capacity to express desire – not necessarily a specific desire (for sex, for love, for protection) but the self as desiring entity. Because of its combination of brevity and extension, the sonnet is both lyrical (exposing a feeling) and dialectic (moving the feeling on to another stage by explanation), so that it both articulates a feeling and moves it towards an end, which will be the end of the sonnet if nothing else. If the culture of an age proposes a particular kind of love – Christian, sexual, Platonic, courtly – as the goal of human endeavour, then the sonnets of the age will focus on that, and be 'about it'. Love, however, is culturally contingent; desire is not, though what it desires specifically is.

Desire, as has been suggested, is the sense of an absence, or, more exactly, a need to abolish an absence. It was Petrarch's extraordinary achievement to find in the sonnet a space where the movement between the desiring /I/ and its goal could be rhetorically mapped, by various linguistic devices that became the currency of poetic Europe. Thereafter, however desire might specifically be focused, the sonnet could express it, and Petrarchan love becomes a master analogy for all desire, and the great myth which Bembo embodied in the Queen of the Fortunate Isles is its narrative presentation. In so far as the sonnet can hold that narrative, it does so, with particular congeniality in Elizabethan England, in an age and in a place where, quite literally, there was a Queen who was prepared to become the living enactment of that myth. Love is thus an analogy of desire for political success, for maximising one's power; and of course, as success in real sexual love is one of the things men and women desire, a love-sonnet may be an analogy of love itself. Equally it may not.

That desire is broader, in a sense, than love is shown by one of the most beautifully balanced sonnets of the period, by an otherwise unremarked writer, Charles Best, in whom for a moment myth and eloquence meet:

> Look how the pale queen of the silent night
> Doth cause the ocean to attend upon her,
> And he, as long as she is in his sight,
> With his full tide is ready her to honour.
> But when the silver wagon of the moon
> Is mounted up so high he cannot follow,
> The sea calls home his crystal waves to wone,
> And with low ebb doth manifest his sorrow.
> So you, that are the sovereign of my heart,
> Have all my joys attending on your will,
> My joys low ebbing when you do depart,
> When you return, their tide my heart doth fill.
> So as you come, and as you do depart,
> Joys ebb and flow within my tender heart.[4]

Nothing prevents this sonnet from being a private tribute of devotion to Best's own mistress or wife, and with its gentle and persistent rocking rhythm, enhanced by careful placing of antitheses and of polysyllables (very few), it enacts both the movement of the tides and the oscillations of feeling to which these correspond. The woman's beauty is delicately signalled by an absence of decoration which draws attention to the very pale colours that are there – 'pale', 'silver' and 'crystal' – and the simplicity of the syntax suggests both the incessant movement of the sea and the diffidence of the speaker. The feminine rhymes (learnt from Sidney) accentuate this, and a very careful control of consonants keeps the voice moving easily forward. The dialectic markers, 'Look how . . .', 'but', 'so', 'so', correspond to the structural divisions of the sonnet, and a sense of 'sweet reasonableness' is created.

But the metaphor which Best chose is one which has resonances far beyond the private world. He himself adopted the discourse of homage to a queen which runs right through the sonnet, and which unifies private human love with the political order and (because of the image of the moon) with the geo-physical order in a wholly characteristic sixteenth-century manner; he may or may not also have known – as a sonneteer of some sophistication, he probably read the lyrics of his day – that this moon-metaphor had already been appropriated by Sir Walter Ralegh in his sonnets and other poems to 'Cynthia', in his incessant and not often successful attempts to keep the favour and financial patronage of Queen Elizabeth. In court circles Ralegh, the 'shepherd of the Ocean', whose

> song was all a lamentable lay
> Of great unkindnesse and of usage hard
> Of Cynthia the Ladie of the sea,
> Which from her presence faultlesse him debard[5]

was known as a 'most loftie, insolent and passionate' poet (in Puttenham's phrase), and his employment of Petrarchan and pastoral forms and conceits for political advantage both complied with the Queen's own mythmaking and helped to establish Petrarchan love-poetry as a political discourse. Such a sonnet as Best's, then, whatever its author's private purposes, produces a passionate /I/ whose whole being is absorbed into making a gesture (in this case a fourteen-line compliment) within the rituals of courtly advancement: his desire is to be closer to the source of all livelihood. As Ralegh himself put it in a letter of 1592 that might almost be a paraphrase of Best's sonnet:

> My heart was never broken till this day, that I hear the Queen goes away so far off, whom I have followed so many years with so great love and desire, in so many journeys, and am now left behind her in a great prison alone.[6]

And the fact that sonnets such as this were copied, circulated and even sung by people removed from the court and quite innocent of any political ambitions does not diminish the force of the discourse: 'for every man hath business and desires', of which the fashionable sonnet could serve as the metaphorical articulation, just as it had articulated a new kind of civic awareness in mid-thirteenth-century Italy.

Very closely linked to passion is what I have earlier called 'pleynt', or 'complaint' in the Elizabethan vocabulary. Naturally anyone desiring what he cannot have will tend to complain of his lack, to 'bewaile and bemoane the perplexities of Love', but the sonnet was also used for 'pleynt' in a rather wider sense, often outside sequences. The penitential structure of Petrarch's *Rime* had introduced, particularly at the end of his sequence, a philosophising /I/, looking back on the folly of earthly love *sub specie aeternitatis*; it is difficult to do this in isolated sonnets, since the new persona is really the converse (or the convert) of the old, and a sequence in two parts (like Watson's) is really required to establish this, or the kind of retrospective division of one's own poetry into profane and divine that John Donne shows in his *Holy Sonnets* (after 1617). Some poets did, of course, simply write sonnets to heavenly love, sometimes adapting or rewriting Petrarch, and sometimes straightforwardly writing to a divine mistress or master, like Henry Lok, in his 'Sundrie Sonnets' of 1597.[7] But there is an intermediate stage, between earth and heaven, when the /I/ becomes a spectator of the world's vanities, either satirically or philosophically, and complains or laments that 'quanto piace al mondo è breve sogno'.

This theme, usually known as the *topos* of mutability,[8] is found in the Bible, and served to power medieval asceticism; it is also a product of court culture, for nothing vanishes faster than courtly favour. To complain of mutability is thus part of the stance of the experienced courtier, but it involves more than simply writing a sonnet to complain of a favour refused. The persona has to look outwards towards the world, and become a generalised authority or a spectator, something which involves the loss or renunciation of the individualised personal passion that characterises the desiring /I/: indeed, the /I/ may disappear from the sonnet altogether, as in many of the sonnets of Guittone d'Arezzo. To get to that point of vantage from the /I/ of passion, so immersed in his suffering that he can only image it, not understand it, often requires a literal withdrawal from the theatre of passion, as here in Sir Walter Ralegh's sonnet usually entitled 'Farewell to the Court':

> Like truthles dreames, so are my joyes expired,
> And past returne, are all my dandled daies:
> My love misled, and fancie quite retired,
> Of all which past, the sorow onely staies.
> My lost delights, now cleane from sight of land,
> Have left me all alone in unknowne waies:
> My minde to woe, my life in fortunes hand,
> Of all which past, the sorow onely staies.
> As in a countrey strange without companion,
> I onely waile the wrong of deaths delaies,
> Whose sweete spring spent, whose sommer wel nie don,
> Of all which past, the sorow onely staies.
> Whom care forewarnes, ere age and winter colde,
> To haste me hence, to finde my fortunes folde.[9]

The two dominant metaphors of this sonnet, life as a dream or a play in the first quatrain, and life as a voyage of discovery in the second quatrain and sestet (a metaphor peculiarly appropriate to Ralegh), allow the time of the mind to be metaphorised as space, so that experience, being old enough to look back on what one remembers and judge it, can be represented as no longer seeing one's country on the horizon, and future hopes as trying to complete a land journey before winter comes. If Ralegh's syntactical control wavers a little at the end – due perhaps to these quatrains having been originally part of a longer lyric, here rather abruptly turned into sonnet form – the economy and compactness of the metaphors show a very fine grasp of the way a good sonnet should move, and of the balance to be struck between repeating a point and trying to make too many points. The movement from past to present to future is easy and definite, and each stage has its metaphorical exposition.

But the discourses of passion and of mutability do not always occupy separate rooms, and the pure Petrarchan perception of ideal beauty and of the suffering of the lover is liable to be disturbed, in the Elizabethan sonnet, by an excursion into the wastes of time, which changes both the nature of the /I/ and the purpose of the rhetoric. For as the /I/ moves from passion to mutability the run of the sonnet becomes concerned less with the drama of feeling and more with the movement of time; and the couplet ending is less a matter of courtly wit than of sober epigram. One begins to notice, in the later sixteenth century, both in France and in Britain, a distinctive kind of opening line which is a sign of this shift: grave, melodious and usually containing a word that, as it were, sounds the tonic of the key of mutability:

> Quand vous serez bien vieille, au soir, à la chandelle . . .
> (Ronsard)
>
> Comme le champ semé en verdure foisonne . . . (du Bellay)
>
> When Winter snows upon thy golden hairs . . . (Daniel)
>
> One day I wrote her name upon the strand . . . (Spenser)
>
> I have not spent the April of my time . . . (Griffin)
>
> I know that all beneath the moon decays . . . (Drummond)
>
> Like as the waves make towards the pebbled shore . . .
> (Shakespeare)
>
> How soon hath Time, the subtle thief of youth . . . (Milton)

While not every sonneteer who starts in this key continues it throughout the sonnet, there is at least an invitation to the reader in such an opening to construct a persona with a certain weight and distance from what he speaks of, as opposed to the intensely present persona of, say, Sidney's *Astrophel and Stella.*

The third main discourse in the sonnets of this decade (and later) is in some ways the strangest, most remote and least explicable: at the end of Shakespeare's *Sonnets* of 1609, the editor printed two sonnets which every reader of the sequence notices as being apart from the rest; they are on the same theme, and this is the first of them:

Cupid laid by his brand and fell a sleepe,
A maide of Dyans this aduantage found,
And his loue-kindling fire did quickly steepe
In a could vallie-fountaine of that ground:
Which borrowd from this holie fire of love
A datelesse lively heat still to indure,
And grew a seething bath which yet men proue
Against strang malladies a soveraigne cure:
But at my mistres eie loues brand new fired,
The boy for triall needs would touch my brest,
I sick withall the helpe of bath desired,
And thether hied a sad distemperd guest,
But found no cure, the bath for my helpe lies,
Where Cupid got new fire; my mistress' eyes.
(Sonnet 153)

The figure of Cupid as Lord of Love (Petrarch's 'nimico signore' – 'lord and foe') is of course in both the classical and medieval poetic traditions; but this Cupid, imagined as the small son of Venus, winged, with bow and/or torch, as here, is in a discourse usually called 'Anacreontic', which entered European poesis at the end of the fifteenth century, with the publication of the collection of late-classical lyric poems in Greek known as the *Greek Anthology* (1494). The poems attributed to Anacreon of Teos were published in 1554, and from these two sources comes the mythology of the boy Cupid and his mother Venus, 'ruler of Paphos and Cyprus, goddess of the dark eyebrows', as Ronsard called her. What was serious human cruelty in the medieval Cupid becomes mischief in the small boy, and playfulness and whimsicality begin to dominate.

Further, the myth has its own topography: Venus' terrain, Paphos, Cyprus or the island of Cytherea, is a country that overlaps the land of pastoral, Arcadia, and the gods of Arcadia, like Diana in Shakespeare's sonnet, come and go in Cupid's world. The really strange feature of this landscape is its ability to incorporate the bodies of the lover and his mistress, which then become sites of narrative action:

Long time I fought, and fiercely waged warre
Against the God of amorous desire:
Who set the senses mongst themselves at jarre,
The hart inflaming with his lustful fire.
The winged boy upon his mother's knee,
Wantonlie playing neere to *Paphos* shrine,
Scorning that I should checke his Deitie,
Whose dreaded power tam'd the gods divine,
Forth from his quiver drew the keenest dart,
Wherewith high *Jove* he oftentimes had wounded:

And fiercely aimed it at my stubborn hart,
But back again the idle shaft rebounded.
Love saw, and frownd that he was so beguiled,
I laught outright, and *Venus* sweetly smiled.[10]
(Watson, *The Tears of Fancie*, 2)

This setting of the sonnet's speaker in a fantastic landscape surrounded by personifications of parts of himself, however whimsically or lightly done, is really a reversion to an older, pre-Petrarchan way of looking at the self: if with its overpretty decorative imagery of bees, flowers and amoretti the Anacreontic mode seems very baroque, it is closer to a medieval way of detaching the /I/ from the self, with now a top dressing of humanist classicism and pastoral. Sidney had a fondness for the Cupid myth, using it some fourteen times in the sonnets of *Astrophel and Stella*,[11] where his habitual ironic detachment accommodates it well enough; everyone, however, feels the two 'Cupid sonnets' at the end of Shakespeare's collection to be at odds with the kind of treatment of self that is going on throughout the cycle. It is worth noticing, in this connection, that in *Romeo and Juliet*, which is a kind of anthology of rhetorics of love, as Romeo moves from his very modish love of Rosaline to his true love for Juliet (though the one is as unexplained as the other), the Anacreontic rhetoric passes to Mercutio, while Romeo takes over the stilnovistic or Petrarchan rhetoric of passion:

[*Mercutio*:] Romeo! humours! madman! passion! lover!
Appear thou in the likeness of a sigh;
Speak but one rhyme, and I am satisfied;
Cry but 'Ay me!' pronounce but 'love' and 'dove';
Speak to my gossip Venus one fair word,
One nickname for her purblind son and heir,
Young Adam Cupid, he that shot so trim
When King Cophetua lov'd the beggar maid! (II.i)

[*Romeo*:] O, speak again, bright angel, for thou art
As glorious to this night, being o'er my head,
As is a winged messenger of heaven
Unto the white-upturned wondring eyes
Of mortals that fall back to gaze on him,
When he bestrides the lazy-pacing clouds,
And sails upon the bosom of the air. (II.ii)

The three discourses, of passion, of mutability and of Anacreontic fantasia, can overlap in many ways – by sharing metaphors, by sharing personifications, by succeeding one another in a single sonnet – but the reader of the sequences of the 1590s will discover many occasions when between one sonnet and another the author has changed voice or stance, moving from one discourse to another. This the sonnet sequence positively invites, just as the epic discourages it; and part of the pleasure of reading the sequences is the variety of voices one hears, and the rapidly changing occasions evoked, which give a sense of the multifaceted nature of human experience in a way that we think of as proper to the novel. Here, for example, are three sonnets from Giles Fletcher's *Licia*, numbers 14, 17 and 18,[12] which offer an Anacreontic whimsy from a detached spectator, a plangent sonnet from a rather sententious personage, and a rapid piece of impassioned argument heard on the stairs:

My Love lay sleeping where birds music made,
Shutting her eyes, disdainful of the light;
The heat was great; but greater was the shade
Which her defended from his burning sight.
This Cupid saw, and came a kiss to take,
Sucking sweet nectar from her sugared breath.
She felt the touch, and blushed, and did awake,
Seeing 'twas Love, which she did think was Death.
She cut his wings, and causèd him to stay,
Making a vow, he should not thence depart,
Unless to her the wanton boy could pay
The truest, kindest and most loving heart.
  His feathers still she usèd for a fan,
  Till, by exchange, my heart his feathers wan. (*Licia* 14)

As are the sands, fair Licia, on the shore,
Or coloured flowers, garlands of the spring,
Or as the frosts not seen nor felt before,
Or as the fruits that Autumn forth doth bring;
As twinkling stars, the tinsel of the night,
Or as the fish, that gallop in the seas,
As airs, each part that still escapes our sight,
So are my sighs, controllers of my ease.
Yet these are such as needs must have an end,
For things finite, none else, hath Nature done:
Only the sighs which from my heart I send
Will never cease, but where they first begun.
  Accept them, sweet, as incense due to thee,
  For you immortal made them so to be. (*Licia* 17)

I swear, fair Licia, still for to be thine,
By heart, by eyes, by what I hold most dear!
Thou check'dst mine oath, and said, these were not mine;
And that I had no right by them to swear.
Then by my sighs, my passion and my tears,
My vows, my prayers, my sorrow and my love,

My grief, my joy, my hope and hopeless fears,
My heart is thine, and never shall remove!
These are not thine, though sent unto thy view;
All else I grant, by right they are thine own.
Let these suffice, that what I swear is true,
And more than this, if that it could be known.
So shall all these, though troubles, ease my grief,
If that they serve to work in thee belief. (*Licia* 18)

There is certainly an increasing ease of movement, in all senses, in the decade. A flourishing theatre must have taught contemporary versifiers much about fitting speech to metre; and also, by satirising current verse fashions, as Shakespeare does in *Love's Labour's Lost*,[13] must have kept them abreast of what was in vogue – the verse miscellanies of the time also represented the age to itself, but could be erratically old-fashioned in their selections. It is rare, however, to encounter sheer cloth-eared incompetence of the order of Soowthern after 1595 (*Zepheria*, which runs him close, is dated 1594); and a certain smoothness and accuracy in rhyming can be taken for granted, so much so that, of course, Donne and others then began to experiment with ways of breaking that smoothness up. Sonneteers complain about the poetry of their rivals –

the bastard sonnets of these Rhymers bace
which in this whiskinge age are daily borne
to their owne shames, and Poetries disgrace[14]

– but the *topos* of dispraising other writers as one introduces one's own writing is common in all centuries, and indicates merely that there were a lot of sonneteers, not that there were a lot of bad ones. It is remarkable, however, given the amount of criticism produced by writers who were practising sonneteers, that no one attempted a detailed account of the principles of sonnet-writing, or even translated some of the Italian practical criticism available. The critical problems – of decorum, of imitation, of rhyme versus classical metre, of national literature – were worked over in Britain as in Italy, and Sidney was quickly enough hailed as 'the English Petrarke' to provide a 'miglior fabbro' for British writers. (One notices, however, that when Sidney, and Spenser, too, are cited in the anthologies of the age as rhetorical examples the *Arcadia* and *The Faerie Queene* are much oftener cited than their sonnets.) Yet no detailed criticism of particular sonnets, with reflection on their principles, emerged to parallel the numerous Italian examples on both older and contemporary writers, from Petrarch to Tasso.[15] The explanation may be that Britain had no municipal academies; for most of the printed practical criticism of sonnets emerges from the lectures given in the numerous academies which were established in Italian cities in the sixteenth century – a sonnet, when one thinks of it, is exactly the right length for a dilettante's paper among literary friends. The aristocratic prejudice against publishing light verse may also have prevented literary coteries, as at Wilton House under Sidney's sister Mary, from putting into print the literary discussions they had.

But the longest sustained comment on the sonnet which we have from this period comes from one of the poets given patronage by Mary, Countess of Pembroke, in the midst of a treatise which, if it is not a record of poetical discussions, certainly reflects the ideas of the Wilton circle: Samuel Daniel's *A Defence of Ryme* (1602?).[16] Writing to defend rhymed verse against the advocacy of classical metres for English by Thomas Campion (*Observations in the Art of English Poesie*, 1602), Daniel gratefully acknowledges his Wilton training in poesis, some fifteen years before:

> having beene first incourag'd or fram'd thereunto by your [William Herbert, Mary's son] most Worthy and Honourable Mother, receiving the first notion for the formall ordering of those compositions at *Wilton*, which I must ever acknowledge to have beene my best Schoole. . . .[17]

In the course of his *Defence*, he attacks the perversions of word order often found in Latin and Greek verse, and is then prompted to reflect upon the human propensity to create 'unnecessary intrications'. This in turn brings the sonnet to mind, and he moves from the intricacy of bad sonneteering to the pleasure of mastering the difficulty of the form – the idea is not new, but is rarely expressed by English writers:

> And indeed I have wished there were not that multiplicitie of Rymes as is used by many in Sonets, which yet we see in some so happily to succeed, and hath beene so farre from hindering their inventions, as it hath begot conceit beyond expectation, and comparable to the best inventions of the world: for sure in an eminent spirit whome Nature hath fitted for that mysterie, Ryme is no impediment to his conceit, but rather gives him wings to mount and carries him, not out of his course, but as it were beyond his power to a farre happier flight. Al excellencies being sold us at the hard price of labour, it followes, where we bestow most thereof, we buy the best successe: and Ryme being farre more laborious then loose measures (whatsoever is objected) must needs, meeting with wit and industry, breed greater and worthier effects in our language. So that if our labours have wrought out a manumission from bondage, and that wee goe at libertie, notwithstanding these ties [of rhyme], wee are no longer the slaves of Ryme, but we make it a most excellent instrument to serve us.

Then it occurs to him that the arbitrary length and structure of the sonnet might be read as an analogy, in the poetry–power equivalence, of tyranny:

> Nor is this certaine limit observed in Sonnets, any tyrannical bounding of the conceit, but rather a reducing it in *girum*, and a just forme, neither too long for the shortest project, nor too short for the longest, being but onely employed for a present passion. For the body of our imagination, being as an unformed *Chaos* without fashion without day, if by the divine power of the spirit it be wrought into an Orbe of order and forme, is it not more pleasing to Nature, that desires a certaintie, and comports not with that which is infinite, to have these clozes, rather than, not to know where to end, or how farre to goe, especially seeing our passions are often without measure: and we find the best of the latines many times, either not concluding, or els otherwise in the end then they began. Besides, is it not most delightfull to see much excellently ordred in a small roome, or little, gallantly disposed and made to fill up a space of like capacitie, in such sort, that the one would not appear so beautiful in a larger circuite, nor the other do well in a lesse: which often we find to be so, according to the powers of nature in the workman. And these limited proportions, and rests of Stanzes consisting of 6, 7, or 8 lines are of that happines, both for the disposition of the matter, the apt planting the sentence where it may best stand to hit, [that] the certaine close of delight with the full body of a just period well carried, is such, as neither the Greekes or Latines ever attained unto.[18]

Daniel's concept of poetic form is, as one would expect from a member of the Sidney circle, influenced by Neoplatonic ideas of natural and divine harmony: artificial forms in art are a means of controlling the 'body of the imagination', just as natural forms in the physical world are God's means of imposing on Nature an order reflective of His divine harmony. 'Et è Iddio sommo poeta e il mondo suo poema' – 'For God is the chief of poets, and the world is His poem.'[19] Probably because the sonnet appears to be the most 'tyrannical' restriction of the imagination, Daniel chooses it as his instance of 'just forme': accepting that it is not a narrative form, but one which enacts a moment of feeling or an immediate state of mind ('onely employed for a present passion'), Daniel sees the sonnet form as circling the thought, bringing it into the characteristically perfect 'Orbe of order and forme', having a kind of intermediate dimension which enables it to accommodate both what is immediately felt and what is discursively developed.

Under the influence of Neoplatonic theories of harmony, Daniel as it were inverts the notion of the sonnet as a place of challenge or trial:[20] the tension between feeling and thought, the lyrical and the discursive, the /I/ of passion and the /I/ of reflection, is seen by him as a reconciling, producing what he very agreeably calls 'the certaine close of delight'. Just as the infinity of potential creation is abridged in the created world of Nature, so the infinity of human passion, 'often without measure', is abridged in the measure of the sonnet (and similar stanza forms). And, though its subject is passion, its art lies in taking advantage of its dimensions to bring that passion to a reflective close, with a 'sentence', that is, a *sententia,* put just where its impact will be greatest. So in fourteen lines, or even in shorter stanzas, a single piece of verse may do what all poetry does to mankind: control the chaos of passion, and draw it to civil behaviour.

The sense that a good sonnet is one in which the endlessly developing imagination is reined in or circumscribed is one that we have noticed before in sonnets on the sonnet. Whether we see this developmental movement as coming from a conceit – the hunting of a metaphor through a thicket of words – or from a dramatic situation, as in Sidney's sonnets, the sonnet must have it, or it cannot represent passion; but it must also control it and conclude it, or it cannot end. The harmony of the universe is echoed in its sweetness, the *dolcezza* of the Italian rhetorical critics; and the wisdom of the universe in its gravity, the two together giving 'the certaine close of delight'.

Daniel's metaphors in his prose seem to suggest that he would have approved this metaphysical extension of his ideas: his own sonnets suggest that he attempted the practical extension of them. The forward movement of his metaphors gives us the mimesis of feeling, but the grave steadiness of his metre gives us the voice of a reflective /I/, involved with the passion but always in control of his perceptions. There is hardly ever, in Daniel, the kind of violent oscillation between different states that one finds in Petrarch or Sidney, and if there is a twist or snap at the end it comes from the wit of a reflective /I/, rather than from the hysteria or desperation of a passionate one. There is no satirical edge to the voice, as there is in Michael Drayton, and the effect is of a kind of passionate tranquillity:

> Beautie (sweet Love) is like the morning dew,
> Whose short refresh upon the tender greene
> Cheers for a time but til the Sun doth shew,
> And straight 'tis gone as it had never beene.
> Soone doth it fade that makes the fairest florish:
> Short is the glory of the blushing Rose,
> The hew which thou so carefully dost norish,
> Yet which at length thou must be forc'd to lose.
> When thou, surcharg'd with burthen of thy yeeres,
> Shalt bend thy wrinkles homward to the earth,

And that in Beauties lease expir'd appeares
The date of Age, the Kalends of our death –
  But ah! no more, this must not be fore-told,
  For women grieve to thinke they must be old.
(*Delia*, 1601, 47)[21]

(When this sonnet first appeared, in 1592, the last two lines were slightly, yet significantly, different:

But ah no more, thys hath beene often tolde,
And women grieve to thinke they must be old.)

Here the note of mutability is sounded at the start, and maintained very lightly in lines that vary very little from normal spoken word order. The frequent use of a two-syllable adjective with a one-syllable noun ('morning dew', 'tender greene', 'blushing Rose') to end the line and give the rhyme brings a folk-song element in, and the first two quatrains seem to belong to that voice of naïve wisdom that we associate with Elizabethan pastoral and also with eighteenth- and nineteenth-century 'tea-table miscellanies'. The problem is, of course, to develop this; a lesser writer, like Fletcher or Bolton, would have repeated himself in piling up more examples of fading things; Daniel develops the sestet by changing the diction. 'Surcharg'd', 'burthen' and the legal imagery belong to a severer and more learned voice, but one still tender towards fragile things; the use of 'homward' is a particularly delicate recall of the *topos* of Earth as the mother of all. But finally, as we expect 'the full body of a just period well carried', this severer, sententious voice interrupts himself, as if he cannot bear his own conclusion, abandons legal terms and inversions of syntax, and returns to the simplicity of monosyllables with which the sonnet started.

Daniel's 1592 (above) version is equally melodious, but lacks wit: the later version involves a kind of metapoetic irony, since what is not to be said is what the poem has just said; and since it cannot be said to women, lest it grieve them, the original addressee ('sweet Love') is replaced by the reader, conspiratorially nodding to the tender-hearted speaker. The later sonnet is thus dramatic, though without any of Sidney's extravagant gestures.

Since by the mid-1590s the sonnet is known to all sonneteers to be a popular form, a certain competitiveness enters into sonnet-writing, when

Sonnets thus in bundles are imprest,
And every drudge doth dull our satiate eare. . . .[22]

The sonneteer is competing for the favour of his beloved (real or imaginary), not with other lovers, but with other writers, and the object of his desire is to write well in order to be read well. To say that the /I/ of the Elizabethan sonneteer is manifested in adequate rhetorical performance – 'to be' is to have spoken well – is in one way just a truism of sonnet-writing: Petrarch is continually aware that his words fall short of describing Laura's perfections, and he cannot 'be' as a lover unless he can say what he loves. There are many fluently written sonnets which say that they cannot express themselves fluently, or wittily make a virtue of being tongue-tied:

> Dumbe Swannes, not chatring Pies, do Lovers prove,
> They love indeed, who quake to say they love.
>
> (*AS* 54, ll. 13–14)

However, the desire to write effectively, which arose, for most of these poets, from the economic necessity of obtaining patronage or protection by showing themselves to be capable of useful eloquence, leads to a preoccupation with the accomplishment of writing itself as an accomplishment of being – the metaphysical point already made in relation to Daniel's *Defence of Ryme*. The same point is neatly made (if we accept speech as a metonymy for writing) in *Twelfth Night*, when Olivia asks Cesario/Viola what she would do, were she Orsino, to win Olivia's love:

> [*Viola*:] Make me a willow Cabine at your gate,
> And call upon my soule within the house,
> Write loyall Cantons of contemned love,
> And sing them lowd even in the dead of night:
> Hallow your name to the reverberate hilles,
> And make the babling Gossip of the aire,
> Cry out *Olivia*: O you should not rest
> Between the elements of ayre, and earth,
> But you should pittie me.

To which Olivia, stunned, replies: 'You might do much.'[23] In saying how she would speak – how, in effect, she would make the whole of Nature into a poem in praise of Olivia – Viola has spoken, and so well that she has won Olivia. If one is speaking about the possibility of speech, or the failure of speech, or the incompleteness of speech, it is essential to speak well. There is therefore in the sonnet sequences of the 1590s a new attention – not by every poet, nor in every sequence – to the accomplishment of speech, and hence to the formal adequacy of the sonnet or sonnet grouping, drawing attention to what Daniel calls 'much excellently ordred in a small roome'. His own sequence, *Delia*, both in its 1592 and later versions, begins with two sonnets which offer contrasting views of his own writing:

> Unto the boundles Ocean of thy beautie,
> Runs this poore river, charg'd with streames of zeale
> Returning thee the tribute of my dutie,
> Which here my love, my youth, my plaints reveale.

Here I unclaspe the booke of my charg'd soule,
Where I have cast th'accounts of all my care:
Here have I summ'd my sighes, here I inrole
How they were spent for thee; looke what they are:
Looke on the deere expenses of my youth,
And see how just I reckon with thine eies:
Examine well thy beautie with my truth,
And cross my cares ere greater summes arise.
  Read it (sweet maid) though it be done but sleightly,
  Who can show all his love, doth love but lightly. (1)

Go wailing verse, the infants of my love,
Minerva-like, brought foorth without a mother:
Present the Image of the cares I prove,
Witnes your father's grief exceeds all other.
Sigh out a storie of her cruel deeds,
With interrupted accents of despaire:
A monument that whosoever reeds,
May justly praise, and blame my loveless Faire.
Say her disdaine has dried up my blood,
And starved you, in succours still denying:
Press to her eyes, importune me some good,
Waken her sleeping pittie with your crying,
  Knock at her hard heart, beg till ye have mov'd her,
  And tell th'unkind, how dearly I have lov'd her. (2)

The second sonnet is the more orthodox: the poem, or in this case the sequence, is addressed as if it were not a text to be read but a person to be heard, and is requested to go as a messenger, like Viola to Olivia, and be 'fortified against any denial'. This preserves the fiction of the sonnet as a letter arguing a case, by way of the metonymy by which we conventionally accept the letter as the person. But the speech of these messengers, the 'infants' of the speaker, is the very opposite of ordered; it is broken, made of sighs, knocks, crying and wailing, preserving the fiction that a poem is the immediate passionate utterance of an /I/ in a state of emotional disturbance. As Petrarch implies in the opening sonnet of the *Rime*, one reads the poem, but imagines that one hears the sigh.[24]

But the first sonnet, which frames the second because it precedes it, takes the unusual course (in the long history of the sonnet) of treating writing as writing. Beginning with the cliché of tears offered as a tribute (and, by the by, touching on the interesting image of a sonnet sequence as a river, to which individual sonnets are contributing streams), Daniel activates the commercial sense of 'tribute', as booty brought back to the Queen or to an entrepreneur by such voyagers as Drake and Ralegh.

This starts a conceit which leads him to suppose that his sonnet sequence stands in relation to his sufferings as an account-book stands in relation to a cargo of merchandise: an exact summary which describes the cargo and the expenses of the voyage but does not, of course, show them other than 'slightly'. The mistress, as reader, is compared to the auditor who can discharge the accounts by crossing off the tally, an exact and exacting scrutineer of the written 'account'.

Certainly some sonneteers continue to represent the sequence as a portrait or a mirror of the mistress, but most of those who supply a metaphor for their own utterance connect it to the speaker, not to the addressee. Among those for whom the sequence is an 'account' are Michael Drayton, in *Ideas Mirrour* (1594) and later in *Idea* (1619); and Edmund Spenser (*Amoretti*, 1595). Drayton's original title is itself nicely poised between self and other, since 'Idea' is simultaneously a possible name for an idealised mistress and a name for the products of the imagination in the self: the mirror both portrays the mistress and frames or circumscribes the 'ideas'. But his two prefatory sonnets, one at the beginning of his career and one at the end, opt for the sequence as self-accounting:

> Reade heere (sweet Mayd) the story of my wo,
> The drery abstracts of my endles cares,
> With my lives sorow enterlyned so;
> Smok'd with my sighes, and blotted with my teares:
> The sad memorials of my miseries,
> Pend in the grief of myne afflicted ghost;
> My lives complaint in doleful Elegies,
> With so pure love as tyme could never boast.
> Receave the incense which I offer heere,
> By my strong fayth ascending to thy fame,
> My zeale, my hope, my vowes, my praise, my prayer,
> My soules oblation to thy sacred name:
>   Which name my Muse to highest heaven shal raise
>   By chast desire, true love, and vertues praise.[25]
>
> (*Ideas Mirrour*, Amour 1)

Hardly an inviting blurb; but the terms of notation – abstracts, memorials and even elegies – metaphorise each sonnet as an item in a larger 'story'. The sense that the sequence is a gift offered to a higher being allows the metaphorical shift in the sestet to the text as incense, proceeding from the sacrifice of the lover – a burnt offering on the altar of beauty; this develops the text-image to suggest the sonnets as prayers in a prayerbook or anthems of praise. This conceptualising of the sonnet sequence is at once religious and courtly, since gift-giving in return for favours is ritualised in both spheres.

Drayton's second sonnet, which began the sequence as he printed it twenty-five years later, offers a different but related view of the lover in the text:

> Like an adventurous Sea-farer am I,
> Who hath some long and dang'rous voyage beene,
> And call'd to tell of his Discoverie,
> How farre he sayl'd, what Countries he had seene,
> Proceeding from the Port whence he put forth,
> Shewes by his Compasse, how his Course he steer'd,
> When East, when West, when South, and when by North,
> As how the Pole to ev'ry place was rear'd,
> What Capes he doubled, of what Continent,
> The Gulphes and Straits, that strangely he had past,
> Where most becalm'd, where with foule Weather spent,
> And on what Rocks in peril to be cast?
> Thus in my Love, Time calls me to relate
> My tedious Travels, and oft-varying Fate.
>
> (*Idea*, 1619, Sonnet 1)

This rather tired sonnet, running a conceit straight through without making use of the quatrain or sestet divisions, likens Love to a sea-voyage, using the Ovidian metaphor of the mistress's body as a landscape; but, though for a reader acquainted with, say, Donne's 'Elegie 18: Love's Progress' (published 1669) there might be a *double entendre* in 'how the Pole to ev'ry place was rear'd', the places mentioned in this introductory sonnet must rather represent moments of experience, and the chapters or sections of the voyage-text that describe those places are the individual sonnets. The sonnets of *Idea* do not assemble into a succession of 'brief encounters' even as much as do the sonnets of *Astrophel and Stella*, but having learnt, as all his age did, from Sidney, and probably also from the manuscript poems of Donne, how to handle outbursts of feeling Drayton is the master of the overheard moment of dramatic conflict:

> Since there's no helpe, Come let us kisse and part,
> Nay, I have done: You get no more of Me,
> And I am glad, yea, glad with all my heart,
> That thus so cleanly I my Selfe can free.
> Shake hands for ever, Cancell all our Vowes,
> And when we meet at any time againe,
> Be it not seene in either of our Browes,
> That we one jot of former Love reteyne;
> Now at the last gasp of Loves latest Breath,
> When his Pulse fayling, Passion speechlesse lies,
> When Faith is kneeling by his bed of Death,

And Innocence is closing up his Eyes,
Now if thou would'st, when all have given him over,
From Death to Life, thou might'st him yet recover.
(*Idea*, 1619, 61)

Anyone who begins a sonnet with 'You get no more of me' is falsifying what he says even as he says it, having at least twelve lines more to give by the rules of the sonnet. There is a pleasing formal wit here in a sonnet that begins with an ending and ends with a beginning; and the rush of ludicrous personifications in the sestet puts a distance between the speaker and his author. Drayton's strong sense of the conventionality of the sonnet makes his voices very varied, and he mimics, at one time or another, practically all of his contemporaries.[26] But his own liking, which grew stronger during the quarter-century in which he worked with *Idea*, for representing 'himself' as some kind of licensed fool – which might be a development in him of Sidney's fondness for making jokes about his own poesis – tends to undercut the whole idea of an emotional journey. Petrarch would never have said, in the middle of the *Rime*:

As other men, so I my selfe do muse,
Why in this sort I wrest invention so,
And why these giddy metaphors I use,
Leaving the path the greater part do go;
I will resolve you; I am lunaticke. . . .
(*Idea*, 1602, 12.1–5)

The presence, in a collection of sonnets, of what in Chapter 6 I called an 'archspeaker', an /I/ who can take an overview of 'his' collection, and thus speak about the act of speaking, means that we have a narrator who both presents his passionate self and stands back from it, taking a wiser, detached, perhaps even cynical or dismissive attitude to that other. In *Tottel's Miscellany*, the persona who emerges from the titles of the miscellaneous poems ('rime sparse') is a courtly lover who has gained moral and philosophical insights into the mutability of things, a persona always popular and particularly congenial, for example, to Sir Walter Ralegh. At the end of the sixteenth century, in an age which had not yet arrived at the diary as a publishable form, which had seen only rare examples of the autobiography, and which completely lacked newspapers and journals in which a self might voice its opinions in short form, the sonnet sequence allowed, as Drayton shows, the presentation of a self in a series of moments of varied perceptions and reflections.[27]

The sonneteer who, after Sidney, has the strongest sense of the sequence as an emotional diary is Edmund Spenser, who like Drayton and Sidney begins his sequence, the *Amoretti* of 1595, with a prefatory sonnet about writing and reading: indeed, the very title has a formal reference, since 'Amoretti' means 'little love-offerings'.

> Happy ye leaves when as those lilly hands,
> Which hold my life in their dead doing might,
> Shall handle you and hold in loves soft bands,
> Lyke captives trembling at the victors sight.
> And happy lines, on which with starry light,
> Those lamping eyes will deigne sometimes to look
> And reade the sorrowes of my dying spright,
> Written with teares in harts close bleeding book.
> And happy rymes bath'd in the sacred brooke,
> Of *Helicon* whence she derived is,
> When ye behold that Angels blessed looke,
> My soules long lacked foode, my heavens blis.
> Leaves, lines, and rymes, seeke her to please alone,
> Whom if ye please, I care for other none.[28]

It is perhaps because one knows Spenser as the author of *The Faerie Queene* that there seems to be an unusual degree of control here, like the casual power that one discerns in the tiny clavichord pieces of Bach. Having written almost six books of the most complicated epic in the English language, Spenser by 1595 had acquired the habit of controlling large tracts of narrative, consisting of huge quantities of discrete nine-line stanzas. Here, at the outset of a mere eighty-nine[29] sonnets, he establishes control not merely by the metapoetic metaphor he uses (that the pages of the text stand like souls in front of a Recording Angel) but by a kind of formal density and discipline that must have been second nature to him, like fugal harmony to Bach.

The way in which the content of the three quatrains is marshalled (and the word is chosen advisedly, given the metaphor of captivity) in the final couplet under its headwords, 'leaves, lines, and rymes', the first two linked by alliteration and the second two by off-rhymes, gives an assurance of mental control, which is important in a sonnet using the rhetoric of passion, as this does. Too much discursive marking makes a sonnet arid; too little can leave it hysterical or bombastic. Spenser's easy control is subtly enhanced by the soft alliteration of the letter 'l', the dominant sound of the poem, which gives a phonic continuity to balance the discursive one.

His distinctive contribution to the sonnet form is also part of his control and steadiness: the so-called 'Spenserian' rhymescheme, ABAB BCBC CDCD EE, used in quantity by no other writers except the Scots sonneteers around James VI. It is a very demanding rhymescheme, at least as difficult as the Petrarchan scheme (ABAB ABAB CDE CDE) from which the Earl of Surrey seemed to have freed English writers, to the satisfaction of all concerned; and Spenser had no imitators among the sequences which followed his. As has already been suggested (p. 104 above), it is most unlikely that he obtained the pattern from Scotland; since the stanza of *The Faerie Queene* runs ABAB BCBC C, and he had written nearly four thousand of them when he wrote the *Amoretti*,[30] he must have had these chained quatrains permanently lodged in his brain, so that to extend nine lines to fourteen cost little effort. No other writer had anything approaching this experience of chained quatrains, and that may explain why Spenser's form was not adopted by anyone else. (Nor was his style; what Samuel Daniel called his 'agèd accents and untimely words',[31] though mightily admired in *The Faerie Queene*, had no imitators in the sonnet.)

Spenser's habit is to divide his sonnets at the quatrains, usually beginning a new sentence, or at least a new main clause, at each quatrain, with another to begin the final couplet. His thought moves in very clearly marked stages, with almost no run-on lines from quatrain to quatrain, and with prominent dialectic markers, such as 'so', 'yet', 'thus' and 'then'. Since he wrote the *Amoretti* at the age of about 40, perhaps we can detect in this methodical structuring a sort of middle-aged deliberateness; however it registers with the reader, it is certainly offset by the continuity of the chained rhymes, which flow across and hold together the conceptual breaks. The movements are at once discrete and continuous, what Wordsworth brilliantly imaged as

> Sweet Spenser, moving through his clouded heaven
> With the moon's beauty and the moon's soft pace. . . .

There is indeed a 'soft pace' kept throughout this sequence, something that only Daniel and Drummond of Hawthornden – both of them very concerned with phonic melody – can accomplish.

But rather oddly, given this massive control and steadiness, Spenser has often been accused of extravagance of one kind or another: Drummond of Hawthornden called the sonnets 'childish',[32] and professed to believe that they were not by Spenser at all; but, then, Drummond had little sense of humour, and might well have thought some of the playful sonnets of the *Amoretti* merely silly. Sidney Lee, who liked English writers to be original, objected to 'strained conceits . . . silently borrowed from foreign literature';[33] and more recently J. W. Lever, persuaded that 'the sonnet exists for the expression of personal and direct perception', found the sequence too theoretical, and 'patch[ed] . . . with conventional irrelevancies'.[34]

But leaving aside for the moment consideration of the coherence of Shakespeare's sonnets, it can be seriously argued that Spenser produced the most coherent and highly developed sonnet sequence of all his contemporaries, and that the /I/ presented in it has a degree of sophistication which one would have to go back to Dante or Petrarch – or forward to Shakespeare – to parallel. To justify this, and conclude this chapter with a satisfactory defence of Spenser, I must recapitulate some earlier material.

The sonnet does not exist 'for the expression of personal and direct perception' as far as any of its sixteenth-century writers are concerned, mainly because the notion of 'personality' which makes us value direct and individual perception only arises gradually in western Europe out of the late-Renaissance writing we are now talking about. It exists, as far as one can determine from those who practised it, to enable the utterance of a passionate self in eloquent – that is, rationally controlled – form; this rational control might be exercised inside the single sonnet, by the pressure of its dialectic structure upon its passionate lexis, or in a longer sequence, by the emergence of countervailing passions – penitence, regret, revulsion, stoic endurance – to oppose the previous ones. If one asks why, since the passionate self has to be controlled, it should be thought necessary to let it utter itself at all, then perhaps no single answer will cover the sonnet from Giacomo da Lentino to Milton: but passions are always the horses of the soul's chariot, and if we no longer desire, then we cease to be. Passions provide the energy and motive of speech itself, and speech well formed then guides the passions. Through the persuasive effect of that speech upon others, the specific ends of one's desires may be obtained:

> Loving in truth, and faine in verse my love to show,
> That the deare She might take some pleasure of my paine:
> Pleasure might cause her reade, reading might make her know,
> Knowledge might pitie winne, and pitie grace obtaine,
>   I sought fit words to paint the blackest face of woe. . . .
>
> (*AS* 1, ll. 1–5)

Sidney's speaker obeys the Muse's injunction to 'looke in [his] heart and write', not because he thinks his own perceptions valuable but because he wishes to persuade – a sonnet sequence is a kind of petition for emotional recognition, which amounts to a recognition of self, in that to the Lady it is the desiring or 'passionate' self that speaks.

The question then arises, in what rhetorics, in what forms, shall the petition be drawn? Or, to change the metaphor from judicial to theatrical, what roles will gain the most applause? Having at first presented his sequence as a book (his self will exist if the leaves are read), Spenser later presents it as a theatrical performance, as Nashe presented Sidney's:

> Of this worlds Theatre in which we stay,
> My love lyke the Spectator ydly sits
> Beholding me that all the pageants play,
> Disguysing diversly my troubled wits.

Sometimes I joy when glad occasion fits,
And mask in myrth lyke to a Comedy:
Soone after when my joy to sorrow flits,
I waile and make my woes a Tragedy.
Yet she beholding me with constant eye,
Delights not in my merth nor rues my smart:
But when I laugh she mocks, and when I cry
She laughes, and hardens evermore her hart.
What then can move her? if nor merth nor mone,
She is no woman, but a sencelesse stone.

(*Amoretti* liiii)

The theatrical metaphor emphasises that what is transacted between them is the *performance* of feeling: the expressions of that feeling are masks, the tragic corresponding to the rhetoric of passion, and the comic to the playful mode associated with Anacreontic rhetoric. The rhetoric of 'pleynt' can also be tragic, but at its most philosophical, as we have seen, creates a persona who withdraws from the 'theatre of the world' – the sonnet can also be a gesture of repudiation of the stage. Petrarch had established the principle of 'overview' in a sequence; in his first sonnet of the *Rime* and periodically throughout, he allows the narrating /I/ to look back upon his own performance, and to conclude that his poetry might have been better than it was, or that it had not the effect he wished. Clearly, to have a speaker in a sequence who is aware that he is writing one, or even just aware that he is writing poems, is to introduce a master of ceremonies, and to make the reader aware that the individual performances are under the control of a supervising /I/. Sidney has an ironic master of ceremonies, who constantly problematises the act of writing/speaking; Drayton has a zany, who pretends to be irresponsible; Spenser has his own epic narrator from *The Faerie Queene*, who enters three (and possibly four) times, not counting the first sonnet of all: once in a sonnet addressed to Spenser's friend Lodowick Bryskett (xxxiii), apologising for letting the *Amoretti* interrupt the writing of *The Faerie Queene*, once praising the three Elizabeths in his life, his mother, his Queen and his future wife (lxxiiii) and once again pleading for a respite from writing his epic (lxxx): unless we take Shakespeare's sonnets about the 'rival poet' as a parallel, this is the only sonnet in a sequence which sets that sequence in a literary context.

After so long a race as I have run
Through Faery land, which those six books compile,
Give leave to rest me being half fordonne,
And gather to my selfe new breath awhile.
Then as a steed refreshed after toyle,
Out of my prison I will breake anew:

And stoutly will that second work assoyle,
With strong endeavour and attention dew.
Till then give leave to me in pleasant mew,
To sport my muse, and sing my loves sweet praise:
The contemplation of whose heavenly hew,
My spirit to an higher pitch will rayse.
But let her prayses yet be low and meane,
Fit for the handmayd of the Faery Queene.

(*Amoretti* lxxx)

The octave of the sonnet deals with the completion of one section of *The Faerie Queene*, probably the six finished books which we now have;[35] and the sestet with the composition of the *Amoretti*. As is normal in Elizabethan criticism, Spenser regards his sonnet-writing as 'sport' in relaxed surroundings ('pleasant mew') and, while still acknowledging the exalted nature of his mistress, insists that the style of the sonnets must be 'low and meane' (that is, written in the low and middle styles of rhetoric as befits material that is sportive or passionate). Given Spenser's interest in Neoplatonic theories of love, and his exaltation of his mistress, Elizabeth Boyle, as 'divine and born of heavenly seed', it is necessary to insist that his narrator is quite clear about the stylistic level of what he oversees: as a handmaid differs in rank from her Queen, so the *Amoretti* differ in rank of style from *The Faerie Queene*.

This is not so very different from Petrarch's sense that his sonnets and *canzoni* to Laura were 'scattered' ('sparse'), 'harsh and dark' ('aspre e fosche'), or 'too low' ('troppo umile') or 'trifling' ('nugae');[36] though he did not explicitly compare his *Rime* to his own epic poem, the *Africa*, his view of their stylistic ranking is clear. Spenser, who had absorbed a good deal from Petrarch and from his own near-contemporary Tasso, like him a producer both of sonnets and of a major European epic, had the characteristic Renaissance reverence for large-scale, continuous, highly decorated narrative, the public and national epic; and therefore regarded the utterance of the private voice as less serious and less worthy. This does not mean that the private voice, in a sonnet, could not deal with serious matters; merely that in a small poem, like the sonnet, or even in a collection of such poems, lacking narrative coherence and elaboration, the seriousness of the voice could not match the seriousness of the epic speaker. Shakespeare probably thought *The Rape of Lucrece* a much more serious work than his own 154 sonnets – certainly he seems to have cared much more about it.

Remembering that for the courtier – and Spenser tried very hard to be a court poet – there was no distinction between play and work, in a culture where ritualised play could be intensely serious and consequential, we might approach a sonnet sequence such as the *Amoretti* as today we would approach a sophisticated dinner-party conversation. In both there are speakers and hearers, and no single voice may speak for very long. In both there is a permissible range of kinds of speech – one may not, for example, be too learned or professional, nor may one be too coarse. To say a thing well or wittily is much appreciated, even if it is not original to the speaker; intimate confessions are permitted, but not at too great length. A certain amount of cultural allusiveness is expected. There is a range of gambits: one may tell anecdotes (briefly) or jokes; one may philosophise, moralise, be satirical or reminisce; one may even be intensely serious about a matter dear to one's heart – but not for too long. And constantly, in both sonnet and table-talk, one is performing for an audience, moving in and out of a series of poses, and watching one's own performance as one gives it (with, perhaps, ironic metaconversational remarks superadded). The aim is not truth, but delight: above all, one is asked to speak well. It is not accidental that the popularity of the sonnet coincides with that of the courtesy manual, often written in the form of aristocratic conversations.

Spenser, then, creates in the *Amoretti* an /I/ who desires one thing (marriage to his Lady) but performs his desire eloquently from various angles and in various voices and registers, within the range conventional to the sonnet discourse. So there is affectionate badinage (lxxi), erotic fantasia (lxxvi), anecdote (lxxv), self-reproach (lxxxiiii), ironic conversation with others (xxix), extravagant addresses to Cupid (x) and moral commonplaces (xxvi); there are sonnets which address the Lady, others which talk about her, others which are private self-communings, even ones which have Sidney's (and Wyatt's) trick of suggesting a conversation in progress (xxxiii, lxv). There is also a variety of emotions directed towards the beloved: exasperation (x), adoration (viii), frustration (xxxvi), rage (xlvii), sexual desire (lxiiii), companionship (lxxv), avuncular consolation (lxvi), loneliness (lxxxvii) and joy (lxxxii). As structuring devices, there are three imitated (even if not directly) from Petrarch: the two-part division *in vita* and *in morte* imitated by Drummond and varied by Watson in *Hekatompathia* is turned by Spenser into a division before and after his acceptance by his Lady, which occurs at lxvii, a sonnet that owes a lot to Tasso and to Petrarch. Second, the whole sequence leads to a climax: for Petrarch, his repentance after Laura's death climaxes in the great *canzone* to the Virgin, *Rime* 366; for Spenser, his acceptance by Elizabeth Boyle climaxes in their marriage, celebrated in *Epithalamion*, which stands after the *Amoretti* in the 1595 volume. And, third, Spenser adopted Petrarch's device of marking the progress of the self by noting the progress of time, not over years, as Petrarch had done, but over two years marked by two New Year sonnets (iv and lxii), two spring sonnets (xix and lxx) and two Lent and Easter sonnets (xxii and lxviii) – a device which calls to mind the use of the seasons in Tennyson's *In Memoriam*.

If the *Amoretti* are unique in proceeding towards a happy marriage, the sequence is also exceptional in its shaping and control. Less extravagant in gesture than Sidney's *Astrophel and Stella*, it manages an amazing variety of moments of desire, or aspects of desire, contained within a Petrarchan frame of a preliminary sonnet and a great climactic ode, with various structural controls along the way. The apparently discordant sonnets of absence at the end (lxxxvii–lxxxix) do no more than image the desolation that absence does indeed bring to those newly, but truly, in mutual love. The last sonnet of lamentation will be followed by a change of key in the first stanza of *Epithalamion*, where Spenser's speaker turns all previous sorrow to joy: for the moment, the *Amoretti* ends with the same confident powerful movement with which it began, and an unforgettable registration of lover's pain in the image of the dove awaiting the return of her mate in the gathering dark:

> Lyke as the Culver on the bared bough[37]
> Sits mourning for the absence of her mate,
> And in her songs sends many a wishfull vow,
> For his return that seemes to linger late.
> So I alone now left disconsolate,
> Mourn to my selfe the absence of my love:
> And wandring here and there all desolate,
> Seek with my playnts to match that mournful dove:
> Ne joy of ought that under heaven doth hove,
> Can comfort me, but her own joyous sight:
> Whose sweet aspect both God and man can move,
> In her unspotted pleasauns to delight.
> Dark is my day, whyles her fayre light I mis,
> And dead my life that wants such lively blis. (lxxxix)

He has little sense of irony, and his long training in allegorical narrative made him unapt to fashion the intricate metaphorical chains of Shakespeare or Donne; but because of his easy control, from couplet up to sequence, and his rich variety of gestures of passion, whether sportive or plaintive, Spenser offers the finest example, in his decade, of that intricate dance of passion and eloquence that was the Elizabethan sonnet sequence.

9

'THEE (MY SELFE)': THE SONNETS OF SHAKESPEARE

In 1609 the London publisher Thomas Thorpe first registered and then published a quarto volume of 154 sonnets, entitled 'SHAKE-SPEARES SONNETS. Never before Imprinted'.[1] In fact, two of them, numbers 138 and 144, had been printed before, in William Jaggard's *The Passionate Pilgrim* of 1599; but the remainder had been unpublished until that date, well after the Elizabethan sonnet vogue was over. At the end of the volume was also a 329-line narrative poem in forty-seven stanzas called 'A Lover's Complaint', in which the main speaker is a woman betrayed by a beautiful young man. No one disputed that Shakespeare had written what Thorpe published, and Shakespeare himself was still alive to object had the volume contained anything he wished to disavow. Nothing of that sort seems to have happened, and so it is very nearly certain that the sonnets in Thorpe's quarto volume (Q) are by William Shakespeare.

If this seems a very toe-in-the-water start to a discussion of what is, after Petrarch, the most famous sonnet collection in European literature, it is because nothing else about this perverse, unique and bewildering collection of poems is certain. The collection creates unique and highly specific situations, full of apparently circumstantial allusions; it addresses two people, a man and a woman, with an intimacy and a ferocity of emotion unparalleled outside the sonnets of Michelangelo; it is the longest single collection of sonnets in the English Renaissance repertoire; and it is by a man who left a very large amount of other work, and about whose life we know a great deal. Yet not a single circumstance or allusion anywhere has been incontrovertibly dated or attached to a definite person; not a single sonnet has itself been dated, while dates anywhere between 1583 and 1609 have been suggested; and about Shakespeare's connection with Q itself nothing whatever is known.[2] Finally, it is not even clear whether the 154 sonnets were intended by Shakespeare to form any kind of a sequence, nor what relation they should have with 'A Lover's Complaint'.[3] It is almost as if some suspicious overseer, imbued with all the deviousness of a Henry James, had set himself to ambiguate the text at all possible points.

This is not as fantastic as it seems: Sidney's *Astrophel and Stella* was subjected to some prudent censorship to avoid offending Lady Rich and her husband,[4] and the accusations against the young man and the so-called Dark Lady in Shakespeare's *Sonnets* do go far beyond anything that Sidney had written. It is thus quite possible (everyone who writes about Shakespeare's sonnets starts to conjecture sooner or later) that Shakespeare declined to publish until he thought it safe, and even then published only on condition that he himself was kept out of the transactions, and that all traceable references were removed. That would explain the late appearance of the *Sonnets*, and their extraordinary ambiguousness.

However, as this chapter will not be much concerned with the biographical or historical aspects of the *Sonnets*, but rather with Shakespeare's use of the sonnet persona, it is as well to state here briefly what is known and what is fairly safely conjectured about the Q-sonnets.

1 They are by Shakespeare; the three that are most suspect are 153 and 154 (the two Anacreontic sonnets referred to in Chapter 8), and 145, a rather naïve sonnet in tetrameter lines quite unlike anything else in Q. However, no one queried this in Shakespeare's lifetime.
2 Shakespeare most probably did not oversee the printing. The clearest indication of this is that 126, which is a twelve-line poem in couplets, was printed in Q with empty brackets for an extra two lines after it, showing that the printer/proofreader noticed its oddity, but could not check the matter with the author.[5] There are several other misprints which a proofreading author would have picked up.
3 Following from 2, it cannot be said that the order of the sonnets in Q is Shakespeare's. As it stands, 1–126 appear to be addressed to, or to concern, a very beautiful young man, and 127–54 similarly to concern a dark-haired lady. The first section comprises poems of praise and passionate devotion, not unmixed with reproach and self-disgust; the second section has mainly poems of rage and reproach, with a few conventional poems of praise and devotion. But the first section contains only about twenty-five sonnets in which the male sex of the person addressed or referred to is clear: many of sonnets 1–126 could have been written to or about a woman. The second section much more clearly concerns a woman, and only one sonnet, 150, seems as if it might have been misplaced from the first section.
4 Many sonnets are paired, in the sense that the phrasing or imagery of the second clearly continues from the first (these are discussed below). It can be assumed that Shakespeare intended these to be read as pairs; there may be others in this case which have become separated – e.g., 48 and 52.
5 There is no prefatory sonnet to show that Shakespeare thought of his

poems as a sequence (and, if there were, it would not prove that these Q-poems were the ones he thought of); but there are a number of 'overview' sonnets in which the speaker is aware of having written a lot of poems to the young man (e.g., 78, 102, 103, 105). Since there are otherwise only two poems outside the Q-sonnets which could, however obliquely, be about the young man, 'A Lover's Complaint' and 'The Phoenix and the Turtle', it seems safe to assume that the 'lays' and 'verses' referred to in 102 and 103 are included in the sonnets of Q.

6 The first seventeen sonnets urge the young man (identified as male in eight of them) to marry and beget a son. This is so extraordinary a topic for sonnets (or indeed for any kind of literary work) that Thomas Thorpe could hardly have found these seventeen scattered about, as he might have found sonnets on Time or the planets. Their collection as a group, though not their placing first in Q, can be assumed to be Shakespeare's doing.[6]

7 There are four 'triangle' sonnets, 42, 133, 134 and 144, in which the young man becomes sexually involved with the woman, this being a double infidelity to the speaker. Sonnets 42 and 134 seem like a pair, but could not be paired in Q because 42 is addressed to the young man, and 134 to the woman. This triangular relation, to say nothing of sexual infidelity itself, again is quite extraordinary in sonnet-writing, and it of course provides a kind of narrative link between 1–126 and 127–54; as this arises from the content of the sonnets, and not merely from their juxtaposition, this triangular relation must be Shakespeare's invention.

8 It is certain that Shakespeare was writing sonnets before 1599: two sonnets, as was said above, in Q appeared in print in 1599, and in 1598 an observer of the literary scene, Francis Meres, referred in print to 'Shakespeare's sugared sonnets among his private friends'.[7] It is theoretically possible that we have lost all the sonnets he wrote before 1598, and that everything in Q dates from 1599–1609; but as British sonneteers did not write enormous quantities of sonnets the supposition must be that many, if not most, of the sonnets in Q are indeed among the ones known to have been circulated 'among his private friends'.

9 The period 1592–9 is the period most favoured by critics for the composition of the *Sonnets*, though no attempt to date any single sonnet by critical, historical or stylistic means has been accepted by everyone.

10 Both the man and the woman are praised in conventional Petrarchan or courtly terms in some sonnets; but others make it clear that the speaker feels himself betrayed by the shameful conduct of the man and the sexual promiscuity of the woman.

There is a precedent for the last aspect in Catullus' disastrous devotion to Lesbia, and hints of it in Wyatt's poetry, but the existence of two deeply flawed and unworthy lovers is fundamentally anti-Petrarchan, and appears nowhere else in the Elizabethan sonnet. If we ask what such an unusual mimesis could signify, the readiest answer, and the one favoured by the majority of critics, is that the situations and feelings presented in the *Sonnets* come from Shakespeare's own life. Certainly, the dramatist who could imagine the torments of Othello and of Hamlet could have invented the speaker of the sonnets, and created his circumstances out of air; but, apart from the fact that nothing in the sonnet convention would have suggested such a mimesis, much of the quasi-circumstantiality is so handled that many of the sonnets are actually obscure.

Allusion to circumstances known to speaker and hearer is one of the marks of real conversation between people, and thus one of the characteristics that poets learn to mimic when they wish to invent conversations between people. But when presenting circumstances 'as if' they were real to the speakers, that is, not having to be explained because they are already known or present, the poet has to explain them to the reader, or enable the reader to handle them 'as if' s/he knew what they were. Here, for example, Sidney imitates a conversation between 'Astrophel' and a friend:

> Having this day my horse, my hand, my launce
> Guided so well, that I obtain'd the prize,
> Both by the judgement of the English eyes,
> And of some sent from that sweet enemie *Fraunce*. . . .
> (*AS* 41, ll. 1–4)

'This day' is a sign of speech (in writing we always specify the day), and needs no addition – we are happy to accept that the speaker and his auditor know what day 'this' is, and accept that we do not need to know ourselves; but thereafter, in order for the reader to understand what is going on, Sidney has to make his speaker speak to an auditor who was not present at the tournament, one who needs to be told that French envoys were there. As it happens, this is plausible, since the whole sonnet can be imagined as spoken by Astrophel as he comes away from the tilt ground; but the slight awkwardness of 'that sweet enemie' is a concession to the need to inform a reader at the cost of distorting the naturalness of speech. By contrast, Shakespeare's Sonnet 86 seems highly circumstantial in a way that baffles the reader:

> Was it the proud full saile of his great verse,
> Bound for the prize of (all to precious) you,
> That did my ripe thoughts in my braine inhearce,
> Making their tombe the wombe wherein they grew?

Was it his spirit, by spirits taught to write,
Above a mortall pitch, that struck me dead?
No, neither he, nor his compiers by night
Giving him ayde, my verse astonished.
He nor that affable familiar ghost
Which nightly gulls him with intelligence,
As victors of my silence cannot boast,
I was not sick of any feare from thence.
But when your countinance fild up his line,
Then lackt I matter; that infeebled mine. [Q: matter,][8]

We can rescue the opening of this sonnet from bafflement by supposing that Sonnet 86 was intended by Shakespeare to be paired with Sonnet 80:

O How I faint when I of you do write,
Knowing a better spirit doth use your name,
And in the praise thereof spends all his might,
To make me toung-tide speaking of your fame. (80.1–4)

The nautical metaphors in both sonnets (86.1–2, 80.5–14) suggest their linkage. But the cryptic references to 'his compiers [compeers] by night' and 'that affable familiar ghost' offer circumstances that cannot be located in the reader's world, though they are pointed to as already known to the addressee. This is an allusive conversation between the speaker and his beloved that excludes the reader. Yet as a practising dramatist Shakespeare was trained precisely to create conversations, particularly at the beginning of plays, which give the audience information while preserving the fiction that this information is already known to the speakers. It can hardly be for lack of skill that Sonnet 86 gives the reader almost nothing of what is evidently known to both speaker and addressee.

Though only a small number of the sonnets show these private circumstances, their presence does suggest that we are reading something not primarily meant for us to read: and the enormous variety of solutions to the circumstantial enigmas that have been proposed by commentators after most diligent research[9] leads one to believe that the circumstances could hardly have been common knowledge in Shakespeare's own day. The collection in Q, which seems tonally and thematically very homogeneous (allowing for the shift from the young man to the lady), might well represent sonnets written by Shakespeare for a variety of quite different purposes, and sonnets written to the young man for his private reading only may now be mixed in with sonnets written for general circulation; so Sonnet 17 ('Who will beleeve my verse in time to come'), which is certainly addressed to the young man, since it mentions his begetting a son, lies next to 18 ('Shall I compare thee to a Summers day') which we read as addressed to the young man also; but we cannot be certain that Shakespeare did not, for example, write it on behalf of an acquaintance called Summers courting a Mistress Day.

This way lies either madness or an enormous book devoted to the historical and biographical possibilities. For my purposes, I think it is fair to assume that the sonnets as we have them are written by Shakespeare out of his own feelings towards a young man and a lady with whom he was involved as the poems suggest: the young man was rich, powerful and unmarried, and in a position to give Shakespeare patronage; at some stage Shakespeare felt himself being supplanted in the young man's affections by the figure known to critics as the Rival Poet. The lady was married to someone else, but had an affair with the young man as well as with Shakespeare. The young man's youth made Shakespeare feel old (he was in his mid-thirties in the late 1590s). Finally, Shakespeare's love for the young man was not physically homosexual, as Sonnet 20 makes quite clear.

To what extent does it matter whether the *Sonnets* are 'true' or not? What Shakespeare does with the sonnet, and what he does with the /I/ that speaks in it, is what it is, whether the events happened in his own life or were imagined: but we can read the sonnets more coherently, using one sonnet to understand another, if we can assume that they all (or almost all) proceed from Shakespeare's narrating self to one other male and one other female. This is particularly relevant to the small number of 'meditative' sonnets, like Sonnet 116 ('Let me not to the marriage of true mindes/Admit impediments'), which are concerned with general mutability, and are spoken to no particular person by a detached voice of authority and experience. Most Elizabethan sonnet sequences – indeed, most sixteenth-century sequences – have such sonnets, since this stance and voice was one of the conventional /I/s available; but if, for example, we can lock this sonnet into the more specific sonnets to the young man we can propose quite a different reading of its final couplet:

> If this be error and upon me proved,
> I never writ, nor no man ever loved.

As a self-contained sonnet in the experiential voice, it would produce a last line of two impossibilities; since 'I' has writ, and since men have loved, then this is not error. But, as occurring in the context of the sonnets to the young man, the line may also mean 'I never writ, nor ever loved any man (which is impossible, since you know I love you)'. And it may have been phrased with deliberate ambiguity to mask a homoerotic construction under a conventional one.

But whether he lived it, or whether he imagined it, Shakespeare has created an /I/ markedly different from anything before him, which makes new demands on and uses of the sonnet (e.g., the appearance of paired sonnets). The difference is in the desired objects, as was said: for the first time in the entire history of the sonnet, the desired object is *flawed*, which leads to a new kind of self-questioning, leading in turn to new employment of the sonnet space.

It had always been crucial to the existence of the /I/ of the sonnet that the cruelty of the mistress (or, if we consider also religious sonnets, of God) is directed to the lover: it is a cruelty which in its exercise gives recognition to the lover, by creating effects in him which, if distressing, are none the less manifestations of *him*. (The worst fate for the courtier is to be ignored.) We see the dramatic image of this in Beatrice's 'disdain' for Benedick in *Much Ado about Nothing*, which dramatically creates Benedick in the play, fills him out and gives him an existence. What is extraordinary in Shakespeare's sonnets, whether because of the circumstances of Shakespeare's own life or out of some unknowable *Angst*, is the recurring sense that the speaker is being brushed aside, by a lover who is insufficient: not interested enough in him even to be cruel. We have here an /I/ not so much tormented as in limbo (to recur to a Dantean parallel): marginalised by the absorption of his patron in other concerns and by the promiscuity of his mistress, and driven to accuse himself of inadequacy, he seeks desperately for a reflex of himself in eyes that will not look (even with disdain) on *him*:

Say that thou didst forsake mee for some falt,
And I will comment upon that offence,
Speake of my lamenesse, and I straight will halt:
Against thy reasons making no defence.
Thou canst not (love) disgrace me halfe so ill,
To set a forme upon desired change,
As ile myself disgrace, knowing thy wil,
I will acquaintance strangle and looke strange:
Be absent from thy walkes, and in my tongue [Q: walkes and; tongue,]
Thy sweet beloved name no more shall dwell,
Least I (too much prophane) should do it wronge:
And haplie of our old acquaintance tell.
For thee, against my selfe ile vow debate,
For I must nere love him whom thou dost hate. (89)

Then hate me when thou wilt, if ever, now,
Now while the world is bent my deeds to crosse,
Joyne with the spight of fortune, make me bow.
And doe not drop in for an after losse:

Ah doe not, when my heart hath scapte this sorrow,
Come in the rereward of a conquerd woe,
Give not a windy night a rainie morrow,
To linger out a purposd over-throw.
If thou wilt leave me, do not leave me last,
When other pettie griefes have done their spight,
But in the onset come, so shall I taste [Q: stall]
At first the very worst of fortunes might.
And other straines of woe, which now seeme woe,
Compar'd with losse of thee, will not seeme so. (90)

Unlike Sidney's sonnet 'Alas, whence came this change of lookes?' (*AS* 86), which appears to place the lover in the characteristic Petrarchan and courtly position of accepting whatever penance the beloved lays upon him, this bitter pair of sonnets starts from a *hypothetical* aversion of the lover, not from a 'real' one: Shakespeare's speaker is constructing himself against a possibility of being 'hated' for some fault which, it is clear from 89.1–4, he would actually commit as a consequence of having been accused of it. Having been forsaken, he would himself become the forsaker (89.8–9), and become his own opponent. To love the other is to hate the self, if the other hates it. The second sonnet, 90, then extends this masochistic logic to ask that this hypothetical hatred should become real instantly, so that his present woes may seem nothing in comparison with the loss of the beloved. The positive semi-proverbial experience expressed in the final couplet (90.13–14) has been generated out of a fantastic hypothetical negativity, in which the beloved plays no actual part.

The exclusion or marginalising of the speaker occurs in the very first sonnet of the collection, the first of the group of seventeen sonnets urging the young man to beget a son. Since the speaker is male (20), the theme by its very nature excludes him; but the humanist tradition of male friendship and eulogy might well have been adapted to celebrate a male bond continued through the marriage of one of the parties. What we have instead from Shakespeare is a curious attack upon his love in a sonnet whose very form and patterns begin to mimic the faults they attribute:

From fairest creatures we desire increase,
That thereby beauties *Rose* might never die,
But as the riper should by time decease,
His tender heire might beare his memory:
But thou contracted to thine owne bright eyes,
Feed'st thy lights flame with selfe substantiall fewell,
Making a famine where aboundance lies,
Thy selfe thy foe, to thy sweet selfe too cruell:

Thou that art now the worlds fresh ornament,
And only herauld to the gaudy spring,
Within thine owne bud buriest thy content,
And tender chorle makst wast in niggarding:
  Pitty the world, or else this glutton be,
  To eate the worlds due, by the grave and thee. (1)

Beginning with a quatrain in the key of mutability, written with a melancholy fluency that half a dozen of his fellow sonneteers could manage, Shakespeare increases the density of his metaphors sharply thereafter, and simultaneously, as is his manner, ambiguates his language (does 'contracted' mean 'pledged in marriage' or 'reduced to small compass' – or both?). The intense concentration of metaphors is accompanied by a concentration of sounds – the sixth and eighth lines are almost tongue-twisting – and of meanings, as in the last line, which must be read slowly to be understood. What one might call the inspissation of rhetoric, the opposite of *copia*, which is a fluent expansion of ideas, is a characteristic of Shakespeare's middle and late plays, and seems also to have been a habit in his sonnet-writing, whenever that occurred. Here the density, the thickening of the discourse, has to do with the fault of which the beloved is accused: that he turns in on himself, and is so self-absorbed, literally spending time gazing at his own eyes (1.8) that, as the word 'absorb' suggests, he eats himself. The seed that he contains remains within the bud, and what he ought to give to the world, in the form of children, is wasted by being hoarded within an unfolded flower. As the last line unpleasantly suggests, he is a kind of grave: he himself will be eaten by the grave, but before that, in hoarding his own seed, he has himself been the grave of his children (the 'world's due'). The restless metaphors of eating and hoarding turn the floral metaphors of mutability into cannibalism and death; and even the spring, the season of begetting, has become 'gaudy'. And this self-eating creature is the object of love of the speaker, the object shown to us right at what we must assume to be the beginning of Shakespeare's text. This 'all-eating shame' (2.8) continues as a motif throughout the seventeen sonnets concerned with begetting a son; and creates a beloved continually reproached for what is, in the fullest sense of the word, *selfishness*, something that excludes the speaker by its very nature.

The self-doubting and existential nervousness that this introduces into the sonnets I shall return to later in this chapter; for the moment, Sonnet 1 will serve as a first specimen of Shakespeare's handling of the sonnet form. Like all his sonnets, including those in the plays, it uses the rhymescheme established by Surrey, ABAB CDCD EFEF GG; in no case does Shakespeare use the ABBA CDDC octave, nor does he ever use an Italian sestet. Nineteen of the sonnets have one of the rhymes of the octave recurring in the sestet, but this never seems to be a deliberate contrivance, except for 135, one of the ferociously bawdy 'Will' poems, which rhymes ABAB BCBC ADAD AA, the A-rhyme being 'Will' itself – 'Will in over-plus' as the sonnet says. One sonnet, 46, has the unusual sestet EFEF FF, and the effect, while certainly intended, is really rather clumsy. Just as Shakespeare was mostly content to use other writers' plots, he was content to use the standard English sonnet, not even varying it as much as his fellow sonneteers did.

The corollary of this is that he must have accepted the 4 + 4 + 4 + 2 structure which that rhymescheme entails; indeed, he not only accepted it but positively co-operated with it, in making almost all his octaves fall into two distinct sense units, 4 and 4, which are also distinct syntactical units; there is almost always a sense break between octave and sestet: Sonnet 89 is one of only four (66, 89, 148 and 151) where the sense of the octave and the syntax cross the 'turn' of the sonnet, and of these 66 is a 'list' sonnet whose procedure anyway turns 4 + 4 + 4 + 2 into 12 + 2.

Compared with almost any of his contemporaries, and particularly with Henry Lok, Spenser, Donne, Herbert and Milton, Shakespeare is formally and structurally remarkably uninventive. His extraordinary metaphorical powers, and his acute and developing sense of the movement of blank verse, seem to have made no novelties in the way he laid out his sonnets formally. There are two 'non-sonnets' in the *Sonnets*: 126 is in twelve lines in couplets (a standard epigram form), and 99 has fifteen lines, rhyming ABABA CDCD EFEF GG, a layout so odd that it looks like an unamended draft. The remaining maverick in the *Sonnets* is 145,[10] a regular sonnet but in tetrameters; and, in the plays, Berowne's own sonnet in *Love's Labour's Lost*, 'If Love make me forsworne, how shall I sweare to love?', is regular but in hexameters, like the first sonnet of *Astrophel and Stella*.

None of this constitutes evidence that Shakespeare experimented with the sonnet form; the uniformity of the *Sonnets* suggests very plainly that he was not interested in formal variants at all. Sonnet 1, wholly conventional in rhymescheme and disposition of parts, is a very fair example of the room he chose to work in throughout his residence in the sonnet. But, if the shape is conventional, the movement imparted to it is not: to change the metaphor (as Shakespeare himself would do), to read such a sonnet is like going for a short drive with a very fast driver: the first lines, even the first quatrain, are in a low gear; then the second and third accelerate sharply, and ideas and metaphors flash past; and then there is a sudden throttling-back, and one glides to a stop in the couplet. Very often, as here, Shakespeare begins with a comparatively easy line or two, where each word is familiar, and word follows word in an expected fashion, predicted both by syntax and by association:

From fairest creatures we desire increase,
That thereby beauties *Rose* might never die. . . .

A slight acceleration, perhaps, in the next line, when instead of '*in* time decease' we have

But as the riper should *by* time decease. . . .

In the second quatrain, the embedded phrase 'contracted to thine owne bright eyes' asks us to hold the subject 'thou' till its verb arrives, while grappling with the wholly novel idea of being contracted to one's own eyes – which is bound also to suggest, especially to a reader of Donne's 'The Canonization',[11] the sense of being contracted *into* one's own eye, as one is when one looks closely into the eyes of another. The completion of the sense involves a coinage, 'self-substantial', which occurs in the midst of a dense consonantal cluster: f/dstth/tsfl/wths/lfs/shlf; from this one exits into paradoxes, 'famine/abundance; sweet/cruel'. The turn of the sonnet sees a return to more familiar language – 'gaudy', though unusual, is not challenging or metaphorically complicated in conjunction with 'herald' and 'spring' – until the moment when the beloved is again accused of self-indulgence, and the conjunction of 'bud' and 'buriest' involves a tangling of metaphors. 'Content' is enabled to have a double sense, 'what you contain as a potential source of seed' and 'that which contents you', and these two senses underlie the next line's oxymorons, 'tender churl' and 'waste in niggarding': what is contained is tender and is wasted (seed), and what contents 'thee' is churlish and miserly behaviour.

At this point of maximum density in the accusations, as it were, Shakespeare's speaker gathers his utterance together into a 'sentence', a verdict on this churlish behaviour and a piece of advice, pithily and epigrammatically phrased as the whole sonnet comes neatly to a halt:

Pitty the world, or else this glutton be,
To eate the worlds due, by the grave and thee.

What has been said above of Sonnet 1 might be said with appropriate changes of dozens of others in the sequence: a melodious and relatively easy start, then a sharp metaphorical acceleration into the midst of the sonnet, and then an epigrammatic braking of the argumentative drive in the final couplet. To achieve what I called 'inspissation', an increase in the frequency with which complications of language and thought come at one along the line, Shakespeare (and indeed anyone who writes lyric verse) has many resources, as, for example:

1 Coinages, unfamiliar words, neologisms, grammatical transformations:

The world will waile thee like a *makelesse* wife (9.4)

By oft *predict* that I in heaven finde (14.8)

The painful warrier *famosed* for [fight] (25.9)

And thou (all they) hast all the all of me (31.14)

2 Repetitions: puns, quibbles, *traductio*:

Suns [sons] of the world may staine, when heavens sun staineth (33.14)

No love, my love, that thou maist true love call (40.3)

And darkely bright, are bright in darke directed (43.4)

How would thy shadowes forme, forme happy show (43.6)

Ruine hath taught me thus to ruminate [ruinate?] (64.11)

3 Abstractions: simple unmetaphorical words describing processes or concepts, giving an illusion of terseness and precision:

And every humor hath his adjunct pleasure,
Wherein it findes a joy above the rest,
But these perticulers are not my measure,
All these I better in one generall best (91.5–8)

Which should example where your equall grew (84.4)

Nor loose possession of that faire thou ow'st (18.10)

That poore retention could not so much hold (122.9)

4 Submerged metaphors: one word or phrase from a metaphorical field not elsewhere represented:

Thy pyramyds buylt up with newer might
To me are nothing novell, nothing strange,
They are but *dressings* of a former sight (123.2–4)

Time doth *transfixe* the florish set on youth (60.9)

Alas 'tis true, I have gone here and there,
And made my selfe a motley to the view,
Gor'd mine own thoughts. . . . (110.1–3)

5 Ambiguations: a word or phrase so placed that it has two or more meanings:

O least the world should *taske* you to recite (72.1)
(= oblige, constrain; = challenge)

Since from thee going he went *wilfull* slow (51.13)
(= intentionally; = stubbornly)

Against that time (if ever that time come) (49.1)
(= in anticipation of; = in opposition to)

I never writ, nor no man ever loved (116.14)
(= no man loved; = I loved no man)

These are merely examples of what the reader can multiply to his or her own satisfaction; by consulting any annotated edition of the *Sonnets*, one can see how massively difficult these conjoining features make the reading of Shakespeare's verse. Only Sidney and perhaps Wyatt at his best offer anything like the same sensation of quick but difficult movement as one reads.[12] The energising of the text by metaphorical shifts and ambiguities keeps the reader constantly moving forward through it, and one has a strong sense of listening to an urgently presented argument.

In a marvellously acute phrase, Rosalie Colie once referred to Shakespeare's 'particularly brainy, calculated incisiveness':[13] while the *Sonnets* contain a good deal of Inns of Court logic-chopping, the persona created as the speaker does give the impression of attacking each sonnet as one might a crossword – a well-defined space inside which a problem must be quickly solved. And, though a very large proportion of the sonnets, 122 out of 154, are directly addressed to the beloved (male and female), the speaker seems often to be less interested in the beloved than in the problem that the beloved creates; and if he is marginalised he repays this by becoming absorbed in his own dialectic, making his addressee an afterthought:

Like as to make our appetites more keene
With eager compounds we our pallat urge,
As to prevent our malladies unseene,
We sicken to shun sicknesse when we purge.
Even so being full of your nere cloying sweetnesse,
To bitter sawces did I frame my feeding;
And sicke of wel-fare found a kind of meetnesse,
To be diseas'd ere that there was true needing.
Thus pollicie in love t'anticipate
The ills that were not grew to faults assured, [Q: were,]
And brought to medicine a healthfull state
Which rancke of goodnesse would by ill be cured.
But thence I learne and find the lesson true,
Drugs poyson him that so fell sicke of you. (118)

This sonnet belongs, in Q, to a loose group, 109 to 125, in which the speaker confesses to some shameful acts not clearly specified ('my harmful deeds' – 111.2) and agonises over his own motives for loving and his deserving. This group contains some of the most difficult sonnets Shakespeare ever wrote, difficult not just because particular words or phrases are obscure, but because entire sonnets seem to mask or ambiguate the attitude of the speaker, while taking the reader through an apparently incisive explanation of it. It is really very hard to understand what Shakespeare meant to say about 'himself' in many of these sonnets, and yet the impression (which the reader may test on the sonnet above) is one of rapid movement, intense concentration, and a kind of economical ruthlessness with language that is usually a sign of precision of thought – or, rather, clarity of thought: Shakespeare may be unclear, but not imprecise. The apex of undecidability is reached in Sonnet 94, described by Ingram and Redpath in their edition, with considerable restraint, as 'somewhat elusive':

> They that have powre to hurt, and will doe none,
> That doe not do the thing, they most do showe,
> Who moving others, are themselves as stone,
> Unmoved, could, and to temptation slow:
> They rightly do inherrit heavens graces,
> And husband natures ritches from expence,
> They are the Lords and owners of their faces,
> Others, but stewards of their excellence:
> The sommers flowre is to the sommer sweet,
> Though to it selfe, it onely live and die,
> But if that flowre with base infection meete,
> The basest weed out-braves his dignity:
>   For sweetest things turne sowrest by their deedes,
>   Lilies that fester, smell far worse then weeds. (94)

This sonnet appears to belong to a small group (87–94) dealing with the withdrawal of love from the speaker by the beloved, consequent upon the event dealt with in 78–88, the supplanting of the speaker as the beloved's poet and eulogiser by another poet. If we can indeed read in groups, 94 also serves as the first sonnet of another group, 94–6, blaming the youth for an unspecified fault, a theme which had appeared before in 67, 69 and 70. The sestet of 94 appears to belong to the material of 95, both metaphorically and thematically; and the octave, dealing with the beloved's capacity to hurt, seems to belong to that preoccupation with unreliable appearances that marks 92 and 93. So little does the sestet have to do with its octave that one is tempted to think of the printer mislaying a sheet, as if the octave originally had another sestet, and the sestet a different octave. Certainly, Shakespeare's habit of writing his sonnets in syntactically discrete quatrains makes this possible, and any poet writing a sonnet sequence would be bound to have fragments of sonnets lying about.

What makes this simple (and quite unprovable) explanation unlikely is that even the octave is at odds with itself, and shows the familiar oscillating undecidability we have noticed before. After the fourth line, 'Unmoved, co[u]ld, and to temptation slow', most readers want to read the next line as 'They *wrongly* do inherit heaven's graces', remembering from the first seventeen sonnets how strongly this speaker condemns holding things back, and refusing to expend nature's riches. But those who have the power to hurt, and do not use it, are on the other hand those who *rightly* inherit heaven's graces, since it is a sign of genuine nobility to have power, but not to use it to harm the weak. Yet, again, if they inherit rightly, why should they be described as 'lords and owners of their *faces*' – an unexpected and sinister phrase suggesting exactly that disjunction of appearance and intention in great ones that baffles and betrays the courtly suppliant or client. Though this sonnet, with its neutral stance and general addressee (the young man is probably being referred to under cover of 'they', but he is not addressed), looks very much like a hundred other Elizabethan sonnets written in the philosophical or experiential voice, moving throughout in suave competent generalisations and maxims, its internal argument is entirely incoherent.

My purpose is not to interpret this sonnet by asking exhaustive questions, but to emphasise that at any point in the collection, even in the section of the *Sonnets* addressed to the woman, where the anxieties of patronage and fortune do not exist, and the commerce (to use a familiar metaphor) is strictly between equals, this /I/ may turn the sonnet into a word- or concept-maze, which looks like a rational argumentative attempt without actually being one:

> Love is my sinne, and thy deare vertue hate,
> Hate of my sinne, grounded on sinfull loving,
> O but with mine, compare thou thine owne state.
> And thou shalt finde it merrits not reprooving,
> Or if it do, not from those lips of thine,
> That have prophan'd their scarlet ornaments,
> And seald false bonds of love as oft as mine,
> Robd others beds revenues of their rents.
> Be it lawfull I love thee as thou lov'st those
> Whome thine eyes wooe as mine importune thee,
> Roote pittie in thy heart that when it growes,
> Thy pitty may deserve to pittied bee.
> If thou doost seeke to have what thou doost hide,
> By selfe example mai'st thou be denide. (142)

Now, in the dance of love, in sonnets, novels and stage comedy, lovers do spend a lot of time riddling one another around, teasing with wordplay, bogus logic and spurious argument, like the courtiers in *Love's Labour's Lost*; but how far this stands from the obsessive bewilderment of 142 can be judged from the 'dance' sonnet in *Romeo and Juliet*, which similarly uses the metaphors of profanity and sin, yet manages to be quite different (it is worth remarking that, though Shakespeare could obviously write dialogue sonnets very well, no other voice ever intrudes upon the speech of the /I/ of the *Sonnets*):

> [*Romeo*:] If I prophane with my unworthiest hand,
> This holy shrine, the gentle sin is this,
> My lips two blushing Pilgrims ready stand
> To smooth that rough touch, with a tender kisse.
> [*Juliet*:] Good Pilgrime, you do wrong your hand too much,
> Which mannerly devotion shows in this,
> For Saints have hands, that Pilgrimes hands do tuch,
> And palme to palme, is holy Palmers kisse.
> [*Rom.*.] Have not Saints lips, and holy Palmers too?
> [*Jul.*:] I Pilgrim, lips that they must use in prayer.
> [*Rom.*:] O then deare Saint, let lips do what hands do,
> They pray (grant thou) least faith turne to dispaire.
> [*Jul.*:] Saints do not move, though grant for prayers sake.
> [*Rom.*:] Then move not while my prayers effect I take. [They kiss][14]
> (*Romeo and Juliet*, I.5.93–106)

Slightly more intricate in rhymescheme than was Shakespeare's wont (ABAB CBCB DEDE FF), this is much simpler in imagery: one conceit animates the entire poem, that of the beloved's body as a shrine, and her lover as the worshipper. Each line merely adds to this idea, without introducing new material or ironising what is there. A little wordplay (palm/Palmer) decorates it. To say 'merely', as if the development of a metaphor were less valuable than changing it, is certainly unfair to what Shakespeare is doing here: the two lovers (instantly, of course, in love) amplify one another delightedly, first by formal answers, four lines to four lines, and then with a more rapid and excited exchange. The arithmetic of the sonnet will give Juliet the last line if they go on alternating, which would be inappropriate to Romeo's wooing: Shakespeare therefore gives him two lines at 11–12 to get him the last line of the sonnet.

The difference between this sonnet and Sonnet 142, or any of the 'undecidable' sonnets discussed above, is not simply a local difference in handling metaphors, but a major difference in rhetorical strategies, in which Shakespeare seems to be doing something at once different from almost all his predecessors, and more recognisably modern, in terms of our own post-Romantic expectations of lyric poetry. In all its long development, and various changes, the sonnet always functions under the arch of Renaissance rhetoric: it is an utterance designed to persuade, either the person it is formally addressed to or the overhearing reader, or both. The /I/ that is created in its space is therefore an /I/ who exhibits himself to convince the hearer that he is passionate, wise, witty, devoted, penitent, full of admiration – all these personae we have already encountered. Visibility, not ripeness, is all, and the sonnet is a small theatre. Shakespeare talks, through his speaker, as if he accepted the necessity 'to allure men to heare or looke on that hee supposeth himself to be excellent in',[15] particularly in the sonnets to the young man, his patron; but he appears to have been troubled by the role of actor in ways that his contemporaries were not (he was, after all, the only sonneteer actually to be a professional actor). In trying to account for that struggle with meaning that makes his sonnets so distinctive and so appealing to us, we have one sonnet in which he notices his own difficulty and makes it the subject of the poem, Sonnet 23:

> As an unperfect actor on the stage,
> Who with his feare is put besides his part,
> Or some fierce thing repleat with too much rage,
> Whose strengths abondance weakens his owne heart;
> So I for feare of trust, forget to say,
> The perfect ceremony of loves right, [so Q; most editors: rite]
> And in mine owne loves strength seeme to decay,
> Ore-charg'd with burthen of mine owne loves might:
> O let my books be then the eloquence,
> And domb presagers of my speaking brest,
> Who pleade for love, and look for recompence,
> More then that tonge that more hath more exprest.
> O learne to read what silent love hath writ,
> To hear wit[h] eies belongs to loves fine wit. [Q: wit eies/fine wiht]

As is normal, this sonnet uses an entirely conventional *topos*, the ineffability *topos* in which the speaker declares that he is made dumb by the beloved's effect on him. If there is an incident to be imagined behind this sonnet, it is that, having been unable to say what he should while in the beloved's presence, he now writes it and sends it. But since in line 10 what he writes is called 'dumb' Shakespeare has activated the metaphor by which writing poetry is called speaking it, which destroys, or at the least blurs, the very distinction between speaking (which fails) and writing (which should succeed) on which the sonnet apparently turns. The final couplet, which would work perfectly well on its own as so many of Shakespeare's do, then compounds this blurring by referring to 'hear with eies'. (At this point the compositor of Q, feeling perhaps that things were still too intelligible, misplaced an 'h', with the result that, for a fraction of a moment, one reads 'to hear wit eyes' – hearing the wit of eyes is the counterpart of reading the silence of speech. Shakespeare cannot be blamed for that, but the error is a reminder that ambiguation is cumulative: starting the process early in the sonnet sensitises the reader to ambiguate for himself or herself later on.)

To return to the start of this sonnet: Shakespeare uses the theatrical metaphor to remind us that to speak of love, in Renaissance poetics, is not what it is for us, a revealing of private individuated feelings, but an acting-out of a ceremony, a rite which (thanks to Q again) we also take to be a right or due of the beloved – he or she is entitled to be spoken to or of in a certain prescribed way. The parallel between beloved and audience is exact: both come, as Samuel Johnson said, to hear lines declaimed with just gesture and elegant modulation. Failure to speak properly is failure to love, which is why Sidney whimsically reminds his audience that

> Dumbe Swannes, not chatring Pies, do Lovers prove,
> They love indeed, who quake to say they love.
>
> (*AS* 54, ll. 13–14)

Now, an actor is two people: the human being who knows that for the moment he is acting, and the persona who speaks the part. If fear of not speaking well enough takes over, the human being separates from the persona ('besides his part', as we still say 'I was beside myself with fear') and the performance fails. Anxiety over one's capacity to perform causes the very failure it fears.

So far we are still within the orbit of the ineffability *topos*, fluent speech about lack of fluency. But the next two lines are wholly original, and destroy any kind of whimsicality that we might have expected. In referring to himself as

> some fierce thing repleat with too much rage,
> Whose strengths abondance weakens his owne heart

Shakespeare makes his speaker involve himself in something quite without parallel (as far as I know) in the sonnet convention. Assuming that this sonnet is addressed to the young man, and that there is therefore no sexual sense in 'thing' or in 'rage', we have the image of the lover as a ravening beast, whose heart bursts from his own ferocious energy. Now, it is common to have the mistress of the lover compared to a cruel beast (cf. Spenser, *Amoretti* xxxi), but not the lover, since this image would effectively reverse the relation of patron and client, sovereign and subject, on which the whole analogue depends; yet Shakespeare offers it here as the successor to the theatrical metaphor without further explanation. Since it is fear that puts the actor 'besides his part', and since it is 'feare of trust' (whatever that exactly means) that 'so' disables the /I/ (line 5), the parallel with the wild beast can only be sustained if we assume that the rage which destroys the beast, as fear destroys the actor and disables the /I/, is rage proceeding from fear – 'fear of trust'.

If so, the octave suddenly coheres round this phrase, which brilliantly explains both the predicament of the lover seen as a phenomenon of courtly clientage, and the baffled obliquity of Shakespeare in so many of the sonnets discussed in this chapter. The phrase is ambiguous, meaning both 'fearing to trust' and 'fearing to be trusted' – we should now speak of 'commitment' in a relationship, but the double edge is the same. The very strength of the lover's desire to love disables him from loving, because his love is too great, 'ore-charged with burthen of mine owne love's might'. Again, there is a crucial ambiguation: both 'the might of the love I feel' and 'the mightiness of the person I love' (who, as we know, is of much higher social rank). The double inadequacy – too great a love to be returned in kind, and too high a person to bestow love so low – is utterly corrosive, and decays the capacity to speak, which is the very existence of the /I/ of poetic discourse and courtly success. This speaker suspects that both his pleas for love (i.e., to be allowed to love) and his hopes of recompense (to be loved in return) will be frustrated, and that suspicion itself destroys his ability to speak, on which the success of being loved and loving crucially depends. (Subsequent sonnets add to this matrix of doubt the agony of both having betrayed and having been betrayed by his beloved.)

After this, the sestet seems to make another conventional gesture: 'accept what I write as if it were what I should say' ('presagers' here has an etymological sense of 'uttering in advance': that is, having failed to speak once, he writes his speech in advance of his approaching his beloved again – cf. Sonnet 26). But just before we relax into the couplet there comes an extraordinary inspissation of the discourse in line 12: 'More then that tonge that more hath more exprest.' Apart from the difficulty of finding the antecedent to 'More' (recompense more than . . ., or plead for and look for . . . more than . . . ?), we have been encouraged by the octave to think of the tongue as saying *less* than it ought, and the sudden effort of accommodating this double 'more' to a tongue that has failed in eloquence is bewildering, at least to this reader. It is possible, in the context of the sequence, that 'that tonge' refers outside this sonnet to the rival poet of Sonnet 80 *et seq.*, who had more often written at greater length than had Shakespeare; or the 'that' may be a generalising 'that', in conformity with Shakespeare's fondness for abstract classes of things: 'more than the kind of tongue which more often says more'. In any interpretation, the result is the same: to use language in a highly difficult and ambiguating way precisely in the act of describing how the speaker's sense of 'self' has become ambiguated and distressed.

This, it seems to me, is what Shakespeare characteristically and uniquely does in his sonnets: he directs the ambiguating and densening resources of language to precisely those places where he considers the insecurity of his own selfhood – seen as reflected in the love or favour of others, or in his own doubtful capacity to give love himself. This does not prevent him from writing clear and lovely sonnets – he seems happiest when considering his power to immortalise his patron – but it makes almost every other conventional stance of the /I/ of the sonnets fiercely problematic, in a way that we, who are conditioned to think of the /I/ of each of us as a locus of conflict, find very appealing.

It is a paradox of speech that very strong emotion, or distress, prompting the desire to speak, disables speech. As the documentary film-maker Denis Mitchell said, on the basis of his own experience of encouraging ordinary people to perform before the camera, 'You can't reproduce it, the passion and the sadness imprisoned within'.[16] If Shakespeare did desire to reproduce his own passion and sadness imprisoned, then he had to get behind, or under, or out from under, the already existing theatrical personae of passion and sadness in the Petrarchan convention, and invent a countersonnet, one which without ceasing to gesture in publicly comprehensible ways still manages to insist that these gestures are inadequate.

The reader will have noticed that very little has been said in this chapter about formal features of the Shakespearian sonnet. Extraordinary even when he is conventional, Shakespeare managed to write some of the finest sonnets in the entire repertoire without, as was said earlier, making any alteration to the conventional form inherited from Wyatt and Surrey, and used by his contemporaries. As we have seen, he never varied the common form, ABAB CDCD EFEF GG, except when he repeated a rhyme sound; he used the simplest of structures, keeping a distinct utterance in each quatrain and in the couplet, and usually making sense pauses coincide with line pauses, or at least with distich pauses. He only once (148) crossed the boundary of the turn between octave and sestet, apart from sonnets using the 'list' form, and the final couplet is hardly ever joined syntactically to the third quatrain. Sonnet 129, quoted above, is one of the very few to have a strong enjambment (lines 2–3) and even in that very disturbed utterance there is only one.

Metrically, he is equally unremarkable. Masterly though he is in fitting speech rhythms to iambic verse, he does not assault the ear as Donne does, and such metrical features as can be measured – frequency of initial trochees, for example, or fondness for pauses immediately after the first, or before the last, syllable of a line – show little difference from his contemporary Samuel Daniel.[17] And finally, in the matter of what might be called sonnet strategy, he almost always writes sonnets addressed to the beloved (though it has never been satisfactorily explained why the young man is sometimes addressed as 'thou' and sometimes as 'you' in no clear pattern). There are no dialogue sonnets, no conversation sonnets, no sonnets with acrostics, anagrams, tails, reversible lines or any of the other games that versifiers elsewhere indulged in. And, most baffling of all, despite all the literary echoes, no single sonnet has been clearly shown to be translated from, adapted from or even to be quoting from any other sonneteer, British or Continental. The clearest literary analogue is, of course, in the two sonnets which seem most at odds with the rest, the Anacreontic sonnets 153 and 154. The explanation of this unique independence may be that he so urgently desired to have the sonnet /I/ express his own concerns that he literally took no notice of anyone else.

But if this self-expression through the created /I/ was so important to him as to make him ignore the sonnets of others, it follows that the conventional sonnet form must have struck him, even after repeated use, as entirely adequate. (He would play with it in the plays, but not in his sonnets.) Why, given the intense difficulty of his rhetoric, did he not attempt a more complicated or fragmented form? Perhaps he did, but not in the compass of a single sonnet: there are twelve pairs of sonnets in the collection, and one of these, 91 and 92, is probably a triplet, including 93. Of these, two are pairs by similarity: 46, 'Mine eye and heart are at a mortal warre', is a conceit obviously antithetical to 47, 'Betwixt mine eye and heart a league is took'; but, other than reversing the conceit, the second does nothing with the ideas of the first. Similarly, 135 and 136 are alike in a virtuoso display of bawdiness on the word 'Will': if the last line of 136, 'Think all but one, and me in that one *Will*', means 'Imagine that all your lovers are me, and that I alone am having intercourse with you', then the first line of 137, 'If thy soul check thee that I come so near', probably refers back to 'in that one will' – i.e., 'so near you as to enter your body'; and would suggest that the two sonnets were to be read together.

The remaining pairs, however, can be called 'developmental pairs', in that the argument of the first sonnet is picked up and extended or reworked in the second. The pairs involved are: 5 and 6; 15 and 16; 27 and 28; 44 and 45; 50 and 51; 67 and 68; 73 and 74; 89 and 90; 91 and 92 (and 93?); and 113 and 114 (46 and 47, and 135 and 136, have already been mentioned). Sometimes the link is verbal, as between 5 and 6:

> But flowers distil'd though they with winter meete,
> Leese but their show, their substance still lives sweet. (5.13–14)

> Then let not winters wragged hand deface,
> In thee thy summer ere thou be distil'd . . . (6.1–2)

sometimes thematic, as between 50 and 51: 50 (one of the few sonnets to image a particular event) deals with the speaker on horseback, plodding wearily away from his beloved; 51 begins very clearly with the same event:

> Thus can my love excuse the slow offence,
> Of my dull bearer, when from thee I speed,
> From where thou art, why shoulld I hast me thence,
> Till I return, of posting is noe need.

But it is not clear that there is a verbal connection, since the word 'thus' may indeed refer to the events of Sonnet 50, but could equally mean 'in the following manner', referring to the excuse given in 51.3–4. Sometimes, were it not for the printing order in Q, we should not think of two sonnets together at all. Here, printed as one poem, are 73 and 74, the first of which is almost always anthologised on its own:

> That time of yeeare thou maist in me behold,
> When yellow leaves, or none, or few doe hange
> Upon those boughes which shake against the could,
> Bare ruin'd quiers, where late the sweet birds sang. [Q: rn'wd]
> In me thou seest the twi-light of such day,
> As after Sun-set fadeth in the West,
> Which by and by blacke night doth take away,
> Deaths second selfe that seals up all in rest.
> In me thou seest the glowing of such fire,
> That on the ashes of his youth doth lye,
> As the death bed, whereon it must expire,
> Consum'd with that which it was nurrisht by.
>   This thou percev'st, which makes thy love more strong,
>   To love that well, which thou must leave ere long.
> But be contented when that fell arest,[18]
> With out all bayle shall carry me away,
> My life hath in this line some interest,
> Which for memoriall still with thee shall stay.
> When thou revewest this, thou dost revew,
> The very part was consecrate to thee,
> The earth can have but earth, which is his due,
> My spirit is thine the better part of me,
> So then thou hast but lost the dregs of life,
> The pray of wormes, my body being dead,
> The coward conquest of a wretches knife,
> Too base of thee to be remembred,
>   The worth of that, is that which it containes,
>   And that is this, and this with thee remaines.

If the first fourteen lines are a single poem, then they are a melancholy meditation upon death, leading to an exhortation (expressed as a statement) to love with greater intensity that which does not last – the great *topos* of 'carpe diem', applied poignantly to himself by a greying Shakespeare. So the poem is usually presented. But, if it is read immediately with what follows, the emphasis alters: the young man is kindly but firmly rebuked for desperately lavishing his love upon what he cannot hold for long, because he is in love with the mortal part, the less valuable body. What matters is the spirit, which the verse that he is now reading preserves for ever. If the first sonnet appears to restate, marvellously, Horace's 'carpe diem', the second corrects this, and substitutes Horace's 'Monumentum exegi aere perennius', echoing the sentiment which Shakespeare probably knew, that

> Non omnis moriar, multaque pars mei
> Vitabit Libitinam. . . .[19]

> [I shall not wholly die, but a great part of me
> Will survive Death. . . .]

This correction gives new meaning to the very first line:

> That time of yeeare thou *maist* in me behold . . .

– not a sad 'It is, alas, quite likely that I look elderly to you' but 'Certainly, I may look old to you, but if all you perceive in me is just the wreckage of time, then remember that . . .'.

Q prints the sonnets apart, and numbers them separately, though there is no doubt that 74 is intended to follow 73. Elsewhere paired sonnets are printed apart, and we must assume that Shakespeare left no instructions for a 28–line sonnet of a new kind. How far the meaning of a sonnet can 'survive' when the succeeding sonnet alters it is a question I do not propose to discuss: it is probably a severer case of what happens to any sonnet when it is read as part of its sequence instead of being presented on its own. There seem to be no precedents for 28–line sonnets: the simple *tenzone* sonnets of the Sicilians and later Italian writers are of course linked as question and answer, and are usually formally linked by rhyme; *corona*-sonnets are linked by line repetitions, and are always to be read as a unit. Petrarch experimented twice with the extended sonnet, in Shakespeare's manner, once repeating his rhymes in what amounts to a three-stanza poem, *Rime* 41–3, rhyming ABBA ABBA CDC DCD (41)/BAAB BAAB DCD CDC (42)/ABBA ABBA CDC DCD (43); and later in two sonnets similarly paired by rhyme, 100 and 101, rhyming ABBA ABBA CDE DCE/ABBA ABBA CDE DCE. In these sets, 41 and 42 make no sense without each other; 43 could stand alone; and 100 and 101 would not, I think, seem at all unusual or difficult if either was read on its own. The evidence, such as it is, suggests that in the Italian tradition anyone trying to pair sonnets would signal it by repeating rhyme words, as Petrarch does.

Shakespeare could have known the paired sonnets of Samuel Daniel, the contemporary to whom he is most often compared, in any one of the six editions of *Delia* issued between 1592 and 1601. Daniel has four pairs, vi and vii, ix and x, xxxi and xxxii, and xlvii and xlviii (in the 1601 numbering); there is also a semi-*corona* group, xxxvi to xl, linked by repetition of the last line (or a portion) in the next first line, but without returning the last sonnet to the first, as a full *corona*-sequence should. Of the pairs, ix and x are linked last line to first line, but otherwise have little necessary connection; the other three pairs are 'developmental', in the Shakespearian sense. Though Daniel never attains the density of word-play and metaphorical alteration that characterises Shakespeare, Sonnets xxxi and xxxii could certainly have suggested to Shakespeare (if he needed prompting) the possibility of the paired form – and that without any Italianate repetitions of rhymes or rhyme-sounds:

The Starre of my mishap impos'd this paine
To spend the Aprill of my yeares in griefe:
Finding my fortune ever in the waine
With still fresh cares, supplide with no reliefe.
Yet thee *I* blame not, though for thee tis done,
But these weake wings presuming to aspire,
Which now are melted by thine eies bright sun,
That makes me fall from off my hie desire.
And in my fall *I* crie for helpe with speed,
No pittying eie lookes backe upon my feares:
No succour find *I* now when most I need
My heats must drowne in th'Ocean of my teares.
  Which still must beare the title of my wrong,
  Caus'd by those cruell beames that were so strong. (xxxi)

And yet I cannot reprehend the flight,
Or blame th'attempt presuming so to soar; [1601: sore]
The mounting venter for a high delight,
Did make the honour of the fall the more.
For who gets wealth, that puts not from the shore?
Danger hath honor, great designes their fame,
Glorie doth follow, courage goes before.
And though th'event oft answers not the same,
Suffize that high attempts have never shame.
The meane observer (whom base safetie keeps)

Lives without honour, dies without a name,
And in eternal darknes ever sleeps.
  And therefore Delia, tis to me no blot,
  To have attempted, though attaind thee not. (xxxii)

Despite his confident swing into a new argument, and the extra intricacy of a Spenserian rhymescheme (ABAB BCBC CDCD EE), Daniel cannot sustain the energy of thought, and relapses into a string of proverbs, all padding out his second fourteen lines. Shakespeare never wrote anything so slack in his sonnet pairs, and (whether or not he knew of Daniel's efforts) seems to have used the form because it allowed him to argue a point at much greater length than one sonnet will ever allow. His natural inclination was to compress rapid movement and shifts of thought into fourteen lines: twenty-eight extended the opportunity to examine the implications of an idea.

If this indeed was Shakespeare's only significant alteration of the sonnet form, then that points to a reason for his seeming contentment with the simple 4 + 4 + 4 + 2 structure in alternating rhymes which he used throughout: his mimesis was to create a speaker who should try to rescue himself from his passion by argument, not by setting a sensual self against a spiritual one, or a past self against a present one, as Petrarch had done; but by setting an apparently rational self against a passionate one. To do that, he needed to keep the simple clarity of the argumentative sonnet visible, holding its boundaries and enhancing its capacity for decisive epigram while letting his fears beat up and down and across inside it. And this he had to do while also maintaining (as no modern poet would feel obliged to do) a persona and a rhetorical stance that would be comprehensible inside the power relations of his own society. When he spoke of the function of his own poems, he always made them much simpler than they are:

Kinde is my love to day, to morrow kinde,
Still constant in a wondrous excellence,
Therefore my verse to constancie confin'de,
One thing expressing, leaves out difference. (105.5–8)

He presents the speaker of the sonnets as one trying to praise and commemorate within the Petrarchan and humanist conventions, and when he criticises his poetry it is because it is unfashionable (76, 82), too simple (85, 79), monotonous (76, 105), not sophisticated enough to do the beloved justice (103). Once only (apart from Sonnet 23, discussed above) does he appear to tackle the problem of writing about himself (instead of the problem of failing to write well about his patron), in Sonnet 62, a sonnet typically replete with puns and ambiguations:

Sinne of selfe-love possesseth al mine eie,
And all my soule, and al my every part;
And for this sinne there is no remedie,
It is so grounded inward in my heart.
Me thinkes no face so gratious is as mine,
No shape so true, no truth of such account,
And for my selfe mine owne worth do define,
As I all other in all worths surmount.
But when my glasse shewes me my selfe indeed
Beated and chopt with tand antiquitie,
Mine owne selfe love quite contrary I read
Selfe, so selfe loving were iniquity.
  Tis thee (my selfe)[20] that for my selfe I praise,
  Painting my age with beauty of thy daies. (62)

But since, as the couplet says, the self is the other, we cannot be quite sure, even here, exactly what he meant, or by what, or whom, he was in life or in verse possessed. It is to presenting that uncertainty, with all the resolution of which the sonnet is capable, that he seems to have bent his energies.

10

THE SEVENTEENTH CENTURY: HERBERT, DRUMMOND AND MILTON

If we knew when Shakespeare wrote his sonnets, we should know whether to consider him the last great sonneteer of the sixteenth century or the first of the seventeenth – the zenith of its zenith, or the leader of its decline. For, though some of the finest, and most influential, British sonnets remained to be written after the accession of James VI to the throne of England in 1603, by Drummond, by Herbert, by Donne and by Milton, the sonnet declined in popularity as the sonnet sequence passed out of favour. At least, one can say that it declined in frequency, since (apart from Donne) only Davies of Hereford, Drummond, Lady Mary Wroth and (probably) Fulke Greville published sequences actually written after the accession of James – sonnets of dedication, elegy and praise continued to appear as prefatory or epilogue material in books.[1]

The crisp explanation for this decline, which did not occur in France or in Italy, is that British poets so identified the sonnet with Petrarchan love that when a queen who governed through the rituals of erotic flattery was replaced by a king who prided himself on his academic learning the Petrarchan mistress was replaced as an ideal by the philosopher king. There is a certain truth in this – Sir Walter Ralegh, for example, curried favour with Queen Elizabeth by writing Petrarchan verse to her; but he curried favour with James VI and I by dedicating his *History of the World* (1614) to him instead (with disastrous results). And one notes that several other things seemed to come to an end with the sonnet sequence and with its century – courtesy manuals are rare after 1600, until the seventeenth century invented its own forms; and poetical miscellanies, of the kind that dispersed the 'honied eloquence' of the Petrarchan poets, almost disappear after *A Poetical Rhapsody* of 1602.

On the other hand, madrigal verse and songbooks, which though not making great use of sonnets made great use of Petrarchan conceits and topoi, continued to appear in an even flow from 1588 to about 1620; and lute-song books (which favoured texts for the single voice) were actually at their most popular immediately after the accession of James VI and I, between 1603 and 1613.[2] Two courtiers of James, both very much concerned to climb the ladder of favour, thought it not amiss to publish their sonnets (admittedly written as juvenile verse in the 1590s): Sir William Alexander's long and chilly sequence *Aurora* in 1604, and Sir David Murray of Gorthie's amiable but wholly unoriginal sequence *Caelia*, in 1611. George Herbert (1593–1633), sending a pair of sonnets to his mother for New Year's Day 1610 (NS), cast a slightly priggish undergraduate eye upon 'the vanity of those many Love-poems, that are daily writ and consecrated to *Venus*', and resolved to run counter to what he observed still to be the poetic fashion:

> My God, where is that ancient heat towards thee,
> Wherewith whole showls of *Martyrs* once did burn,
> Besides their other flames? Doth Poetry
> Wear *Venus* Livery? only serve her turn?
> Why are not *Sonnets* made of thee? and layes
> Upon thine Altar burnt? Cannot thy love
> Heighten a spirit to sound out thy praise
> As well as any she? Cannot thy *Dove*
> Out-strip their *Cupid* easily in flight?
> Or, since thy wayes are deep, and still the same,
> Will not a verse run smooth that bears thy name?
> Why doth that fire, which by thy power and might
> Each breast does feel, no braver fuel choose
> Than that, which one day Worms may chance refuse?
>
> Sure, Lord, there is enough in thee to dry
> Oceans of *Ink*; for, as the Deluge did
> Cover the Earth, so doth thy Majesty:
> Each Cloud distills thy praise, and doth forbid
> *Poets* to turn it to another use.
> *Roses* and *Lillies* speak thee; and to make
> A pair of Cheeks of them, is thy abuse.
> Why should I *Womens eyes* for Chrystal take?
> Such poor invention burns in their low mind
> Whose fire is wild, and doth not upward go
> To praise, and on thee, Lord, some *Ink* bestow.
> Open the bones, and you shall nothing find
> In the best *face* but *filth*, when, Lord, in thee
> The beauty lies in the *discovery*.[3]

Written at the end of the year in which Shakespeare's sonnets were published (it is hugely tempting to think that, since no other new sonnets had been printed since 1605, it was a reading of Shakespeare's that provoked the young Herbert), these two sonnets are, formally, much more inventive than Shakespeare's, and, indeed, than any written thitherto (except for those of the very forgettable Henry Lok). Any reader of seventeenth-century verse will hear John Donne's voice in these two sonnets, and in the first particularly; if the style owes something to Sidney's colloquial immediacy, it has even more of Donne's manner, because of the extensive enjambment. The agitated questions, running across line boundaries and creating sense pauses in the middle of lines instead, are something we associate with Donne's mature manner – for example, in Holy Sonnet 18, 'Show me, deare Christ, thy Spouse'; but the second sonnet, which more calmly answers the questions, is also innovative. Previous sonneteers, while often willing for fluency's sake to extend a sentence across the line-end or even through a quatrain, respected the major divisions. Sidney, who enjambs fairly freely in his sestets, tends to keep the octaves regular; Shakespeare, as we have seen, hardly ever passes over a conventional boundary. This first sonnet of the 17-year-old Herbert is quite remarkably transgressive:

> My God,
> where is that ancient heat towards thee
> Wherewith whole showls of *Martyrs* once did burn,
> Besides their other flames?
> Doth Poetry
> Wear *Venus* Livery?
> only serve her turn?
> Why are not *Sonnets* made of thee?
> and layes
> Upon thine Altar burnt?
> Cannot thy love
> Heighten a spirit to sound out thy praise
> As well as any she?
> Cannot thy *Dove*
> Out-strip their *Cupid* easily in flight?
> Or,
> since thy wayes are deep and still the same,
> Will not a verse run smooth that bears thy name?
> Why doth that fire,
> which by thy power and might
> Each breast does feel,
> no braver fuel choose
> Than that,
> which one day Worms may chance refuse?

The marvellous turn of this sonnet, at the word 'Or' (what else?) occurs not between line 8 and line 9, but between 9 and 10; this leaves only five lines for the 'sestet', and since by a piece of metrical onomatopoiea lines 10 and 11 'run smooth', and also rhyme, a couplet emerges there also, as well as at the end. Even if one allows that the first quatrain does, after all, 'turn' with the words 'only serve her turn', the sonnet still breaks into 4 + 5 + 2 + 3, the couplet rhymes suggesting that the rhymescheme should be grouped ABAB CDCDE FFEGG.

The second sonnet is similarly free: its sentences end in the middle of lines, not at the end, and the first quatrain is five lines long. This sonnet divides 5 + 3 + 3 + 3, and as before, in the sestet, each triplet seems to have its own couplet, giving 5 + 3 + [1 + 2] + [1 + 2].

Retrospectively, of course, we can be quite sure from Herbert's later craftsmanship that this is not the wildness of incoherence, but what it is also in Donne, the dramatising of the pressure of speech in a new way. There are signs that this pair of sonnets is highly controlled: the witty parallel of the opening lines, question and answer:

My God, where is . . .
Sure, Lord, there is . . .

the repeated quasi-proverbial turns of phrase (Herbert was unusually fond of proverbs and maxims):

Doth Poetry wear *Venus* Livery?
Cannot thy *Dove* out-strip their Cupid?
Thy ways are deep, and still the same . . .
Each Cloud distills thy praise . . .
Roses and *Lillies* speak thee . . .
Nothing . . . in the best *face* but *filth* . . .
The beauty lies in the *discovery*

and the accuracy with which the stresses arrive, sometimes against the dominant iambic rhythm, to accentuate pronouns and connectives as required:

/ x x / x / x / x /
Why are not *Sonnets* made of thee? and layes
x / / x x / / x / /
Upon thine Altar burnt? Cannot thy love

/ / x / / x / x x
Each Cloud distills thy praise, and doth forbid

Since John Donne was a close friend of Herbert's mother, Lady Magdalene Herbert, from 1604 until her death in 1627, and must have been acquainted with the young Herbert while he lived in London (1604–9), it is overwhelmingly likely that the resemblance between these two early sonnets of Herbert and the sonnets of Donne arises from Herbert's having seen some of Donne's verse; if not the Holy Sonnets themselves, then perhaps the *corona*-sequence, 'La Corona', which Donne may have sent to Herbert's mother in 1607.[4] The urgently disturbed dramatic rhythms, and the constant enjambment and medial sense pauses that mark Donne's verse appear on a very high level of competence here, in what are probably the very first sonnets Herbert wrote; what does not appear, and what therefore will distinguish a sonnet by Herbert from one by Donne, is violent eclipsis (omission of normally necessary words), a kind of compression which Herbert did not like, perhaps because it made against his beloved plainness of style. Extreme hyperbaton (distortion of normal word order) often accompanies eclipsis in Donne, and Herbert uses it with much more restraint. Donne's fifth sonnet in 'La Corona' is a showpiece of these schemes:

> *By miracles exceeding power of man,*
> Hee faith in some, envie in some begat,
> For, what weake spirits admire, ambitious, hate;
> In both affections many to him ran,
> But Oh! the worst are most, they will and can,
> Alas, and do, unto the immaculate,
> Whose creature Fate is, now prescribe a Fate,
> Measuring selfe-lifes infinity to a span, [1633: to span]
> Nay to an inch. Loe, where condemned hee [1633: inch, loe]
> Beares his owne crosse, with paine, yet by and by
> When it beares him, he must beare more and die;
> Now thou art lifted up, draw mee to thee,
> And at thy death giving such liberall dole,
> *Moyst, with one drop of thy blood, my dry soule.*[5]

The trick of accentuating an afterthought ('Nay to an inch') by letting it carry the eighth line into the ninth had been used by Petrarch (*Rime* 254);[6] the real originality in this sonnet comes from the force of repeated pauses, introduced by the twisted and compressed word order, working with enjambments against the normal iambic line and its tendency to match phrasing to line. As was said in discussing the anarchic comic sonnets of Cecco Angiolieri (Chapter 2) the sonnet is a remarkably strong form, and as readers of a sonnet like this almost always can be relied upon to have read regular sonnets the anterior discourse controls the present text: there is, however, in Donne's octave here a strong sense of energy trying to burst its bounds.

The /I/ which is created is certainly passionate and immediate (whence perhaps the echoes of Sidney's sonnets that one notices now and again) but also expostulatory: if the sonnet is a cage, this speaker is beating at the bars. It is natural to connect this with Donne's own religious struggles and anxieties; but as we find it in Herbert, so we also find it routinely in seventeenth-century dramatic verse. Deliberately not aligning sense pauses with line pauses (which in drama has the effect of suggesting very close-paced conversation) can be in a way introduced into the sonnet, by making the first line open with an abrupt medial caesura:

Oh my blacke Soule! now thou art summoned
By sicknesse. . . .

This is my playes last seene, here heavens appoint
My pilgrimages last mile. . . .

Death be not proud, though some have called thee
Mighty and dreadfull. . . .

Batter my heart, three person'd God; for, you
As yet but knocke, breathe, shine, and seeke to mend. . . .

This has the effect of beginning the sonnet with fervour and directness, and then launching it into fluency as the longer sentence overrides the line-end. This rhythmic pattern seems to have stuck in the British ear:

Avenge, o Lord, thy slaughter'd saints, whose bones
Lie scatter'd on the Alpine mountains cold. . . .

O Friend! I know not which way I must look
For comfort. . . .

Rebuke me not! I have nor wish nor skill
To alter one hair's breadth in all this house
Of Love. . . .[7]

To anticipate the end of this chapter a little, one of the easiest ways of thus throwing the sonnet 'out of phase' is to open with an apostrophe, which naturally carries its own pause after it; now, Milton found this particularly appealing, and it is to him rather than to Donne that we owe the reappearance of this strongly expostulatory pattern in the nineteenth-century sonnet, though it is anchored in the speech mimesis of the early seventeenth century.

Herbert himself, though not normally thought of as a sonneteer, remains one of the most interesting users: he wrote seventeen sonnets, all of which (except the two to his mother, quoted above) appeared in the posthumous printing of his poems, *The Temple. Sacred Poems and Private Ejaculations*, 1633.[8] The word 'ejaculations', though not specifically referring to sonnets, does suggest the attraction of the expostulating /I/ for contemporary readers. Like Shakespeare, Herbert favoured a very simple rhymescheme: ABAB CDCD EFEF GG (10) and ABAB CDCD EFFE GG (7). Two sonnets, 'Love (1)' and 'The Holdfast', have a repeated rhyme, giving ABAB CDCD EFFE FF and ABAB CDCD EDED FF respectively. But, unlike Shakespeare, Herbert did not also favour a simple structure; nor, like Donne, did he favour violent alterations of word order. The passionate, struggling or expostulating self, the Christian sinner, was always in Herbert's poetry subject to a preaching and teaching self – a conjunction which the sonnet, containing both lyrical and dialectic elements, is well suited to handle. Donne, one might think, reversed the domination of one self by the other, and by accentuation, eclipsis and hyperbaton created a dominant passionate /I/ barely restrained by the reason of Christian dogma. Herbert's speaker is not so disturbed:

The Answer.

My comforts drop and melt away like snow:
I shake my head, and all the thoughts and ends,
Which my fierce youth did bandie, fall and flow
Like leaves about me: or like summer friends,
Flyes of estates and sunne-shine. But to all,
Who think me eager, hot, and undertaking,
But in my prosecutions slack and small;
As a young exhalation, newly waking,
Scorns his first bed of dirt, and means the sky;
But cooling by the way, grows pursie and slow,
And setling to a cloud, doth live and die
In that dark state of tears: to all, that so
Show me, and set me, I have one reply,
Which they that know the rest, know more then I.[9]

This accomplished and beautifully controlled sonnet seems in some ways much more Petrarchan than the conceit-studded love-sonnets of the 1590s: until Milton, one could hardly find a better example of the peculiar *gravità* so admired in Petrarch than this stately but simple movement, using without distortion the ordinary syntax of speech, but intensifying it with metaphors of a plain but profound compression ('means the sky'; 'setling to a cloud'). Such a plain style, as Swift later shows, will accommodate both learned and vulgar terms ('prosecution', 'exhalation', 'bandie', 'pursie'); it naturally involves proverbs and maxims, which give authority and a kind of wise distancing to the voice; and it controls the errors of a past self with the acquired experience of the present speaker. There are two dangers, which Herbert's predecessors (including Shakespeare) do not always avoid: that the sonnet's structure will split the utterance up into a set of Polonius-like commonplaces; and that the lure of the final couplet will suddenly produce a clever ending. Herbert uses enjambment quietly but persistently to override each main boundary, so that the stages of the argument slightly overlap the stages of the rhymescheme – 4 + 4 + 4 + 2/4½ + 2½ + 4½ + 2½ (how many readers, looking at the sonnet, assume before counting that the sestet begins with the words 'As a young exhalation'?); and then, about to conclude, he begins to gather his poem together before the final couplet, at 'to all, that so/ Show me . . .'.

What with hindsight we can call the Romantic sense of the pressure of energy against form ('The cistern contains; the fountain overflows', said Blake) is really begun in the sonnet when its practitioners learn to run syntax against metrics: Petrarch, who made a powerful appeal to the Romantic poets, has this skill, but it does not reappear as a style of discourse in the sonnet in English until Donne and Herbert. (Shakespeare offers us the pressure of energy against *meaning*, which is distinctive and probably inimitable.) Now, the sonnets of Donne and Herbert were not available in print until after their death, appearing in the same year, 1633;[10] Donne's style in lyric poetry influenced his contemporaries through the circulation of his manuscripts, but Herbert's could not, since he kept his poems to himself until his death; nor can it be seriously suggested that Donne or Herbert was influential as a model for Romantic poets. If there is continuity – and by the beginning of the eighteenth century an editor of Spenser's works had to remind his readers what a sonnet was[11] – then it comes from Milton, whose few and scattered sonnets are in the mainstream of English lyric poetry at least partly because they were written by the author of *Paradise Lost*.

It would be very neat for critics if we could establish that Milton read the poems of Donne and Herbert; since Herbert was a Cambridge lecturer, and his poems were published in Cambridge, this is actually quite likely; but if one is hunting for congenial kinds of discourse in the sonnet, then the British sonneteer most likely to have influenced Milton is Drummond of Hawthornden. His sonnets, at once old-fashioned and modern, deserve consideration in their own right – if Donne's and Herbert's sonnets show a reaction against 'Venus Livery', Drummond's show an absorption of Petrarchanism more thorough than any other writer's, together with a modernisation of it.

William Drummond of Hawthornden (1585–1649) gathers together in his sonnets almost everything that the sonnet had been doing since its invention: this quiet-living, unambitious Scottish laird, rarely moving from his country home just south of Edinburgh, made himself into a kind of anthology of the European sonnet and, being assisted by a naturally good ear and a staggeringly good private library, distilled the literature of six languages (Greek, Latin, Italian, French, Spanish and English) into two sonnet collections, his *Poems* of 1616 and *Flowres of Zion* of 1623.[12]

He inherited sonnets and befriended them: his uncle, William Fowler, wrote one of the first British sonnet sequences, *The Tarantula of Love*, of about 1590, which though not printed until modern times was known to and used by the nephew; a lifelong friend was Sir William Alexander, author of *Aurora*, 1604, and he also knew well Sir David Murray of Gorthie, author of *Caelia*, 1611, Michael Drayton, with whom he corresponded, and Ben Jonson, who visited him at Hawthornden. He also seems to have read and admired the sonnets of the only female sonneteer of the century, Lady Mary Wroth (*Pamphilia to Amphilanthus*, 1621), though it is not known whether he met her.[13]

If he never met or knew of Milton, whose political and religious views he would violently have disagreed with, the connection is still strong, for it was Milton's nephew, Edward Phillips, who in 1656 edited and published *Poems, by that most famous Wit, William Drummond of Hawthornden*, an excellent edition for its day, incorporating poems thitherto unpublished. Attempts to find echoes of Drummond in Milton are probably doomed to failure;[14] for it is the nature of Drummond's verse to be so echoic of others' that anything 'found' in Milton could well have been obtained elsewhere – and Milton, like Drummond, read contemporary Italian poetry in the original.

There could hardly be a better demonstration, as we come to the end of the British Renaissance sonnet, of the cumulative nature of the sonnet's /I/ – the property of what I have called its 'anterior discourse' – than the sequence in Drummond's *Poems* of 1616. This is modelled, like his friend Sir William Alexander's *Aurora*, on Petrarch's *Rime*, in that it consists of sonnets interspersed with much longer poems; it is in two parts, the first consisting of poems addressed to or about a living woman, and the second of poems lamenting her death. After a reprint of Drummond's elegy for Prince Henry, 'Teares, on the Death of Moeliades', comes what looks like a third part, 'Urania, or Spirituall Poems', renouncing earthly love in favour of divine love. Excluding occasional sonnets in the volume, Drummond's sequence has seventy-five sonnets, five songs (some very long), eighteen madrigals and two sestinas ('sextains' to Drummond), all very irregularly spaced. Though the sonnets are sonnets, the sextains sestinas, and the madrigals madrigals, there is no attempt to make the songs into *canzoni* – they are long poems in couplets.

Yet Drummond certainly wrote with a close eye upon Petrarch; if the remark attributed to him a century later is correct, that 'he was the first in the isle that did celebrate a Mistress dead, and Englished the madrigal',[15] then he knew that despite Petrarch's being 'in every mans mouth',[16] no one had actually followed him in writing part of a sonnet sequence following the imaged death of the mistress, or tried to incorporate the short poems the Italians called madrigals (not the same as the madrigal of the British song-books). And since his first sestina is very closely adapted from Petrarch's sestina 'Non a tanti animali il mar fra l'onde' (*Rime* 237, a text not available to him through an intermediary) his Petrarchan imitation was seriously meant.

The phrase 'a Mistress dead' raises acutely the question of who the speaker of Drummond's sequence is supposed to be. Since the records of Drummond's life furnish good evidence of his affection for Euphemia

Cunninghame (or Kyninghame) of Barns in Fife, who died before they could marry, Drummond's first modern editor, William Kastner (1913), and some later critics have wished to read the sequence as autobiographical: where Drummond is plain and melodious, he is conceived to be speaking 'simply and directly from the heart' and where he is imitative and echoic, then 'his model . . . has misled him into thinking more of his conceits than his grief'. The idea that elegiac poetry gains merit by expressing genuine private grief, and that it should do so simply, would have been incomprehensible to a Renaissance poet, even in the act of writing a poem protesting his grief and asking for a simple language to do it in. (Consider *Lycidas*.) Fortunately, perhaps, scholarship has found a date for Miss Cunninghame's death too late for the *in morte* poems in Drummond's 1616 text to have been composed in response to it.[17] Certainly, since Drummond was not a courtier or in need of patronage or wealth, he had no other motive for writing than self-gratification; but that does not make his sonnets personal confessions. Like every other sonneteer of his age (and before) he saw the sonnet, and its attendant other forms, as a repertoire of voices or gestures which expressed characteristic human attitudes, many of which might be, or have been, or might in the future be, his own as well. Poetry is a sweet, witty, passionate, sharp, learned or ornamental expression of what is human, to show that man is possessed of reason, eloquence and wit: a passionate sonnet does not reveal that the author is passionate, but that he is eloquent. If the passions of the author's life when he writes happen to be those he writes about, then he may write the better for it; but no poetic theorist troubles overmuch about that.

Drummond's verse is not readable on the assumption that lyric ought to be the private speech of an individuated mind: half the love-poets of Europe wander about in his lines, and authorise his verses. Again and again a sonnet which might be thought particular turns out to be full of other presences:

> When *Nature* now had wonderfully wrought
> All Auristella's Parts, except her Eyes,
> To make those Twinnes two Lamps in *Beauties* Skies,
> Shee counsell of her *starrie Senate* sought.
> *Mars* and *Apollo* first did Her advise
> In Colour Blacke to wrappe those Comets bright,
> That *Love* him so might soberly disguise,
> And unperceived Wound at every Sight.
> Chaste Phebe spake for purest azure Dyes,
> But Jove and Venus greene about the Light
> To frame thought best, as bringing most Delight,
> That to pin'd hearts *Hope* might for ay arise:

> *Nature* (all said) a *Paradise* of Greene
> There plac'd, to make all love which have them seene.
> (1616: xviii)[18]

The verb 'have seene' in the last line locates 'Auristella' in the speaker's present time, and since this sonnet clearly shows her to have green eyes it is natural to assume that Drummond's mistress did indeed have green eyes. So it may be; but if this is the thought, then the purpose of the sonnet is to gild it with fiction's ore (to recall David Murray's phrase). So the mistress is named, not for herself, but for resemblance to others: '-stella' plainly refers back to Sidney's *Astrophel and Stella*; and, less certainly, the prefixed 'Auri-' may refer to 'Aurora', Sir William Alexander's mistress in his 1604 sequence (Alexander appears in Drummond's poetry frequently as 'Alexis' to Drummond's 'Damon'). Drummond then executes a variation upon two of Sidney's sonnets: he begins and ends with a verbal echo of *AS* 7, as well as using several of its rhyme words:

> When Nature made her chiefe worke, *Stella's* eyes
> In colour blacke . . .
> . . . she minding *Love* should be
> Placed ever there, gave him this mourning weed,
> To honor all their deaths, who for her bleed.
> (*AS* 7, ll. 1–2, 12–14)

And in the middle he echoes the conceit of *AS* 20, where Love hides in Stella's eyes:

> So Tyran he no fitter place could spie,
> Nor so faire levell in so secret stay,
> As that sweet blacke which vailes the heav'nly eye:
> There himselfe with his shot he close doth lay.
> (*AS* 20, ll. 5–8)

So far, Drummond is paying homage to Sidney; but behind Sidney's sonnet, at some distance, lie Petrarch's opening lines of *Rime* 248:

> Chi vuol veder quantunque po Natura
> e 'l Ciel tra noi, venga a mirar costei. . . . (248, ll. 1–2)

[Whoever would behold how much Nature and Heaven can do among us, let him come to gaze on her. . . .]

The conceit of the beloved as the apex of Nature's creation under God gives the mistress a fanciful but powerful mythical status, as the creation of the Godhead, even if at one remove. And associated with that is another myth (which Petrarch does not use) whereby the beloved is represented as being assembled from component parts by the gods, a myth that appears in Hebrew literature in *Genesis* 2.7 and 2.22, and in almost all creation myths elsewhere. George Herbert has his own echo of this in 'The Pulley':

> When God at first made man,
> Having a glasse of blessings standing by;
> Let us (said he) poure on him all we can. . . . (ll. 1–3)

The deployment of this myth, even in so whimsical a fashion as Drummond uses, makes the speaker a kind of hierophant, and the sonnet a public invitation, a call to come and witness a holy truth.

In this sonnet, as in many of Drummond's, there are at least three layers of reading: a surface texture of narrative or description; behind that the voices of other speakers of the sonnet or of lyric verse (Horace, Ovid or other European poets, particularly the very fashionable Giovanbattista Marino, 1569–1625);[19] and behind those again mythical resonances, so that the myth is reached through a receding series of statements of it focused in the present text. Who speaks here? is a question rather hard to answer. Certainly one's sense of an immediate presence, as in Sidney or Shakespeare, is attenuated, as if one listened to a choir, not to a single voice.

Lacking Shakespeare's metaphorical power, and with no taste for the deconstructive energies of pun and irony, Drummond is perhaps nearest to Petrarch, with his sense of the emblematic landscape, the flowing syntax, and the antitheses of emotions and of times. A late (and posthumously published) sonnet entitled 'Saint Peter, after the denying his master' uses the Petrarchan topos of 'Solo e pensoso i più deserti campi/Vo misurando' ('Alone and pensive I trace my steps through the most deserted places'):

> Like to the solitarie pelican
> The shadie groves I hant and Deserts wyld,
> Amongst woods Burgesses, from sight of Man,
> From earths delights, from myne owne selfe exild.
> But that remorse with which my falle beganne
> Relenteth not, nor is by change beguild,
> But rules my soule, and like a famishd chyld
> Renewes its cryes, though Nurse doe what shee can.
> Look how the shricking Bird that courtes the Night
> In ruind walles doth lurke, and gloomie place:
> Of Sunne, of Moone, of Starres I shune the light,
> Not knowing where to stray, what to embrace:
> How to Heavens lights should I lift these of myne,
> Since I denyed him who made them shine?[20]

The pelican and the owl should not be there, one thinks: they are a bad inheritance from a Scots love of classical and curious learning; but the second quatrain is grave and fluent, much in Petrarch's vein, and the dangerous last couplet has a bitter self-mocking precision that effectively ends both the plaint and the sonnet. Before Milton wrote, Drummond had discovered how to make the sonnet move, as this does, with a kind of intense ceremoniousness: this man who was not a courtier, and Milton, probably manage Italianate courtliness in English better than any.

When Milton, most famously, said that poetry should be 'simple, sensuous and passionate' he produced a Janus-faced epigram that, as far as the sonnet at least is concerned, looks both forward and back. The phrase comes from his 1644 *Letter on Education* to Samuel Hartlib, where he is concerned with teaching his pupils 'to discourse and write perspicuously, elegantly and according to the fittest style, of lofty, mean [i.e., middle] or lowly'.[21] Poetry, though a 'sublime art', as he says, is more simple than logic because its function is to display man's passions, and these are inherently less subtle and fine than his reason. The sensuous is lower in the hierarchy of importance and value than the logical and rational, even though 'glorious and magnificent use might be made of poetry, both in divine and human things'. Removed from its comparison with logic inside an educational curriculum, and quoted absolutely, the epigram becomes an endorsement, from the greatest of English epic poets, to make the simple portrayal of human feelings with sensuous richness the goal of art. Curiously, though Milton himself did not intend it that way, that view of poetry was congenial both to Marino and to Drummond; and, had a massive repudiation of passion in favour of elegance and wit not occurred in the mid-seventeenth century, the sonnet might have continued in Britain as in France and Italy. But it was too closely associated both with Petrarchanism on the one hand and with passionate excess on the other to find much favour after 1660 – Edward Phillips's 1656 edition of Drummond is the last printing of the works of a major Renaissance sonneteer in the seventeenth century.

John Milton (1608–74), whose sonnets are the last to be considered in this book, used the sonnet for the other main purpose for which, from the start, it had been employed: comment upon public affairs, and praise of friends. He wrote twenty-four sonnets in his lifetime, including a 'tailed' sonnet (*sonnetto caudato*) which is unique in English;[22] he is the only Renaissance sonneteer to make consistent (though not exclusive) use of the Italian form of the sonnet, and also the only one to write sonnets in Italian. He made no attempt to write a sonnet sequence, whether sacred or secular; but used the form for occasional pieces throughout his adult life, between 1629 and his second wife's death in 1658. He thought well enough of his sonnets to print some in his *Poems* of 1645, and even added later ones when, at the end of his life, he reprinted the volume in 1673.

Milton's sonnets stand in a different relation to his life from those of his Elizabethan and Jacobean predecessors, with the possible exception of Drummond. Milton was not a courtier, nor seeking any patron's favour; and therefore the humble petitionary or pleading /I/ is not one he uses. On the other hand, he was determined to be a poet from an early age, and the question 'What kind of poetry shall I write?' inescapably involves asking 'What kind of voice shall I adopt?'

Before we answer that, it is probably best to look at the kind of sonnets Milton chose to write, since they are remarkably unlike any others before in the British repertoire. The twenty-four sonnets, with one fifteen-line *canzone* stanza, fall into two groups, seven written in his youth, between 1628 and 1632, and the remainder during his political life and early blindness, between 1642 and 1658, when the death of his second wife produced his last sonnet, 'Methought I saw my late espoused saint'.[23] In the first group there are two sonnets in English, and five, with the *canzone* stanza, in Italian: this is a British first, for though Italian was studied and read with reasonable fluency by Elizabethan and Jacobean writers (there was, remarkably, no English translation of Petrarch's *Rime* in this period) no one had published other than occasional dedicatory sonnets in Italian before – even Drummond did not try to write in it.

The six Italian poems seem to record Milton's literary, if not personal, adoration of a young Italian girl, whose name was probably Emilia – it is concealed, *senhal*-fashion, in 'Donna leggiadra'.[24] As he also wrote a sonnet about his fascination with her to his close friend Charles Diodati ('Diodati, e te'l dirò'), it is probable that she really existed, and that, as he was learning Italian anyway, he doubled his efforts in order to impress and please her by addressing her in her own tongue:

> Così Amor meco insù la lingua snella
> Desta il fior novo di strania favella,
> Mentre io di te, vezzosamente altera,
> Canto, dal mio buon popol non inteso,
> E'l bel Tamigi cangio col bel Arno.
> Amor lo volse. . . . (ii.6–11)[25]

[Thus Love in me, beyond my easy language, brings on the new flower of a foreign utterance, while I sing of you, so charmingly proud, in a way not understood by my own folk, and change the fair Thames for the fair Arno. Love willed it. . . .]

He praised her dark eyes and, in a very graceful compliment, her singing:

> Quel sereno fulgor d'amabil nero,
> Parole adorne di lingua più d'una,

E 'l cantar che di mezzo l'hemispero
Traviar ben può la faticosa Luna. . . . (iv.9–12)

[That clear flash of lovely black, eloquence in more than one tongue, and singing that can well beguile the labouring Moon from the mid sky. . . .]

Like Stella, young Emilia may have been responsible for more than she knew; for in his efforts to handle the language of the Arno with becoming elegance Milton was drawn into serious study of Italian poetry. He read Dante (probably not the *Vita Nuova*), Petrarch, Ariosto, Tasso and also two rather less usual poets, one of whom at least seems permanently to have affected his sonnet-writing. This was Giovanni della Casa (1503–56), whose poems, along with those of Benedetto Varchi (1503–65), he purchased about the time of his sonnets to Emilia.[26] Della Casa, who became archbishop of Benevento and a cardinal, rose to be secretary of state to Pope Paul IV, and an eloquent defender of the latter's Spanish policies, a career not unlike Milton's own. Like Milton, too, he was a gifted orator, scholar, poet and aesthete, in whom there was a perpetual struggle between the moralist and the poet. Though he wrote much love-poetry (something not considered incompatible with being a cardinal archbishop), he was chiefly famous for his austere, grave, dignified and learned style, and in particular for his use of enjambment, which, if he did not invent, he was reckoned to have established in Italian poetry.[27] This, which we have already noticed as a novelty in the sonnets of Donne and Herbert, struck Italian critics as the essence of *gravità*:

There is hardly a line that does not move on one into another, and this breaking of the lines, as all the masters tell us, confers the highest gravity; and the reason is that this breaking of the lines runs its course through the whole utterance, and causes it to slow down; slowing down is appropriate to gravity.[28]

Others noticed how della Casa's poems seemed to behave like little speeches, with exordium, exposition and conclusion, and how his rhythms seemed to have an almost tragic grandeur.

Now, Milton did not translate della Casa, nor, like Drummond, did he use him 'paraphrastically'; but throughout his sonnet-writing he chose rhymeschemes that della Casa favoured. Both poets use the ABBA ABBA octave, though that is common enough; but della Casa, in addition to the CDECDE and CDCDCD sestets, heavily favoured asymmetrical sestets, in particular CDEDCE and CDECED (as opposed to, say, CDC CDC, CDC DCD or CDD DEE). Milton's sestets are as follows:

CDCDCD	7
CDECDE	5
CDCDEE	4
CDEDCE	4
CDDCDC	2
CDEDEC	1
CDCEED	1

Despite the occurrence of four with rhymed couplets at the end (the sonnet to Cromwell, and three of the sonnets in Italian), this looks like a determined and lifelong attempt to avoid symmetry, and to introduce thereby the kind of slowing down in the reader's movement as s/he reads that goes with *gravità*. When we add to that Milton's consistent enjambments and deliberate transgressions of the sonnet's quatrains and tercets, and his cultivation of spare, terse and unusual words and word order, such as he could have found in almost no British sonneteer except Donne, there is a strong case for suggesting that even when writing his love-sonnets to Emilia he had turned his back on the British sonnet as insufficiently grave and eloquent, and returned to the Italian humanist civic sonnet that had always run alongside the Petrarchan. To illustrate this other mode, as well as any single example can, let us place a sonnet by della Casa, in austere mode, alongside Milton's own sober self-assessment:

Or pompa e ostro e or fontana ed elce
Cercando, a vespro addutta ho la mia luce
Senza alcun pro, pur come loglio o felce
Sventurata, che frutto non produce.
E bene il cor, del vaneggiar mio duce,
Vie più sfavilla che percossa selce,
Sì torbido lo spirto riconduce
A chi sì puro in guardia e chiaro dielce,
  Misero; e degno è ben ch'ei frema e arda,
Poi che 'n sua preziosa e nobil merce
Non ben guidata danno e duol raccoglie.
  Né per Borea già mai di queste querce,
Come tremo io, tremar l'orride foglie:
Sì temo ch'ogni amenda omai sia tarda.[29]

[Seeking now the pomp of purple, and now the fountain and the oak, I have brought my light to evening profitless, like wretched weeds or bracken, that bear no fruit.

And well does my heart, lord of my vanities, more and more spark like struck flint, so anxiously the soul leads it back to Him who, pure and bright, keeps it in ward, in its misery; and indeed just it is that it shiver and burn, since in its precious and noble freight, so badly handled, it reckons grief and loss.

Nor has the North Wind ever shaken the dark leaves of these oaks as I tremble, fearing that all repentance comes too late.]

Like Shakespeare's 'That time of year thou may'st in me behold', this sombre sonnet uses an autumnal evening landscape – a man looking out over dark oaks, bracken and weeds in a winter wind – as an emblem of past life; but it does not then turn back to secular love, but to repentance. The oak ('elce') is a symbol of worldly achievement; and also gives della Casa a very difficult rhyme word, making the octave a struggle with words as well as with the world. The powerful agitation, both controlled and urgent, which is presented by, for example, overrunning the octave by a single word 'misero' into the ninth line, is well imitated by Milton in his own sonnet of life-reckoning:

When I consider how my light is spent,
Ere half my days, in this dark world and wide,
And that one Talent which is death to hide
Lodg'd with me useless, though my Soul more bent
To serve therewith my Maker, and present
My true account, lest he returning chide,
Doth God exact day-labour, light deny'd,
I fondly ask; But patience to prevent
  That murmur, soon replies, God doth not need
Either man's work or his own gifts, who best
Bear his milde yoak, they serve him best, his state
  Is Kingly. Thousands at his bidding speed,
And post o're Land and Ocean without rest:
They also serve who only stand and waite. (xix)

This sonnet is dominated by the verb 'consider': its protest is not excited, or passionate, but thoughtful: and the speaker is maturer than his own speaking self, since he can call his questioning 'fond' (line 8). The speaker is answered by the greater authority of Patience, speaking with the weight of generality and maxim (the last line of this sonnet has actually become a British proverb). But, if there was any danger of a collapse into trite moralising, Milton has checked it by running his sense pauses against the sonnet divisions. There are six enjambments; the pauses at 'useless' and 'ask' break the first quatrain before the end of its fourth line, and the second before the end of the eighth. The first tercet runs into the second, and only at the end, when the speaker is properly answered, does an epigram coincide with a line. The impression of sobriety is reinforced by the steady beat of monosyllables, always a mimesis of plain speech when used in quantity.

Closely connected with enjambment as another way of slowing the reader down and making the sonnet appear weighty, is the device that my own sentence is using at this moment: grammatical or syntactical suspension. By turning the normal order of words round (hyperbaton) or by inserting sub-clauses, one delays completing the sense: the reader is aware that he or she has only part of a grammatical or syntactic construction, and reads on looking for the missing part. The difficulty of holding what one already has while absorbing sub-clauses and trying to match each new item with the existing parts of the sentence, as the reader is now doing while waiting for me to give him or her the main verb, slows down (there it is) the absorption rate. Milton loved this device, and it is almost a constant of his style in his major poems as well as in his sonnets: since very often the completion is delayed by putting in extra words, the utterance is likely to overflow the single line, and thus enjambment and suspension can work together. But suspension, particularly when protracted, is a baffling device, and Herbert, for example, who enjambs a great deal, rarely suspends. It is very much opposed to the kind of limpid and singing clarity that, for example, the *stilnovisti* cultivated: it may enhance *gravità*, but it makes against sweetness.

The reader with some knowledge of Italian will find at least five suspensions in della Casa's sonnet above, none of any great length: Milton's sonnet has one enormous suspension in the octave, since the main clause, 'I fondly ask', is delayed until line 8, while a huge 'when'-clause winds its way down the sonnet. Inside that clause, a suspension combines with enjambment at 'that one talent which is death to hide/ Lodged with me useless'; and the eclipsis of 'is' between 'my soul' and 'more bent' must momentarily cause the reader to expect a main verb for 'my soul' somewhere further on, perhaps after 'chide', and revise expectations when it does not arrive. The later enjambments, in the sestet, occur in sentences that are proceeding normally.

Both enjambments and suspensions make the reader move forward, but give a sense of confronting obstacles. There is obviously a danger point – just as a rhyme will not work as a rhyme if its completion is delayed too long (about six lines in English verse), so a suspension will break down if too long sustained. Readers do have an enormous drive to make sense of what they read, and poets can bank on it; but there is nice judgement to be used in developing momentum and acceleration in the reader by tantalising, lest one simply confuse and lose him or her. The opening lines of *Paradise Lost*, a six-line suspension which immediately propels the reader into another one, are a famous Miltonic instance.

This quest for weight through suspension and enjambment probably accounts for the most obvious feature of Milton's sonnets, when read in a group. Of Milton's twenty-four sonnets, sixteen are apostrophic, that is, addressed to a person or thing whose name is called out; in thirteen of these the name is the first word; and in eleven of those thirteen the name is followed by a 'who'-clause or equivalent, suspending the sense. This is a very high proportion of apostrophes. What from Petrarch's first sonnet one might call the 'voi che' formula entered sonnet-writing when the sonnet began to be used as a letter or a public statement in the civic affairs of the Italian cities of the thirteenth century[30] – when one is *genuinely* writing a letter, even if in verse, to a friend one does not of course need to attach a long 'che'/'who' clause to his or her name or pronoun, explaining who the friend is; to do so implies a reader or a hearer for whose benefit the addressee's identity or quality is spelt out. It belongs to the public rhetoric of praise (or reprobation), and identifies the speaker as either a courtier or a citizen obliged by necessity to speak out (gratitude, penury, adoration, indignation, wrath . . .). Friends and equals may of course use this trope, but even to praise an equal thus implies a circle of hearers for whom the rhetoric of praise has a social function. Now, of course, anyone using the sonnet as an occasional poem, a mimic letter or speech to mark an occasion, would be bound to fall upon this trope sooner or later, and Drummond, for example, uses it a number of times; it is also used inside Petrarchan sonnet sequences when the lover assumes the role of praise-poet to his mistress. But Milton seems to have noticed, relished and cultivated it for another reason as well.

If one begins a sonnet with 'X, who . . .', one introduces a suspension, almost necessarily of fair length – it would be tactless to praise one's addressee in two or three words. Thus the opening not only signals the /I/ of the sonnet as a public speaker, demanding to be heard inside his social group, but also gives that speaker the means of speaking with great weight. And, one might add, claiming the privilege of being favourably heard, as Milton did in his sonnet entitled 'When the Assault was intended to the City',[31] in which, by a not over-modest comparison of himself to Pindar and Sophocles, he claims the status, idealised in humanist ideology, of city poet:

> Captain or Colonel, or Knight in Arms,
> Whose chance on these defenceless dores may sease,
> If deed of honour did thee ever please,
> Guard them, and him within protect from harms,
> He can requite thee, for he knows the charms
> That call Fame on such gentle acts as these,
> And he can spread thy Name o're Lands and Seas,
> Whatever clime the Suns bright circle warms.
> Lift not thy spear against the Muses Bowre,
> The great *Emathian* Conqueror bid spare
> The house of *Pindarus*, when Temple and Towre

Went to the ground: And the repeated air
Of sad *Electra's* poet had the power
To save th' *Athenian* walls from ruine bare. (viii)

Since the assault – feared in November 1642 – did not materialise, the sonnet was never actually nailed to Milton's door; it is difficult to imagine a pillaging Parolles effectively distracted by solving the identity of the Emathian conqueror. What is significant is that Milton should wish to proclaim himself a public speaker for his city and his cause. The tremendous stateliness (in all senses of the word) that the sonnet can be got to acquire by deft use of apostrophe and suspension is nowhere better illustrated than in the sonnet to Cromwell (the only mature sonnet in which Milton conceded the power of the final couplet, and used the English sonnet form, ABBA ABBA CDDC EE):

Cromwell, our cheif of men, who through a cloud
Not of warr onely, but detractions rude,
Guided by faith and matchless Fortitude
To peace and truth thy glorious way hast plough'd,
And on the neck of crowned Fortune proud
Hast reard Gods Trophies, and his work pursu'd,
While *Darwen* stream with blood of Scotts imbru'd,
And *Dunbarr feild* resounds thy praises loud,
And *Worsters* laureat wreath; yet much remaines
To conquer still; peace hath her victories
No less renownd then War, new foes arise,
Threatning to bind our soules with secular chaines:
Helpe us to save free Conscience from the paw
Of hireling wolves whose Gospell is their maw. (xvi)[32]

In this superbly controlled sonnet, the octave runs over by half a line into the sestet, as if the cup of Cromwell's triumphs overflowed; but is instantly checked by the main clause, 'yet much remains', for which we have waited through eight and a half lines. With the turn from octave to sestet comes a turn from past to future (Petrarch also used the structure of the sonnet to control time); and this brings a change of mode, since the past can be talked about narratively, but the future cannot. The speaker, who has been a laudatory historian up to this point, now turns first to maxim ('Peace hath her victories . . .') since proverbs and maxims are one way of handling the future, and then to petition, which is another way. He is by turns historian, counsellor and petitioner, and these three utterances correspond to the classical division of the oration: exordium (lines 1–8: praise through narration); exposition (lines 9–12: generality and maxim); and conclusion (lines 13–14: request for help). The suspension of the main clause for eight lines generates momentum and excitement, assisted by the repeated 'ands' and the fall of the rhymes. The enjambment in the sestet presents the advice fluently and with dignity, and the couplet gives the strength of epigram to the closing request. This is civic eloquence, from an /I/ in the persona of a wise, experienced but respectful adviser – just such a person as Petrarch, della Casa and Milton, good scholars and humanists all, attempted to be.

Though Milton could not have known it, he at the end of the Renaissance sonnet's career in Britain was returning it to its beginnings. Guittone d'Arezzo would have recognised in Milton's civic moralism a kindred attitude; whether satirical or laudatory, it comes in both men from a created persona who is morally experienced, and talks even to social superiors with avuncular compliment or, if need be, reproof. This is, of course, one of the functions of the occasional sonnet at any time: Drummond wrote a number of sonnets in that mode. But Milton is exceptional in his direct adoption of an Italian pattern, an Italianate rhetoric and a persona neither conventionally Petrarchan nor penitentially religious: the civic humanist, servant and adviser, and also poet and moralist, is his projected /I/ throughout. Because this is a persona designed to sound like a guide, philosopher and friend, and because Milton himself stood in something like that relation to later poets, the sonnets are easily read as intimate poems, and their mode of discourse became congenial to Romantic poets in Britain.

His last sonnet, surely one of the world's greatest, is an almost stilnovistic vision of his *donna angelicata*, his second wife, Catherine Woodcock;[33] but because she was his *wife*, not an unattainable mistress, he speaks of her in the domestic and familial intimacy of childbearing and companionship, evoking not Laura, but that humanist paragon of married happiness, Euripides' Alcestis. Petrarch approaches this peculiar intimacy only after Laura's death, when he imagines her returning to his bedside to comfort him: but the mode of that great poem, *Rime* 359, 'Quando il soave mio fido conforto', is one of penitence for sexual desire, not of regret for the lost intimacy of marriage. Marriage is so wholly excluded from the Petrarchan sequences (Spenser can continue the *Amoretti* after his betrothal only by conjuring up separations and jealousy) that the sonnet reads as something private and unique; its only predecessor is Drummond's sonnet in the Second Part of his *Poems*, 'Sith it hath pleas'd that First and onlie Faire', which Milton seems to have known, for he echoes the line 'Made pure of mortall spots which did it staine' in his own sonnet.[34] But Drummond's mellifluousness dissolves into conventional piety, whereas Milton's terse, compressed and intense sobriety works against the patterning of the sonnet, as always, to give the impression of a mind struggling to impose order upon the wildness of its own loss. It is appropriate that what is probably the last sonnet of the British Renaissance should be also one of the greatest syntheses of eloquence and desire, the essentials, from the start, of the European sonnet:

> Methought I saw my late espoused Saint
> Brought to me like *Alcestis* from the grave,
> Whom *Joves* great son to her glad Husband gave,
> Rescu'd from death by force though pale and faint.
> Mine as whom washt from spot of child-bed taint,
> Purification in the old Law did save,
> And such, as yet once more I trust to have
> Full sight of her in Heaven without restraint,
> Came vested all in white, pure as her mind:
> Her face was vail'd, yet to my fancied sight,
> Love, sweetness, goodness in her person shin'd,
> So clear, as in no face with more delight.
> But O as to embrace me she enclin'd,
> I wak'd, she fled, and day brought back my night. (xxiii)

Almost four and a half centuries after the inventor of the sonnet imagined himself 'vegiendo la mia donna in ghiora stare' – 'beholding my lady fixed in glory' – the sonnet is still the place where Desire confronts its Other, and in a small room some fixity is given to the restlessness of being.

APPENDIX

Publication Dates of British Sonnet Sequences

For the purposes of this list, a 'sonnet sequence' is a collection of poems in which sonnets dominate; it includes two sequences, Watson's and Habington's, which do not contain true sonnets at all.

1560	Anne Lock, *A Meditation*	5 + 21 sonnets
1582	Thomas Watson, *Hekatompathia*	100 18-line poems
1584	John Soowthern, *Pandora*	13 + 5 sonnets
1585	James VI of Scotland, *Essayes of a Prentise*	12 sonnets
1591	Sir Philip Sidney, *Astrophel and Stella*	108 sonnets
	[with 28 sonnets by Samuel Daniel and others]	28 sonnets
	Edmund Spenser, *Complaints*	34 sonnets, 12 + 15 + 7
1592	Samuel Daniel, *Delia*	50 sonnets
1593	Barnabe Barnes, *Parthenophil and Parthenope*	104 sonnets
	Thomas Lodge, *Phillis*	40 sonnets (some irregular)
	Giles Fletcher, *Licia*	52 sonnets
	Thomas Watson, *The Tears of Fancie*	60 sonnets
1594	Henry Constable, *Diana*	86 sonnets (8 are by Sidney)
	Henry Constable, *Spirituall Sonnettes*	16 sonnets (printed in 1815)
	Michael Drayton, *Ideas Mirrour*	51 sonnets
	William Percy, *Sonnets to . . . Coelia*	20 sonnets
	Zepheria (anonymous)	40 sonnets (some irregular)
1595	Barnabe Barnes, *A Divine Centurie*	100 sonnets
	E.C., *Emaricdulfe*	40 sonnets
	George Chapman, 'A Coronet for his Mistress'	10 sonnets
	Edmund Spenser, *Amoretti*	88 sonnets (with 'Epithalamion')
1596	Bartholomew Griffin, *Fidessa*	62 sonnets
	R[ichard] L[inche], *Diella*	39 sonnets
	William Smith, *Chloris*	49 sonnets
1597	Richard Barnefeilde, *Cynthia*	20 sonnets
	R[obert] T[ofte], *Laura*	60 sonnets (alternating with 60 dixains)
	Henry Lok, 'Sundrie Sonnets' and 'Affectionate Sonets' from *Ecclesiastes*	181 sonnets (121 + 60)

1604	Sir William Alexander, *Aurora*	106 sonnets
1605	John Davies of Hereford, *Wittes Pilgrimage*	101 sonnets
	Joshua Sylvester, 'Corona Dedicatoria' in du Bartas, *Divine Weekes and Workes*	11 sonnets
1609	William Shakespeare, *Sonnets*	154 sonnets
1611	Sir David Murray of Gorthie, *Caelia*	26 sonnets
1616	William Drummond, Sonnets from *Poems*	71 sonnets
1620	Lady Mary Wroth, *Pamphilia to Amphilanthus*	83 sonnets (with 20 songs)
1623	William Drummond, *Flowers of Zion*	26 + 3 sonnets
1633	Fulke Greville, *Caelica*	40 sonnets (out of 109 poems)
1634	William Habington, *Castara*	49 14-line poems (in couplets)

Samuel Daniel issued six editions of *Delia* between 1592 and 1601, adding and subtracting sonnets: there are 57 sonnets in the 1601 edition. Michael Drayton published new editions of *Ideas Mirrour*, retitled *Idea*, in 1599 and again in 1602 and 1605, and finally in his *Works* of 1619, adding sonnets. There are also reprints in 1600, 1603, 1608, 1610, 1613 and 1631, making Drayton the most often reprinted British sonneteer. William Habington also produced new editions of *Castara* with additional poems in 1635 and 1640.

Several important sequences and collections remained in manuscript in this period:

c. 1578–85	Alexander Montgomerie (a miscellany of Spenserian sonnets, first printed in 1887)	70 sonnets
c. 1580–5	John Stewart of Baldynneis (a miscellany of sonnets and other poems, first printed in 1913)	28 sonnets
c. 1590	William Fowler, *The Tarantula of Love* (a sequence of Petrarchan sonnets, first printed in 1914)	75 sonnets
c. 1595	Robert Sidney, *Poems* (first printed in 1984)	35 sonnets
c. 1597–8	William Alabaster (religious sonnets, first printed entire in 1959)	79 sonnets
after 1617	John Donne, 'Holy Sonnets', 'La Corona' (printed in 1633)	26 sonnets (19 + 7)

NOTES

1 THE SONNET AND ITS SPACE

1 Since there will be references to Italian sources in this book, it is worth noting that in Italian a century is referred to by the number *after* 1000: thus, the thirteenth century, all the years from 1200 to 1299, is the 'Duecento', literally the 'two hundreds'. The sixteenth century is the Cinquecento, sometimes written as '500, the eighteenth century is the Settecento ('700) and so on.
2 In Spain, the first sonnets were written by the Marqués de Santillana between 1438 and 1458; in France, by Clément Marot, probably in 1529; in Britain, by Sir Thomas Wyatt, about 1525; and in Germany by Martin Opitz about 1624. For the diffusion of the sonnet, see E. H. Wilkins, 'A general survey of Renaissance Petrarchanism', *Comparative Literature*, vol. 2, 1950, pp. 327–42, and also Leonard Forster, *The Icy Fire*, Cambridge, 1969, pp. 32–56.
3 Alistair Fowler, *Kinds of Literature*, Oxford, 1982, p. 31.
4 The word 'reinvented' is used here in fair recognition of a very minor Italian poet, Nicolò de'Rossi (*c.*1285–1335), who wrote many sonnets in the form ABBA ABBA CDCDEE, with such consistency that he undoubtedly chose and preferred the final couplet. Even he, however, rarely makes his last two lines into a unit of thought. With that qualification he, and not Sir Thomas Wyatt, must be regarded as the discoverer of the final couplet in the sonnet. See the edition by F. Brugnolo, *Il canzoniere di Nicolò de' Rossi*, 2 vols, Padua, 1977.
5 Heather Dubrow, *Shakespeare's Captive Victors*, New York, 1987, p. 170.
6 Robert Elbaz, *The Changing Nature of the Self*, London, 1988, p. 12.
7 Folgore wrote two sequences, one of sonnets on the months of the year, and one on the days of the week, describing the pleasures appropriate to each. See *Le rime di Folgore de San Gemignano*, ed. G. Navone, Bologna, 1880.
8 A useful translation of Dante's *De Vulgari Eloquentia* is by Sally Purcell (trans.) *Dante: Literature in the Vernacular*, Manchester, 1981.
9 *De Vulgari Eloquentia* III; see Purcell, op. cit., p. 41.
10 Torquato Tasso, for example, in praising the sublimity of a sonnet by Giovanni della Casa, argued against Dante's ranking of the form. See Bernard Weinberg, *A History of Literary Criticism in the Italian Renaissance*, 2 vols, Chicago, Ill., 1961, vol. 1, p. 176.
11 This sonnet and the two following can be found in G. Getto and E. Sanguinetti, *Il sonetto*, Milan, 1957, pp. 80, 336 and 504.
12 Iain Crichton Smith, 'Studies in power (2)', *Selected Poems*, Edinburgh, 1981, p. 25 (permission to quote from this poem kindly granted by the author.).

13 Questo breve poema altrui propone
Apollo stesso, come Lidia pietra
da porre i grandi ingegni al paragone.

Benedetto Menzini, 'Arte poetica', Book iv, ll. 289–91, *Poetica e satire*, Milan, 1808, p. 105. Menzini (1646–1704) was a Florentine, whose 'Arte poetica' is a useful compendium of the ideas of poetic theory common at the time. Unlike the British, the Italians did not abandon the sonnet in the eighteenth century.

2 SICILIANS AND CITIZENS: THE EARLY SONNET

1 G. Getto and E. Sanguinetti, *Il sonetto*, Milan, 1957, p. 80.

2 The two most important manuscripts of early sonnets are the Codex Vaticanus 3793, and MS. Laurenziano-Rediano 9, now in the Vatican Library. Both were written in the north of Italy in the latter half of the thirteenth century, and present sonnets roughly grouped by author. The scribes usually normalised the dialect in which they presumably had the sonnets in front of them into their own north Italian dialect.

3 The figures are from the catalogue of Sicilian poems by E. Langley, 'The extant repertory of the early Sicilian poets', *PMLA*, vol. 28, 1913, pp. 454–520.

4 The poems of Giacomo da Lentino, with translations, are available in a modern critical edition by Stephen Popolizio: 'A critical edition of the poems of Giacomo da Lentino', PhD thesis, 1975, Ann Arbor University Microfilms, Ann Arbor, Mich., 1980. I am much indebted to this edition, and I have used its versions of Lentino's texts.

5 It is tempting to think, because of this peculiarity, that this is the very 'first sonnet'; but it is in many ways a quite sophisticated poem. See Popolizio's edition, p. 167.

6 South of a line from Blaye in the west of France to Grenoble in the east, the French language took the form known as the 'langue d'oc' or Provençal, because the word for 'yes' was 'oc', not 'oui'. The district now known as Provence has given its name to the speech of the whole region south of that line.

For an excellent introduction to this body of poetry and to its theory, which was quite sophisticated, see R. T. Hill and T. G. Bergin (eds), *Anthology of the Provençal Troubadours*, 2nd edn, New Haven, Conn., 1973.

7 It is not quite fair to accuse the Sicilian poets of ignoring the world of politics, when we remember that most of their poetry survives in anthologies over which they had no control. But their few extant references do not suggest an active political interest.

8 See above, Ch. 1, p. 8. See also Anna M. Clausen, *Le origini della poesia lirica in Provenza e in Italia*, Copenhagen, 1976, and F. Catenazzi, *L'influsso dei Provenzali sui temi ed immagini della poesia Siculo-Toscana*, Brescia, 1977.

9 The origin of the sonnet and the competing theories (largely with a nationalist bias) are discussed by E. H. Wilkins, 'The invention of the sonnet', *Modern Philology*, vol. 13, 1915, pp. 463–94. The *strambotto* is discussed on pp. 478–80.

10 Popolizio, op. cit., p. 159.

11 Towards the end of the thirteenth century Venice had about 100,000 inhabitants, Florence about 95,000. Second Division cities like Padua had about 35,000. The onslaughts of the Black Death, above all in 1348, reduced these

numbers considerably, sometimes by as much as two-thirds. See John Larner, *Culture and Society in Italy, 1290–1420*, London, 1971, pp. 14–20, 122–7.

12 Getto and Sanguinetti, op. cit., p. 10.

13 At this time, and for long after, northern Italian civic politics was racked by the quarrel between two great parties: the Guelphs, who on the whole supported the Papacy and its ambitions, and the Ghibellines, who supported the Emperor and his ambitions. Individual cities, such as Florence, were subject to coups and massacres as one or other group seized control and ousted its rivals. Rustico's sonnet refers to the anguish of the Ghibelline party, which saw its previous supremacy abruptly reversed at the Battle of Benevento in 1266, when Charles of Anjou, with the backing of Pope Urban IV, defeated Manfred, son of the Emperor Frederick II.

14 The phrase means 'the sweet new style', and it refers to the poets discussed in Chapter 3, mainly the Florentine poets of the age of the young Dante. They felt themselves to be pioneers of a new and more melodious poetry, and Dante imagines in his *Divine Comedy* an encounter with a disciple of Guittone who admits that the Sicilians and Guittonians had not attained that sweetness (*Purgatorio*, xxiv, ll. 52–7).

15 The numbers of Guittone's poems, where given, are those in the edition of Francesco Egidi, *Le Rime di Guittone d'Arezzo*, Bari, 1940, whose text follows as faithfully as possible the original manuscripts. The punctuation is Egidi's, but the spellings are those of the manuscripts, which explains the presence of non-standard Italian forms.

16 Ibid., nos 87–110, pp. 182–94; nos 175–202, pp. 235–48.

17 Ibid., p. 238.

18 Ibid., p. 254.

19 Ibid., p. 248.

20 References to Cecco Angiolieri's poems are to the text of G. Cavalli: *Le Rime di Cecco Angiolieri*, Milan, 1959. This sonnet is no. cxx, p. 136.

21 Rosalie Colie, *The Resources of Kind*, Los Angeles, Calif., 1973, p. 103.

22 *Rime di Cecco Angiolieri*, no. xlvii, p. 59.

23 Getto and Sanguinetti, op. cit., p. 82.

24 This translates the phrase, 'la memoria scema', which may mean either 'an empty head' or 'an exhausted memory'; if the latter, the implication would be that fashionable young men stored up sonnets to impress their ladies, and when they ran out they hired poets like Pucci to furnish new ones. This practice continued into the Elizabethan period in Britain.

3 'MAKING THE AIR TREMBLE WITH CLARITY': THE *STILNOVISTI*

1 A *tenzone* is a group of poems on the same subject contributed either by two poets exchanging poems or by a group all contributing. There might be rules to make it more interesting, such as that each poet had to use the same rhymewords. *Tenzoni* were written from the Sicilian period on, but were never popular in Britain.

2 'His' because all the poets of the century whose works survive were men. There is one woman poet who appears in the anthologies of the Duecento, known simply as 'La Compiuta Donzella', 'the Accomplished Maiden'. The manuscripts assign her three sonnets, two of which lament her father's intention to marry her off against her will. Two contemporaries, Torrigniano of Florence and Guittone d'Arezzo, wrote to her, which seems to place her existence beyond doubt, but nothing is known of her save that she was a

Florentine. Two of her sonnets are printed in G. Getto and E. Sanguinetti, *Il sonetto*, Milan, 1957, pp. 36–7.

3 Mario Marti, *Storio dello Stil Nuovo*, Lecce, 1972, pp. 159–60 (trans.). This excellent critical account of the stilnovist school is unfortunately not available in English.

4 The texts of this and the other stilnovist lyrics quoted are taken from Mario Marti, *Poeti del Dolce Stil Nuovo*, Florence, 1969, a massive anthology with full scholarly notes. Guinizelli's poem is on p. 70.

5 The last line of Dante's *Divine Comedy*. For the full text of Guinizelli's poem, see Marti, *Poeti del Dolce Stil Nuovo*, pp. 57–62. A translation of the *canzone* is included in Sally Purcell (trans.), *Dante: Literature in the Vernacular*, Manchester, 1981, pp. 78–80. It is, however, an old translation, by D. G. Rossetti, and not accurate at all points.

6 Marti, *Poeti del Dolce Stil Nuovo*, p. 133.

7 D. G. Rossetti, *Dante and His Circle, 1100–1200–1300*, rev. edn, London, 1874, p. 134. This is one of the very few anthologies which make early Italian poetry available in translation to the English reader. Rossetti set himself to translate into verse preserving the rhymeschemes of his originals, and sometimes sacrifices accuracy to this. It is still an excellent introduction to the poets of the period.

8 But we are still very grateful to scholars who collect and tabulate them. For the metrics of the *stilnovisti*, see Adriana Solimena, *Repertorio metrico dello Stil Novo*, Rome, 1980.

9 'A lover begging for mercy from his mistress produces a lot of words and arguments, and she defends herself in her reply . . . so then, there is an implicit debate between them, and thus all letters and love poems are in debating mode, either implied or expressed.' Brunetto Latini (1220?–1294), *La rettorica Italiana*, ed. A. Maggini, Florence, 1915, pp. 100–2.

10 *Dante Alighieri: Vita Nuova, Rime*, ed. F. Chapelli, Milan, 1965, p. 111.

11 For a brief and non-specialised account of this sub-genre, see C. S. Lewis, *The Allegory of Love*, Oxford, 1936, pp. 66–83.

12 Marti, *Poeti del Dolce Stil Nuovo*, p. 465.

13 The standard critical edition of the *Vita Nuova* is by Domenico de Robertis: *Dante: Vita Nuova*, Milan and Naples, 1980. A very readable version is Mark Musa (ed. and trans.), *Dante's 'Vita Nuova'*, Bloomington, Ind., 1973, which contains an interpretative essay. D. G. Rossetti also produced a translation in the volume referred to in note 7 above.

14 See the brief account by M. Pazzaglia in the *Enciclopedia Dantesca*, 1976, under the heading '*Vita Nuova*: Fortuna'.

15 Some idea of the complexity of reading the *Vita Nuova* can be gained from Jerome Mazzaro, *The Figure of Dante: an Essay on the 'Vita Nuova'*, Princeton, NJ, 1981, and the scholarly bibliography in Robertis' edition (see above, n. 13), pp. 20–3.

16 Robertis, op. cit., p. 225.

17 Ibid.

18 The distinction between the /I/ in the *énoncé* or narrative and the /I/ in the *énonciation* or act of narrating derives from French narratological theory, and has no generally agreed English terms: the *narrated /I/* and *narrating /I/* might serve. See O. Ducrot and T. Todorov, *Encyclopedic Dictionary of the Sciences of Language*, Oxford, 1981, pp. 323, 329.

19 Robertis, op. cit., pp. 169–71.

20 Dante's first sentence is 'In that part of the book of my memory before which very little is readable, there is a heading which says, "Here begins 'The New Life'." '

21 The Petrarch quotation is from the first sonnet of his *Rime*: see Chapter 4, p. 47. Sidney's sonnet ending with this line is quoted and discussed in Chapter 7, p. 114.
22 Robertis, op. cit., p. 197.
23 Ibid., pp. 181–4.
24 Ibid., pp. 245–6.

4 PETRARCH: 'THE GOOD WEAVER OF LOVE VERSES'

1 Dante il mover gli diè del cherubino,
e d'aere azzurro d'or lo circonfuse. . . .

te co' fiori
colga il Petrarca lungo un rio corrente. . . .

Carducci, 'Il sonetto', ll. 1–2, and 'Al sonetto', ll. 3–4, in G. Getto and E. Sanguinetti, *Il sonetto*, Milan, 1957, pp. 483–4. Carducci was the editor of the best nineteenth-century edition of Petrarch's poems (see n. 4 below).

2 'Canzoniere' is the ordinary word for a collection of poems in Petrarch's time, and is sometimes used by critics, as is his own title, *Rerum vulgarium fragmenta* (*Miscellaneous Italian Poems*). Modern practice is to take the title from the first line of Petrarch's first sonnet, and call the collection the *Rime sparse*, or simply the *Rime*. Of the other forms that appear in the collection, the *canzone* is a long poem much like the *ode*, having an indeterminate number of stanzas usually of between seven and twenty lines in length. Once established, the stanza pattern recurs throughout. The *sestina* was a display piece popular with Provençal poets, which passed over into Italian. It consisted of six unrhymed stanzas, each of six lines, and each succeeding stanza had to use the ending words of the previous stanza in a set order. If one uses numbers to denote the six words at the ends of the lines of stanza one, the order went: 123456/615243/364125/532614/451362/246531. The rule is, reverse words 1 and 6 – 61; reverse 2 and 5 – 52; reverse 3 and 4 – 43, giving 615243. Repeat this until stanza six, when doing this to 246531 would produce 123456. Petrarch liked to add a *congedo* or valedictory stanza of three lines in which all six words appeared again, two to a line. See for example *Rime* 80.

The *ballata* was variable in length, as short as seven lines or as long as fifty; its requirement was a refrain, because it was originally danced to (*ballare*). The refrain was announced at the start, and then repeated at the end of each stanza, sometimes words and rhymes, sometimes only rhymes. Petrarch wrote a seventeen-line *ballata* as *Rime* 55, rhyming ABB CDCDCBB EFEFFBB, in which the BB rhyme makes the refrain. The madrigal, which was supposed to have bucolic associations, was a short form of six to ten lines, using tercets, e.g. ABA CBC DEDE (*Rime* 54). Later, and particularly in England, it acquired its musical sense of 'a short verse composition for a group of voices'.

3 Joseph Fucilla, 'The present status of Petrarchan studies', in A. Scaglione (ed.), *Francis Petrarch, Six Centuries Later: A Symposium*, Chapel Hill, NC, 1975, pp. 48 ff.

4 For the reader new to Petrarch, a good place to start is Robert Durling (ed. and trans.), *Petrarch's Lyric Poems*, Cambridge, Mass., 1976, a beautifully printed dual-language text, sensitively translated and lightly annotated. A very readable life of Petrarch is Morris Bishop, *Petrarch and His World*, Bloomington, Ind., 1963; and, for a densely informative short study of

Petrarch's major works, with a biography and an account of the making of the *Rime* included, Kenelm Foster's *Petrarch: Poet and Humanist*, Edinburgh, 1984. Foster's study has an excellent bibliography. For the reader who reads Italian, it is well worth consulting the scholarly edition by G. Carducci and S. Ferrari, *Le Rime di Francesco Petrarca*, Florence, 1899, reprinted G. Contini, Florence, 1965, which has a very useful preface and helpful notes to each poem.

5 See the preface to Carducci's edition of the *Rime* (n. 4 above), p. iv.

6 The classic study is E. H. Wilkins, *The Making of the 'Canzoniere' and Other Petrarchan Studies*, Rome, 1951. See also Foster, op. cit., pp. 92–105.

7 The Latin note was transcribed by the best of Petrarch's early biographers, Ludovico Beccadelli, in his *Vita del Petrarca*, 1569–71, which has been edited by G. Frasso, *Francesco Petrarca e Ludovico Beccadelli*, Studi sul Petrarca 13, Ente Nazionale Francesco Petrarca, Padua, 1983, pp. 61–2. In English, it says:

> Laura, famous through her own virtues and long celebrated in my poems, first appeared to my sight in the first years of my youth, in the year 1327, 6 April, in the church of St Claire in Avignon, at matins; and in that same city, in the same month, on the same sixth day at the same early hour, but in the year 1348, that radiance was taken from our day, when I by chance was in Verona, alas! unaware of my fate. The unhappy news caught me at Parma in a letter from my friend Ludovico [del Brabante], the same year in the morning of 19 May. That most chaste and fair body was laid to rest in the ground of the Friars Minor, towards evening on the day of her death.

The astounding coincidence of the time of Laura's death raises doubts: see Foster, op. cit., pp. 53–5. The speed of her burial was due to the plague: the 1347–8 Black Death was the worst single outbreak in European history.

8 Numbers and line numbers after quotations from Petrarch are from Robert Durling's edition, but the numbering of the *Rime* is standard in modern editions. Translations are my own.

9 The interpretation of these lines is not certain, but the most obvious meaning is 'if she had desired to love me, that would have caused my death and stained her reputation' – because adultery was a serious crime, possibly carrying a death sentence for the man and seclusion from the world for the woman. It is hard to believe that Petrarch would have falsified his own sexual transgression, if any, in a penitential prayer to the Virgin Mary.

10 His son Giovanni was born in 1337, his daughter Francesca in 1343. Beccadelli (see n. 7) relates that Francesca's mother was Milanese, but no evidence has been found.

11 Mario Fubini, *Metrica e poesia: dal Duecento al Petrarca*, Milan, 1962, p. 238.

12 See Chapter 2, pp. 23–5.

13 Except, perhaps, by Dante in a mysterious group of four poems known as the 'Rime Petrose' ('Stony Poems'), which are reprinted at the end of Durling's edition.

14 Ovid's verse collection, *The Metamorphoses* (first century BC), was a sourcebook for Graeco-Roman mythology right through the medieval and Renaissance period. Ovid is mainly concerned with stories in which people are transformed into beasts, birds or plants, but his range of reference was very wide and, as his Latin is not very difficult, his text was used in schools.

15 Two features of the musicality of Petrarch's verse which are not particularly relevant to the English sonnet may be mentioned here. First, he was sensitive

to the distinction beween consonantal and vocalic rhymes – 'sparsi/farsi' would be a consonantal rhyme, and 'viso/riso' a vocalic one. Second, Italian verse is usually written in lines which have an odd number of syllables, and most sonnets have eleven in a line. The caesura, therefore, wherever it occurs, must divide the line into two unequal parts. If there are fewer syllables before the caesura than after it, the line is called a line *a minore*; if the reverse, a line *a maiore*. A good writer took care to vary the balance from *a minore* to *a maiore* and back, unless he deliberately sought an effect of monotony. English writers likewise take care not to have the caesura fall in the same place in the line for too long.

16 'Noi siàn le triste penne sbiggotite', in Mario Marti, *Poeti del Dolce Stil Nuovo*, Florence, 1969, p. 163.

17 Horace, *Carminum Liber III*, final poem. The idea that paper, which is one of the most fragile of things, can make speech, one of the most transitory of things, outlast bronze or stone is woven into a great deal of verse which talks about making verse: it is a metatextual conceit, since it inevitably draws attention to the textual quality of the text in which it occurs.

18 A *senhal* was a secret name bestowed on a Lady (or on himself) by a Provençal poet – the name of a flower, for example, so that the poet could praise the flower as covert praise of his Lady. Laura is certainly the right kind of name for a *senhal*.

5 THE FORTUNATE ISLES: THE SONNET MOVES ABROAD

1 For Chaucer's relations with Italy and Italian authors, see Pietro Boitani (ed.), *Chaucer and the Italian Trecento*, Cambridge, 1983. There is a useful bibliography. Boitani's collection has little to say about Chaucer and Petrarch: for the use Chaucer made of *Rime* 132, see E. H. Wilkins, 'Cantus Troili', *English Literary History*, vol. 16, 1949, pp. 167–73, and the later and fuller article by Patricia Thomson, 'The *Canticus Troili*: Chaucer and Petrarch', *Comparative Literature*, vol. 11, 1959, pp. 313–28.

2 For the little that is known about Chaucer's first visit to Italy, and the possibility of his having met Petrarch, see G. B. Parks, 'The route of Chaucer's first journey to Italy', *English Literary History*, vol. 16, 1949, pp. 174–87.

3 Wilkins, and Thomson after him (see n. 1 above), ascribe a number of misunderstandings of Petrarch's Italian to Chaucer. Of these, only two could be judged failures to comprehend the language: in l. 13 of Chaucer's text, he very clumsily translates 'Come puoi tanto in me' as 'How may of the in me swich quantite'; but the clumsiness is independent of the misunderstanding, since 'potency' or even 'may swich power be' would restore the accuracy but not eliminate the awkwardness of the line. Moreover, though 'potere tanto' certainly means 'to have so much power', 'tanto' by itself means 'so much' either in quantity or in power. The clearest blunder is 'if harm agree me' in l. 10, for 's'a mal mio grado' ('if in spite of myself'). Wilkins ('Cantus Troili') demonstrates that Chaucer could not have got his English version from a faulty *written* copy; it remains possible, however, since the blunder is a gross one, that Chaucer used a manuscript of the poem which had at some stage incorporated a *dictation* error: 's'a mal mio grado' would be very easily misheard as 'Se 'l mal mi è grato' ('if harm is pleasing to me'). The creative use which Chaucer elsewhere makes of Dante and Boccaccio makes it unlikely that his Italian was so poor that he would misunderstand a fairly common idiom.

4 Carlo Muscetta and Daniele Ponchiroli, *Poesia del Quattrocento e del Cinquecento*, Turin, 1959, p. vi (trans.).
5 *Los Sonetos 'Al Italico Modo' de Inigo López de Mendoza, Marqués de Santillana*, ed. Maxim Kerkhof and Dirk Tuin, Madison, Wis., 1985, p. 54 (trans.).
6 The numbers, and the text, of the Marqués' sonnets are taken from the edition in n. 5 above.
7 The anthology by Muscetta and Ponchiroli (n. 4 above) has a section devoted to the female poets of the age (pp. 1257–1309), with short biographical introductions.
8 The text is taken from ibid., p. 1338.
9 A useful edition of Bembo's principal works, with a good introduction, is by Carlo Dionisotti, *Pietro Bembo: Prose della volgar lingua, Gli Asolani, rime*, Turin, 1989. For Bembo's ideas and influence, see Giorgio Santangelo, *Il Petrarchismo del Bembo e di altri poeti del '500*, Rome and Palermo, 1967.
10 John Houston, *The Rhetoric of Poetry in the Renaissance and Seventeenth Century*, Baton Rouge, La, 1983, p. 25.
11 Quoted by Santangelo, op. cit., pp. 79–80 (trans.).
12 Translated from *Gli Asolani* in Dionisotti's edition (n. 9 above), pp. 493–5.
13 The word 'prince' was used in the Renaissance to refer to any crowned head of a state, of either sex, as well as to the male sons of such crowned heads, as now. It was used as we should now use 'ruler'.
14 George Puttenham, *The Arte of English Poesie*, 1589, Book III, ch. 5, pp. 148–9 in the standard edition by G. D. Willcock and A. Walker, *The Arte of English Poesie*, Cambridge, 1936. Because of its constant linking of poetry and courtliness, Puttenham's book has become a key text in modern reading of Renaissance poetry. See Gary Waller, *English Poetry of the Sixteenth Century*, London and New York, 1986, *passim*; Daniel Javitch, *Poetry and Courtliness in Renaissance England*, Princeton, NJ, 1978, chs 2 and 3; and Louis A. Montrose, 'Of gentlemen and shepherds: the politics of Elizabethan pastoral form', *English Literary History*, vol. 50, 1983, pp. 433–50.
15 The texts referred to here are Dante's *De vulgari eloquentia*, c.1315; Bembo's *Prose della volgar lingua*, 1524; Joachim du Bellay, *Défense et illustration de la langue française*, 1549; James VI of Scotland, *The Essays of a Prentise in the Divine Art of Poesie*, 1585; and Puttenham's *Arte of English Poesie*.
16 Puttenham, *Arte of English Poesie*, p. 60.
17 For a more detailed study of this very vexed question, see Ruth Kelso, *The Doctrine of the English Gentleman in the Sixteenth Century*, Urbana, Ill., 1926. See also Lawrence Stone, *The Crisis of the Aristocracy, 1588–1641*, Oxford, 1965.
18 In his *La Poetica* of 1536, Bernardino Daniello complains that the moderns are trivial because they lack the appropriate role model for heroic writing:

> niuno ve ne ha che allo scrivere eroicamente si dia, ma solamente sonetti, capitoli e novelle. Il che se ben si riguarda, non per altro avviene se non perchè essi non hanno chi s'imitare nel verso se non il Petrarca, e Dante, e nelle prose il Boccaccio . . . e non avvenne così a' latini uomini, perciò che essi ebbero nel loro Vergilio grandissimo di tutti poeti.

> [there is no one committed to heroic writing, but only to sonnets, tercets and romances. If one considers it carefully, the only reason is that they have no poetic model but Petrarch and Dante, and Boccaccio in prose . . . which didn't happen to the Latin writers, because they had in Virgil the greatest of all poets.]

Reprinted in Bernard Weinberg (ed.), *Trattati di poetica e rettorica del Cinquecento*, 4 vols, Bari, 1970–4, vol. 1, p. 314.

19 Mario Equicola, *De natura d'amore*, 1525, in G. Spagnoletti, *Il Petrarchismo*, Milan, 1959, p. 109.

20 Bembo, in listing opposed terms, sets the qualities that belong to the professional conduct of the prince against terms of recreation:

> dico che egli si potrebbe considerare, quanto alcuna composizione meriti loda o non meriti, ancora per questa via; che perciò che due parti sono quelle che fanno bella ogni scrittura, la gravità e la piacevolezza . . . E affine che voi meglio queste due medesime parti conosciate, come e quanto sono differenti tra loro, sotto la gravità ripongo l'onestà, la dignità, la maestà, la magnificenza, la grandezza, e le loro somiglianti; sotto la piacevolezza restringo la grazia, la soavità, la vaghezza, la dolcezza, gli scherzi, i giuochi, e se altro è di questa maniera.
>
> [I say that you could judge how much a work deserves praise or not also by this method: in that there are two criteria that determine beauty in any writing, gravity and the power to please . . . And to give you a better understanding of these two, in what ways and to what extent they differ, I include under *gravity* probity, dignity, majesty, magnificence, grandeur and similar qualities; and under *the power to please* I place gracefulness, smoothness, delicacy, sweetness, humour, wordplay, and anything else like those.]
>
> (*Prose della volgar lingua*, Book 2, ch. 9; in Dionisotti's edition (n. 9 above), p. 146)

21 At the end of the chapter quoted in the previous note, Bembo remarks that Dante can often be grave without sweetness, and Cino da Pistoia conversely sweet without gravity, whereas

> il Petrarca l'una e l'altra di queste parti empié maravigliosamente, in maniera che scegliere non si può, in quale delle due egli fosse maggior maestro.
>
> [Petrarch fulfils both of these criteria astonishingly well, in such a fashion that it's impossible to decide in which of the two he has the greater mastery.]
>
> (Ibid.)

22 'I quali, questi tali ragionamenti leggendo et in essi, se non tutti quei precetti, ammaestramenti o regole del arte del dire, almeno i principali e più necessari ritrovando, chi sa che et essi ancora per avventura allo scrivere non solamente novelle, sonetti et amorose canzoni, ma più alti, più gravi e più gloriosi poemi che questi non sono, non si diano?' Reprinted in Weinberg, op. cit., vol. 1, p. 232.

23 Puttenham, *Arte of English Poesie*, pp. 44–5.

6 WYATT, SURREY AND THEIR LEGACY

1 Hugues Vaganay, *Le Sonnet en Italie et en France au XVIe siècle*, Louvain, 1899, reprinted Geneva, 1966.

2 Ibid., p. xv.

3 James VI of Scotland, in his *Ane Schort Treatise conteining some Reulis and Cautelis to be Observit and Eschewit in Scottis Poesie* (1585), recommends the sonnet for this purpose only: 'For compendious praysing of any bukes, or the

authoris thairof, or ony argumentis of uther historeis . . . use *Sonet* verse, of fourtene lynis, and ten fete in every lyne' (*Ane Schort Treatise* in G. Gregory Smith (ed.), *Elizabethan Critical Essays*, 2 vols, Oxford, 1904, vol. 1, p. 223).

4 One would have to decide, for example, whether to include what Thomas Watson calls 'sonnets' in his *Hekatompathia* of 1582, which have eighteen lines; or, sixty years later, whether the fourteen-line poems of William Habington's *Castara* qualify, though they are in couplets throughout.

5 For Wyatt's life and poetry, see Patricia Thomson, *Sir Thomas Wyatt and His Background*, Stanford, Calif., 1964; and also Kenneth Muir, *The Life and Letters of Sir Thomas Wyatt*, Liverpool, 1963. For Henry Howard, Earl of Surrey, see *Henry Howard, Earl of Surrey: Poems*, ed. Emrys Jones, Oxford, 1964.

6 David H. Darst, *Juan Boscán*, Boston, Mass., 1978, pp. 17–26 and 50–80. Boscán's poems were not published until 1543, after his death and Wyatt's; but his poems circulated in manuscript, and Wyatt could certainly have seen his Petrarchan sonnets. Boscán does not, however, use the couplet ending.

7 The connections between humanist rhetoric and courtly rhetoric are discussed by Daniel Javitch, *Poetry and Courtliness in Renaissance England*, Princeton, NJ, 1978, particularly in ch. 1. For a more extended examination, see Frank Whigham, *Ambition and Privilege*, Los Angeles, 1984.

8 Quoted by L. A. Montrose, 'Of gentlemen and shepherds: the politics of Elizabethan pastoral form', *English Literary History*, vol. 50, 1983, p. 441.

9 Wyatt, who married young, separated from his wife, Elizabeth Brooke, about 1525, and on Anne Boleyn's return to Court in that year seems to have become involved with her, until warned off by the obvious infatuation of Henry VIII with her. Had he indeed written poems and sent them to her about that time, it would have been in the highest degree compromising and dangerous to circulate them after the King began to pay his attentions to Anne; Wyatt was imprisoned in fear of his life in 1536, when Anne and five men supposedly implicated in her promiscuity were executed. He escaped, and formed a lifelong attachment to Elizabeth Darrell, who bore him a son, and who may well be 'Phillis' to Anne Boleyn's 'Brunet' in Wyatt's poem 'If waker care, if sodayne pale Coulor'.

10 Numbers after poems or lines by Wyatt refer to the edition by Kenneth Muir: *Sir Thomas Wyatt: The Collected Poems*, Muses' Library, London, 1960 (3rd impression).

11 Anne Ferry, *The 'Inward' Language*, Chicago, Ill., 1983, ch. 2.

12 For a detailed discussion of this aspect of Wyatt's verse, see Stephen Greenblatt, *Renaissance Self-Fashioning*, Chicago, Ill., 1980, ch. 3, 'Power, sexuality and inwardness in Wyatt's poetry'.

13 The terms used here all denote brief expressions of moral or practical advice, but they may be roughly distinguished as follows: a *proverb* is metaphorical and very often alliterative or rhythmical ('A stitch in time saves nine'); an *adage* is unmetaphorical and abstract ('Rule is enemy to quietness') but may have rhetorical enhancement ('*Memento mori*'); the *apophthegm* or *sententia* is a wise saying, usually brief and normally attributable, as proverbs are not, to a single person. The word *maxim* is probably the most useful general term: it suggests that the utterance (proverb, adage or *sententia*) is to be remembered as a guide to future conduct. Since 'maxim' does not have a convenient adjective, a style impregnated with maxims is usually called a proverbial or sententious style. The terms overlap considerably, and were used almost interchangeably in the sixteenth century.

14 Rosalie Colie, *The Resources of Kind*, Los Angeles, Calif., 1973, p. 33.

15 Thomas Dekker, *The Guls Hornebooke*, 1609, edited by E. D. Pendry in *Thomas*

Dekker, Stratford-upon-Avon Library 4, London, 1967, p. 72. Thomas Whythorne, who is mentioned more than once in this book, was a professional musician and occasional poet who left a manuscript autobiography, written about 1576 and only recently edited. He is interesting to linguists because he wrote in a highly idiosyncratic phonetic orthography; to students of biography because he was habitually introspective and frank; and to students of literature and music because he shows very clearly how music and poetry worked in households on the fringe of gentle society. See *The Autobiography of Thomas Whythorne*, ed. James M. Osborn, Oxford, 1961. Osborn edited a modern spelling edition the following year.

16 Anne Lock's sequence is titled 'A Meditation of a Penitent Sinner: Written in Maner of a Paraphrase upon the 51 Psalme of David', and is a separate gathering ([A]-A_9) added to *Sermons of John Calvin, upon the Songe that Ezechias made . . . Translated out of Frenche into Englishe*, printed by John Day, London, 1560. A flyleaf inscription in the British Library copy records that it is 'Liber Henrici Lock ex dono Anne uxoris suae 1559'. Anne Lock was a zealous Protestant and a Marian exile, as was the patroness to whom she dedicated the volume, Catherine Bertie, Duchess of Suffolk. The sonnets may well have been written in 1559, after the return of the Duchess, and Anne Lock, to England on the death of Mary Tudor. Anne Lock has been noticed as a devotional figure (see Patrick Collinson, *The Elizabethan Puritan Movement*, London, 1967, p. 134), and her poetry is briefly mentioned under her husband's entry in *DNB*, sv. 'Lok, Henry', but I know no modern discussion of it.

17 The standard scholarly edition is by Hyder Rollins: *Tottel's Miscellany*, 2 vols, Cambridge, Mass., 1965. The name 'Tottel's Miscellany', which Rollins also uses, was given to Tottel's *Songes and Sonettes* by Edward Arber, in his edition in the English Reprints series, London, 1870, and has stuck, though the word *miscellany* is not even a sixteenth-century word. The differences between the various editions of the *Miscellany* are explained fully by Rollins. The problem of the editor's identity is discussed by Rollins (vol. 2, pp. 85–101); in what follows, I assume for simplicity's sake that Tottel was the editor.

18 The early miscellany, *A Handefull of Pleasant Delites*, London, 1584 (but probably first printed in 1566), advertises itself as containing 'sundrie new Sonets and delectable Histories', but all the entries are broadside ballads. It is made clear in 'The Printer to the Reader' that, whether sonnets or histories, these poems are 'such pretie thinges/As women much desire'; the implication is that sonnets are a light kind of poetry appropriate to women readers. The fact that 'sonets' are distinguished from 'histories' suggests that strong narrative content removes a poem from the category of sonnet; and as a long poem is likely either to be narrative or to develop its theme to the point where it clearly fits into another generic category, such as eclogue or satire, the identification of sonnet with short poems would be customary.

19 *Autobiography of Thomas Whythorne*, p. 174.

20 True sonnets were not commonly set to music in Britain, in contrast with the large number of Petrarchan settings in continental Europe. Of the more than 1,500 musical items reprinted in E. H. Fellowes (ed.), *English Madrigal Verse, 1588–1632*, Oxford, 1920, only twenty-seven are sonnets, with a very few more irregular or unrhymed fourteen-line stanzas. This does not include portions of sonnets: it was not uncommon for an octave or first quatrain to be detached for setting to music. This contrasts with the large number of sonnets set by European musicians, though they, too, would detach parts of a sonnet, or obscure its distinctive structure by using refrains and reprises – a

famous example is Claudio Monteverdi's setting of Petrarch's 'Vago augelletto' (*Rime* 353) in his *Madrigali Guerrieri et Amorosi* (Venice, 1638). In looking more closely at the distribution in Fellowes's collection, one sees that nine of these twenty-seven sonnets were set by William Byrd in his *Psalmes, Sonets and Songs of Sadnes and Pietie* (1588) and his *Songs of Sundrie Natures* (1589), and four, all by Fulke Greville, were set by Martin Peerson in his *Mottects or Grave Chamber Musique* (1630). Though the sonnets chosen by both composers are not in fact all serious, the collections in which these thirteen sonnets occur are among the most serious in the Elizabethan and seventeenth-century repertoire, suggesting that the 'through-composed' style which the non-stanzaic form of the sonnet required was too declamatory and heavy for the majority of composers in Britain. William Byrd solved the problem by setting the octave and sestet separately. The madrigal and lute-song composers were very willing to use all the kinds of subject matter and of rhetoric that appear in sonnets, but not at sonnet length: shorter stanzas, particularly of six to eight lines, were preferred; the argumentative development intrinsic to the sonnet form seems to have been inimical to them. For a short but still useful and informative discussion, see Lisle Cecil John, *The Elizabethan Sonnet Sequences*, New York, 1938, pp. 14–15, 210–12. For more specialised musical studies, see Louise Scheiner, 'Recent studies in poetry and music of the English Renaissance', *English Literary Reniassance*, vol. 16, 1986, pp. 253–86.

21 George Gascoigne, *Certayne Notes of Instruction*, 1575, in *Elizabethan Critical Essays*, ed. Gregory Smith, 2 vols, Oxford, 1904, vol. 1, p. 55.

22 James VI, *Ane Schort Treatise*, in Smith, op. cit., p. 223.

23 Thomas Watson, *Hekatompathia* (1582), in H. M. Klein (ed.), *English and Scottish Sonnet Sequences of the Renaissance*, 2 vols, Hildesheim, 1984, vol. 1, pp. 51, 54.

24 Thomas Campion, *Observations in the Arte of English Poesy* (1602), in Smith, op. cit., vol. 2, p. 331.

25 The only sequence which is markedly different is the prudently anonymous 'Zepheria' of 1594, in which the sonnets are numbered, but called 'canzons'. Six of the forty poems are extended sonnets, the remainder regular, but extremely incompetent.

26 There were ten editions of the *Miscellany* in all: three in 1557, two in 1559, one in 1565, in 1567, in 1574, in 1585 and in 1587. Interesting evidence of what the poets who came immediately after Wyatt and Surrey were making of the sonnet is provided by the rhymeschemes of the twelve regular sonnets and seven quasi-sonnets in the *Miscellany* written by Nicholas Grimald and the 'uncertain authors' (poem numbers from R = Hyder Rollins's edition, referred to in n. 17 above):

R 137: ABAB CDCD EFEF GG (Grimald)
R 146: ABAB CDCD EFEF GG "
R 156: ABAB CDCD EFEF GG "
R 173: ABAB CDCD EFEF GG (Uncertain)
R 179: ABAB CDCD EFEF GG "
R 186: ABAB CDCD EFEF GG "
R 218: ABBA ABBA EFEF GG "
R 219: ABBA CDDC EFEF GG "
R 233: ABBA CDDC EFFE GG "
R 241: ABBA ABBA CDE CDE "
R 257: ABAB CDCD EFEF GG "
R 300: ABAB CDCD EFEF GG "

Only one of these, R 241, is an Italian sonnet; the others follow the rhymescheme of Surrey, and all except one, R 257, which is in tetrameters, have the standard ten-syllable line. The seven quasi-sonnets show a certain amount of experimentation, or perhaps just vagueness:

R 105: ABABAB CDCD EDE GG (Grimald)
R 135: ABAB BCC DEDE EFF (Uncertain)
[Two strambotti joined together, each ending with a rhyme couplet which is also a sense couplet]
R 187: ABAB BCC DEDE FF
[Almost the same, but one line short]
R 200: ABAB BCC DEDE EFF
[The same, but in fourteeners: the writer of this poem, whose initial letters make the acrostic 'EDWARDE SOMERSET', is so far away from the sonnet form that he would have no reason to connect it with his poem.]
R 299: ABAB BCBC BCBCB DD
[The octave and the final couplet suggest that the writer had sonnet form in mind, and the couplet carryover from the first quatrain (ABA {B B}CBC) hints at the Spenserian sonnet form.]

Finally, two sonnets of Petrarch, *Rime* 1 and 3, are translated into fourteeners in couplets, corresponding as is shown to the sections of Petrarch's originals:

R 276: AABB CCDD EEFF GG
[*Rime* 1: ABBA ABBA CDECD E]
R 277: AABB CCDD EEFF GG
[*Rime* 3: ABBA ABBA CDC DCD]

The close matching of sections shows that the writer is thinking in sonnet form, but not observing sonnet rhymes.

What is particularly to be noticed is that, either because they did not exist or Tottel chose to exclude them, there are no French sonnets (ABBA ABBA CC DEDE) and only one Italian sonnet.

27 What, never? Well . . . hardly ever! See n. 28 below.

28 Louise Labé (1526–66), the best woman sonneteer of the age, has a fondness for making the medial couplet into a sense couplet, which then has to be qualified or countered, as in this example:

Predit me fut que devois fermement
Un jour aymer celui dont la figure
Me fut descrite, et sans autre peinture
Le reconnus quand vy premierement.
Puis, le voyant aymer fatalement,
Pitié je pris de sa triste aventure,
Et tellement je forçay ma nature
Qu'autant que luy aimay ardentement.
Qui n'ust pensé qu'en faveur devoit croitre
Ce que le Ciel et destins firent naitre?
Mais quand je voy si nubileus aprets,
Vents si cruels et tant horrible orage,
Je crois qu'estoient les infernaux arrets,
Qui de si loin m'ourdissoient ce naufrage.

[It was foretold me that I should one day deeply love one whose form was described to me, and with no further depiction, I knew him the instant I saw him.

Then, seeing him smitten with love, I took pity on his sad misfortune, and so worked against my own nature, that I loved as strongly as he. Who would not have thought that fair growth should come of that which Heaven and the Fates had produced? But when I see such threatening clouds, such savage winds, so fierce a storm, I think it was the powers of hell, that from so far destined me this shipwreck.]

29 The whole function and effect of titling poems needs much more study than it has received, particularly as regards titles by editors. Briefly, titles serve as a means of locating poems, especially when combined with tables of contents; but, beyond that, they suggest ways of reading the poems both individually and in aggregate. Even simple numbers, such as most writers of sonnet sequences favoured, suggest that the reader is in some way progressing, perhaps in time or psychological development: Tottel's kind of title (which one is tempted to call a 'totle', since it was widely imitated) provides a very small summary of the poem, and thus a criticism of it; the next stage is to provide an initial gloss, as Thomas Watson did in his *Hekatompathia* which expands the title into a kind of narrative; and finally, as in Dante's *Vita Nuova*, one may integrate the poems into a large prose narrative, when the concept of 'title' has disappeared.
30 *Tottel's Miscellany*, ed. Rollins, vol. 2, pp. 107–24.
31 Richard Harrier, *The Canon of Sir Thomas Wyatt's Poetry*, Cambridge, Mass., 1975, p. 3.
32 The Petrarch madrigal 'Or vedi, Amor' (*Rime* 121), rhyming ABB ACC CDD, was turned by Wyatt into the rondeau 'Behold, love' (No. 1 in Muir's edition) rhyming AABBAAABx AABBAx (x = refrain), and by Tottel into the sonnet 'Behold, love' (no. R 69 in Rollins's edition), rhyming very irregularly AABB AAAB AAA BBA. Similarly the rondeau 'What vaileth truth?' (Muir, no. 2) became the sonnet 'What vaileth troth?' (R 70), with the same rhymescheme; and the rondeau 'Goo burnyng sighes' (Muir no. 20), freely adapted from Petrarch, *Rime* 153, becomes the sonnet 'Go, burning sighes' (R 103), with the same rhymescheme as before.
33 In Italian, /io/ and /occhio/ might, but do not, suggest a pun. But, by pure chance, English homophonies give the poet /I: eye/, /dear:deer/ and /hart:heart/, thus suggesting metaphorical explorations of optics, forests and hunting which English Petrarchans eagerly embarked on.
34 *Tottel's Miscellany*, ed. Rollins, p. 95.
35 Ibid., p. 110.

7 'I AM NOT I': THE SONNETS OF SIDNEY

1 The title '*Astrophel and Stella*' is not Sidney's, but was given as far as is known by its first publisher, Thomas Newman, in 1591. Sidney refers to himself as 'Astrophil', the correct Greek coinage for 'lover of a star', twice in *Astrophel and Stella* and, though we have no spelling of the name in Sidney's writing, everyone who uses the name before Newman's edition spells it with an 'i'. Modern practice is to use the 'i' form: however, it is customary to refer to Renaissance texts using the spelling of the original printed title, and all printed editions of Sidney's sequence use the 'e' form, so that strictly '*Astrophil and Stella*' is a nonexistent book!

2 Thus Sidney Lee's fourteenth chapter is entitled 'French light and English gloom' (*The French Renaissance in England*, Oxford, 1910, p. 65); see also J. W. Lever, *The Elizabethan Love Sonnet*, 1956, reprinted London, 1968, p. 93.

3 The relationship of these 'mid-Tudor poets' to Sidney's poesis is discussed by Germaine Warkentin, 'The meeting of the Muses: Sidney and the mid-Tudor poets', in Gary Waller and Michael Moore (eds), *Sir Philip Sidney and the Interpretation of Renaissance Culture*, London, 1984, pp. 17–33.

4 Spenser's contribution to van der Noodt's volume is reprinted, with the original woodcut illustrations, in Spenser's *Minor Poems*, ed. E. de Selincourt, Oxford, 1910, reprinted 1966, pp. 483–504.

5 Watson's *The Hekatompathia* and Soowthern's *Pandora* are reprinted in facsimile, with critical introduction and notes, by H. M. Klein (ed.), *English and Scottish Sonnet Sequences of the Renaissance*, 2 vols, Hildesheim, 1984. Klein does not include James VI's sequence, which appeared as one of the items in James's *The Essayes of a Prentise, in the Divine Art of Poesie*, 1585, ed. Edward Arber, English Reprints series, London, 1869.

6 Ibid., p. 14.

7 The question of who first invented the Spenserian sonnet is discussed by Murray F. Markland, 'A note on Spenser and the Scottish sonneteers', *Studies in Scottish Literature*, vol. 1, 1963, pp. 136–40. Spenser seems to have used the form first about 1580 or 1582, and again in 1586, but not with any consistency until his *Amoretti*, written at the beginning of the 1590s, and first published in 1595. James's volume contains twenty Spenserian sonnets, mainly by himself.

8 Soowthern, *Pandora*, Sonnet 2. The Greek poet Anacreon, whose works and attributed works were first published by Henri Estienne in 1552, was supposed to have loved the boy Bathyllus, here politely called 'her'; Ovid wrote about Corinna, Petrarch about Laura, Ronsard about Cassandra (Cassandre Salviati) in his *Amours* of 1552; and Philippe Desportes (1545–1606) published his sequence *Diane* in 1573. The word 'Tien' refers to Anacreon, who was born in the Greek city of Teos.

9 The standard edition is *The Poems of Sir Philip Sidney*, edited by W. A. Ringler, Oxford, 1962. This edition is immensely informative, and has a meticulous account of Sidney's connections with Penelope Devereux in the notes, pp. 435–47. I have used Ringler's text throughout.

10 Abraham Fraunce, *The Arcadian Rhetoric*, 1588; John Hoskins, *Directions for Speech and Style*, ed. from British Museum MS Harleian 4604 by H. H. Hudson, Princeton, NJ, 1935. See also the review of contemporary appreciations of Sidney by Dennis Kay, 'Sidney – a critical heritage', in Dennis Kay (ed.), *Sir Philip Sidney: An Anthology of Modern Criticism*, Oxford, 1987, pp. 3–29.

11 The *Old Arcadia* is the name given to the version of the novel which Sidney composed between 1577 and 1580, before he wrote *Astrophel and Stella* in 1582. It was much copied and circulated before and after Sidney's death. After writing *Astrophel and Stella*, he embarked on a revised version, left only half-finished at his death; this version was entrusted to his friend Fulke Greville, who printed it as *The Countess of Pembroke's Arcadia* in 1590, presumably thinking that the *Old Arcadia*, though not printed, was sufficiently well known. When Greville's version was reprinted in 1593, Books 3, 4 and 5 of the *Old Arcadia* were added to complete it, though they do not match at all well. The *Old Arcadia* remained unknown in its entirety until rediscovered by Bertram Dobell in 1907. This state of affairs has the confusing consequence that Elizabethan writers writing about 1590 or before about the '*Arcadia*' will

have the *Old Arcadia* in mind; after that date, the two printed versions of 1590 and 1593 with the various reprints of the 1593 'completed' text are the versions likely to be known, until the twentieth-century recovery of the *Old Arcadia* in its entirety.

12 '*AS* 2' and other such numbers refer to the *Astrophel and Stella* sequence as printed in Ringler's edition (see n. 9 above).

13 The omissions are detailed in *Poems of Sidney*, ed. Ringler, pp. 447–8.

14 The term 'deconstructive' is used here to denote texts which explicitly, though not necessarily deliberately, make what Paul de Man, in *Blindness and Insight* (New York, 1971), calls 'the statement about language, that sign and meaning can never coincide' (p. 17). For a reading of *Astrophel and Stella* which works from this angle, see Ronald Levao, *Renaissance Minds and Their Fictions*, Los Angeles, Calif., 1985, ch. 6, 'Astrophil's poetics'. For a discussion of deconstruction and a subsequent application to Shakespeare's sonnets, see Howard Felperin, *Beyond Deconstruction*, Oxford, 1985, chs 4 and 5. The terms 'metafictional', 'metapoetic' and 'metatextual' mean, respectively, 'pertaining to fiction which draws attention to its own fictionality'; 'poetry which deals with the production of poetry'; 'texts which deal with their own status as texts'.

15 Sidney was, however, aware of the *canzone* as a form, and indeed, among his many other innovations, wrote the first *canzone* in English, modelled on Sannazaro, author of *Arcadia*: 'The lad Philisides' (*Poems of Sidney*, ed. Ringler, pp. 256–9 and 496–8). It is interesting, given the third-person songs in *Astrophel and Stella*, that Sidney says that Philisides, 'to shew what a straunger he was to himself, spake of himself as of a third person'. It is tempting to think that Sidney inserted the third-person songs into his sequence with this in his recollection.

16 The kinds of poetry that Bottom admires, and that the mechanicals write, are those that were old-fashioned in the late 1590s, the time of *A Midsummer Night's Dream*. Though extravagant apostrophes are a sign of rant and bombast in general, there are indications in Bottom's part in the mechanicals' play (V.i) that Shakespeare had been looking at at least the last section of *Astrophel and Stella* (published in its authorised version in 1598): not only is there a heavy stress upon night, darkness and absence from Song iv (after Sonnet 85) onwards, with a number of extremely wild apostrophes (e.g., Sonnet 88, 93, 100), but in Bottom's 'I see a voice: now will I to the chink,/To spy an I can hear my Thisby's face', there seems to be a reminiscence of Song vi, 'O you that heare this voice,/O you that see this face', and of Sidney's triple curse on the page, the night and the coachman when Stella disappears in the darkness in Sonnet 105 there may be a parody in Bottom's 'O wicked wall, through whom I see no blisse,/Curst be thy stones for thus deceiving me', particularly since the sonnet has a rather odd conceit of being unable to see through a transparent object, the eye, in lines 3–4. There is also in this section of *Astrophel and Stella* a strange and very old-fashioned sonnet, no. 89, rhyming entirely on the words 'night' and 'day' – cf. Bottom's 'O night, which ever art when day is not'. His later line, 'Sweet Moon, I thank thee for thy sunny beams', which opens a sonnet quatrain of Sidney's favourite pattern, ABBA, is a very good take-off of Sidney's manner, but not sufficiently specific by itself to prove conscious parody. But the Duke's comment after Pyramus' death that 'she will finde him by starre-light./Here she comes, and her passion ends the play' seems to recall Nashe's marvellous line in the 1591 preface to *Astrophel and Stella* that it is 'a tragi-comedy of love . . . performed by starlight'.

17 'Prodnose', the nervous, finicky busybody acquaintance, was the invention of J. B. Morton in his 'Beachcomber' column in the *Daily Express*. Sidney seems to have been the first British writer to use an anonymous busybody dramatically. There are of course sonnet pairs, in which one poet replies to another, as in Sidney's reply to Edward Dyer, printed in his own 'Certain Sonnets' (*Poems of Sidney*, ed. Ringler, pp. 144–5); dialogue sonnets or sonnets answering a question that isn't there could be regarded as collapsed *tenzoni*. See Warkentin, op. cit., p. 24.

18 Discussed above, Ch. 4, pp. 47–9.

19 Alan Hager, 'The exemplary mirage', in Kay (ed.), op. cit., p. 56.

20 The *canzone* which Philisides sings in the 1593 edition of the *Arcadia*, 'The lad Philisides', is a ten-stanza poem on the theme of absence, in which the word appears several times. *AS* 60 ('When my good Angell guides me') plays with the idea that Sidney's presence makes Stella wish him absent and vice versa, concluding:

> Then some good body tell me how I do,
> Whose presence, absence, absence presence is:
> Blist in my curse, and cursed in my bliss.

The pun on 'good body' (obliging friend/entity possessing substance) shows Sidney alert to the metaphysics of the absence/presence paradox.

21 Quoted by J. E. Neale, *Queen Elizabeth I*, 1934, reprinted Harmondsworth, 1960, p. 361.

22 'Watch us, please, and give us your hearty applause.' Reprinted in G. Gregory Smith (ed.), *Elizabethan Critical Essays*, 2 vols, Oxford, 1904, vol. 2, p. 223.

23 *The Poems of Robert Sidney*, ed. P. J. Croft, Oxford, 1984, p. 175. The sonnet is quoted in the editor's modernised spelling and punctuation.

24 There were a number of sonnets beginning with 'Chi vuol veder' or its French equivalent, and the resemblance between Petrarch's sonnet and Sidney's is not so close that one must be adapted from the other. The sonnet which begins Ronsard's *Amours* of 1552, 'Qui voudra voir comme un Dieu me surmonte', has even less resemblance to Sidney's sonnet, but it does contain the sentence, 'Qui voudra voir un sujet de malheur/Me vienne lire' – cf. 'Let him but learne of Love to reade in thee . . .'. Sidney, like Shakespeare, seems to have assimilated motifs and themes without ever borrowing directly. For a short list of his attributions, see Janet G. Scott, *Les Sonnets élisabéthains*, Paris, 1929, pp. 303–7, and the notes to each sonnet in *Poems of Philip Sidney*, ed. Ringler. In the 1580s, Sidney's disinclination to translate or even adapt is remarkable.

25 George Puttenham, *The Arte of English Poesie*, 1589, ed. G. D. Willcock and A. Walker, Cambridge, 1936, pp. 154–5.

26 Smith, op. cit., vol. 2, p. 157.

8 THE ELIZABETHAN SONNET VOGUE AND SPENSER

1 George Gascoigne, *The Posies*, 1575, preface 'To the reverend Divines'.

2 *Ben Jonson*, ed. C. H. Herford and P. Simpson, Oxford, 1927, vol. 3, p. 228. The version of Matheo's speech in the 1616 Folio text is slightly different.

3 J. W. Lever, *The Elizabethan Love Sonnet*, London, 1956, reprinted London, 1968, p. 141.

4 Reprinted from *A Poetical Rhapsody*, 1602, by Norman Ault (ed.), *A Treasury of Unfamiliar Lyrics*, London, 1938, p. 92.

5 Edmund Spenser, 'Colin Clouts Come Home Again' (1595, written 1591), ll. 164–7. The poem is dedicated to and much concerned with Ralegh, but is also a longer allegory of Elizabethan court poetry and its operation. See the useful discussion of Ralegh in Gary Waller, *English Poetry of the Sixteenth Century*, London and New York, 1986, pp. 118–27. See also Leonard Tennenhouse, 'Sir Walter Ralegh and the literature of clientage', in G.F. Lytle and S. Orgel (eds), *Patronage in the Renaissance*, Princeton, NJ, 1981, pp. 235–58.

6 Quoted by Waller, op. cit., p. 125.

7 Perhaps because they were not separately printed as a sequence, Lok's sonnets have received very little attention. They appeared in 1597 as 'sundrie Sonets of Christian Passions' annexed to *Ecclesiastes . . . compendiously abridged and paraphrastically dilated in English Poesie*, with 'other affectionate Sonets'. There are 121 Christian sonnets, and sixty others, each one dedicated to a prominent man or woman. Lok is a dull writer, except in one respect; he has a fondness for very intricate and unusual rhymeschemes. His sonnets are reprinted in *Miscellanies of the Fuller Worthies Library*, ed. A. Grosart, 4 vols, Blackburn, 1871, vol. 2.

8 There is a distinction, though a fine one, to be drawn between Christian *contemptus mundi* and the topos of mutability: Spenser's line 'For all that moveth doth in *Change* delight' (*The Faerie Queene*, VII.viii.2) points to a difference of emphasis, whereby the *topos* involves the speaker in the processes of natural change, however melancholy his view of them may be; the Christian ascetic simply rejects the pleasures of the world as false, without becoming fascinated by their changeability.

9 *The Poems of Sir Walter Ralegh*, ed. Agnes Latham, London, 1929, p. 36.

10 *Elizabethan Sonnets*, ed. Lee, I, p. 139. Sonnets 1–7 of this sequence form a continuous Anacreontic narrative poem.

11 I suggest *AS* 8, 9, 11, 12, 13, 16, 17, 19, 20, 43, 46, 49, 53 and 73; the extent to which the Anacreontic discourse dominates is of course arguable, and *AS* 14, 31, 35, 52, 54, 72 and 79, 80 and 81 (the 'kiss' sequence) might also be included.

12 Sidney Lee (ed.), *Elizabethan Sonnets*, 2 vols, London, 1904, vol. 2, pp. 41, 43.

13 The sonnets composed by the courtiers of the King of Navarre in *Love's Labour's Lost*, Act IV, sc.iii, are meant to be both fashionable and silly: without being wildly ridiculous, they parody the mannerisms of contemporary sonnet-writing. One of them, Longueville's 'Did not the heavenly Rhetoricke of thine eye . . .' was reprinted (with minor variations) in William Jaggard's anthology *The Passionate Pilgrim*, 1599, along with Shakespeare's sonnets 138 and 144 – obviously taken quite seriously.

14 The manuscript of Sir John Davies's 'Gullinge Sonnets' is reproduced in H. M. Klein (ed.), *English and Scottish Sonnet Sequences of the Renaissance*, 2 vols, Hildesheim, 1984, vol. 2, pp. 271–84. The standard edition of the poems is *The Poems of Sir John Davies*, ed. Robert Krueger, Oxford, 1975; the text of the dedicatory sonnet is taken from this.

15 A number of these lectures appear in the four–volume collection of Italian Renaissance criticism by Bernard Weinberg (ed.), *Trattati di poetica e rettorica del Cinquecento*, Bari, 1970–4. Their content varies, from offering general observations on poetry and the sonnet to minute practical criticism of particular sonnets.

16 Daniel's *Defence* is printed in G. Gregory Smith (ed.), *Elizabethan Critical*

Essays, 2 vols, Oxford, 1904, vol. 2, pp. 356–84. My quotations are taken from this edition. A useful anthology of Daniel's work, containing the 1592 version of *Delia* and his *Defence* is *Poems and A Defence of Ryme*, ed. A. C. Sprague, University of Chicago Press, 1930, repr. Phoenix Books, 1965. A facsimile of the 1601 edition of *Delia* is printed at the end of Lars-Hakan Svensson's detailed sonnet-by-sonnet study of the sequence, *Silent Art: Rhetorical and Thematic Patterns in Samuel Daniel's 'Delia'*, Lund Studies in English 57, 1980.

17 Daniel, *Defence*, in Smith, op. cit., p. 358.

18 Ibid., pp. 365–6.

19 Cristoforo Landino, *Dante . . . con l'espositioni di Christoforo Landino et d'Alessandro Velutello*, Venice, 1578, p. 2, quoted by Nesca Robb, *Neoplatonism of the Italian Renaissance*, London, 1935, p. 223.

20 In Ben Jonson's *Conversations* with Drummond of Hawthornden (not fully printed until 1842), Jonson apparently 'cursed Petrarch for redacting [reducing] verses to sonnets; which he said were like that Tirrant's bed, where some who were too short were racked, others too long cut short'. (Quoted in *The Poetical Works of William Drummond of Hawthornden*, ed. L. E. Kastner, 2 vols, Manchester, 1913, vol. 1, p. xxxi.)

21 Sonnet numbers refer to the 1601 edition of *Delia*, available in facsimile in Lars-Hakan Svensson's study (see n. 16 above).

22 Michael Drayton, *Idea* (1599), Sonnet 31, ll. 9–10.

23 *Twelfth Night*, Act I, Scene iv.

24 'Voi ch'ascoltate in rime sparse il suono/Di quei sospiri . . .' ('You who hear in the scattered poems the sound/of those sighs . . .') ignores the written status of the text, but Petrarch's manuscript activity indicates that he knew his poems would be read.

25 The text of *Idea* is a challenge to editors, because of the many alterations and additions that Drayton made to his sequence in his long life. My text is from the early but very clear and useful selection of *Minor Poems of Michael Drayton*, ed. Cyril Brett, Oxford, 1907, which prints the whole of *Ideas Mirrour* of 1594, followed by all the additional sonnets up to 1619, with the numbers they had in the editions in which they were introduced. For a more thorough account of the variations, see the checklist in vol. 5 of *The Works of Michael Drayton*, ed. J. W. Hebel, K. Tillotson and B. H. Newdigate, 5 vols, Oxford, 1931–41.

26 Since Drayton was proud both of his variety and his originality, it is tempting to try to catch him in mimicry. Readers will hear different voices, but I might suggest the following as echoic sonnets:

'Stay, stay, sweet Time' (*Ideas Mirrour*, Amour 7): Daniel
'Oft taking pen in hand' (*Ideas Mirrour*, Amour 10): 'Zepheria'
'Cleere *Ankor*, on whose silver-sanded shore' (*Ideas Mirrour*, Amour 13): Lodge
'Some wits there be' (*Ideas Mirrour*, Amour 28): Sidney
'Truce, gentle love' (*Idea*, 1599, Sonnet 55): Spenser
'An evill spirit' (*Idea*, Sonnet 22): Shakespeare

27 For the very complicated matter of the emergence of the sense of an interior self in the Renaissance, see particularly the first chapter of Anne Ferry, *The 'Inward' Language*, Chicago, Ill., 1983; and also Stephen Greenblatt, *Renaissance Self-Fashioning*, Chicago, Ill., 1980.

28 My texts are from *Spenser's Minor Poems*, ed. E. de Selincourt, Oxford, 1910, reprinted 1966. In marked contrast to the splendid Oxford edition of Sidney's poems by Ringler, de Selincourt's text is very niggardly with infor-

mation, both biographical and textual. Spenser married Elizabeth Boyle of Kilcoran on 11 June 1594, and the *Amoretti* with *Epithalamion* were published in 1595 by William Ponsonby while Spenser was not in London to oversee the printing. There are some pretty clear blunders, such as the repetition of one entire sonnet (xxxv, repeated as lxxxiii), and an intrusive title 'By her that is most assured to herselfe' for lviii; the punctuation is very rigid, and sometimes makes nonsense of the meaning. If Spenser did not oversee the printing, then we cannot know that the order of the sonnets is his, nor the apparent pairings that occur. Spenser had marked the order in various ways, which were noticed, but critical judgements based on placings of single sonnets must be treated with care.

Since we do not know for certain that Spenser was born in 1552, the usually assigned year, the statement in Sonnet lx that forty years of his life were past does not help us to date the *Amoretti*; but it seems most probable that they were written between 1591 and 1593, prior to his marriage in 1594. Since one sonnet (viii) has a quite different rhymescheme from the others, it is probably earlier, and it is quite possible that some sonnets which appear to be directed to Elizabeth Boyle may originally have been written to someone else – or to no one in particular. However, the opening sonnet clearly envisages a sequence, and what Ponsonby publishes must have been intended by Spenser to form one, even if not in exactly the order of the 1595 text (there appears to be no good reason for the placing of the five Anacreontic poems between *Amoretti* and *Epithalamion*).

29 Strictly, 88, since one sonnet is printed twice (see note above).

30 Sonnet lxxx refers to his having compiled six books of *The Faerie Queene* – which of course does not mean that any other sonnet was written after Book VI.

31 Daniel, *Delia*, 1601, Sonnet 52:

> Let others sing of Knights and Palladines
> In aged accents, and untimely words:
> Paint shadowes in imaginarie lines,
> Which wel the reach of their high wits records. . . .

Lars-Hakan Svensson, in *Silent Art* (see n. 16 above), in discussing this sonnet, points out that the formula 'Let others sing of war; I shall sing of love' is used in other Renaissance sonnets and in classical poetry; but the reference to '*aged* accents and *untimely* words' in 1592 (when this sonnet first appeared) must have brought to mind the archaisms of lexis and pronunciation in Spenser's *Faerie Queene*, the first three books of which had appeared in 1590.

32 'As to that which *Spencer* calleth his *Amorelli* [sic], I am not of their Opinion, who call them his; for they are so childish, that it were not well to give them so honourable a father' (*The Works of William Drummond of Hawthornden*, ed. Thomas Ruddiman and John Sage, Edinburgh, 1711, 'Character of Several Authors').

33 'But, despite all his metrical versatility and his genuine poetic force, the greater part of Spenser's sonneteering efforts abound, like those of his contemporaries, in strained conceits, which are often silently borrowed from foreign literature without radical change of diction' (Lee, *Elizabethan Sonnets*, vol. 1, p. xciv).

34 Lever, op. cit., p. 137.

35 Books IV–VI of *The Faerie Queene*, with a second edition of Books I–III, were published in 1596.

36 The sonnets in which these terms occur are *Rime* 1, 293 and 247.

37 The belief that a widowed dove betook itself to a leafless tree to mourn for its mate supplied an emblem of fidelity to the Renaissance: cf. Paulina's remark in *The Winter's Tale*, after the death of her husband, that

> I (an old Turtle)
> Will wing me to some wither'd bough, and there
> My Mate (that's never to be found againe)
> Lament, till I am lost. (V.iii)

Spenser does not of course say, nor even imply, that his mate is *dead*.

9 'THEE (MY SELFE)': THE SONNETS OF SHAKESPEARE

1 The 1609 Quarto of the *Sonnets* is reproduced (without 'A Lover's Complaint'), page by page facing the modern edited text, in Stephen Booth's edition: *Shakespeare's Sonnets*, New Haven, Conn., 1977. The texts of Sonnets 138 and 144 in *The Passionate Pilgrim* are slightly different from those in Q, and are reproduced in Booth's notes to the respective sonnets.

2 The number of editions of the sonnets is very large, and the critical literature intimidatingly so. Stephen Booth's edition, referred to above, is an interpreter's delight, offering 400 pages of notes containing almost every conceivable (and not a few inconceivable) readings of the text; for general use, *Shakespeare's Sonnets*, ed. W. G. Ingram and T. Redpath. London, 1964, revised 1978, is plainly printed, with judicious notes on facing pages for each sonnet, which help interpretation without inflicting overall theories on the reader. A more portable and recent edition is the New Penguin Shakespeare, edited by John Kerrigan, *The Sonnets and A Lover's Complaint*, Harmondsworth, 1986; this edition has a deeply learned but freshly written introduction setting the poetry in the context of the poetry of the age, and interestingly has an appendix giving sonnets which are variants of, or connected with, the sonnets of Q. The scholar's variorum edition is *A New Variorum Edition of Shakespeare: The Sonnets*, ed. H. E. Rollins, 2 vols, Philadelphia, Pa, 1944. The reader should note that any edition which modernises punctuation and/or spelling will by doing so have introduced silent interpretations into the text.

For biographical and related matters, a very useful compendium of what has been suggested over the years by scholars and critics is Hugh Calvert, *Shakespeare's Sonnets and Problems of Autobiography*, Merlin Books, Devon, 1987. This is written in a rather abrupt and ill-organised way, but has helpful tables and lists. A more even-paced survey, with concentration upon metrical questions, is Paul Ramsey, *The Fickle Glass*, New York, 1979. Ramsey's bibliography is excellent, and divided into convenient sections. The most intense examination of the subjectivity created in the sonnets is Joel Fineman, *Shakespeare's Perjured Eye*, Los Angeles, Calif., 1986.

3 Since the main speaker of 'A Lover's Complaint', though female, seems to be ravaged by age and sorrow, and has been betrayed by a well-born youth, the parallel is obvious. John Kerrigan points out in the introduction to his edition (see above, n. 2) that Samuel Daniel's *Delia* of 1592 seems to have begun a sub-genre of sonnet sequences in which the sonnets were followed by other lyrics and a long poem (Kerrigan, p. 13); Spenser's *Amoretti* is one example. However, the passionate erotic complaint, with or without a narrative component, was a popular genre on its own, deriving from Ovid's *Heroides*, and Shakespeare had himself written two examples, in *Venus and Adonis* and *The Rape of Lucrece*. Shakespeare's contemporaries would read these and sonnets

as 'passionate' or Ovidian poetry (see n. 7 below) without necessarily supposing a narrative connection.

4 See Chapter 7, p. 107 and note.

5 If the sonnets do form a sequence – or if at least 1–126 do – then 126 may be what it is because it was intended as the last poem of the set addressed to the young man. If so, the printer did not know this. And if 'A Lover's Complaint' was supposed to be separated from the sonnets by some lyrics different in form or tone, then 153 and 154, which do this admirably, should have been accompanied by 145 and (possibly) 146.

6 The topic of family succession is quite proper in praise poetry; but a sequence explicitly urging someone to beget a child is, as far as I know, unique.

7 'As the soule of Euphorbus was thought to live in Pythagoras: so the sweet wittie soule of Ovid lives in mellifluous and hony-tongued Shakespeare, witnes his *Venus and Adonis*, his *Lucrece*, his sugred *Sonnets* among his private friends' (Francis Meres, *Palladis Tamia*, 1598, printed in G. Gregory Smith (ed.), *Elizabethan Critical Essays*, 2 vols, Oxford, 1904, vol. 2, p. 317). This does suggest that by 1598 Shakespeare had a reputation for erotic verse, and, since Meres prints the word 'sonnets' in italics, that his sonnets were circulating as a collection.

8 In this chapter, I have reproduced the text of Q; since I have much to say about the ambiguities of Shakespeare's verse, there seems no point in using a modernised text which will have already ironed out some of them. I have, however, used 'j' for 'i' and 'v' for 'u' where appropriate; and if Q produces a reading which seems likely to confuse the reader completely I have altered it and set the Q-version immediately alongside. Obviously the Q-printers, in punctuating the copy, had to make decisions about meaning, but it is surprising how seldom what they do is plainly wrong – and even then the error sometimes suggests an interesting train of thought. Since the printers simply put an arabic numeral above each sonnet, it is convenient to refer to sonnet and line thus: (123.4–5).

9 See Calvert, op. cit., sections II–IV.

10 Number 145 is one of the many Elizabethan lyrics that delights in twisting the meaning of phrasing (cf. Sidney's *AS* 63, 'O Grammer rules, o now your vertues show'). We have lost the taste for this, and think it childish. It is certainly light verse, and in tetrameters; it is not likely to have been a song, but it could well have been written for a play, like the silly poem about 'The prayfull Princesse' in *Love's Labour's Lost*. The sonnet immediately after this, 146, is 'Poore soule the center of my sinfull earth', the only unambiguously spiritual sonnet in the collection, which might suggest that at this point in the manuscript the sonnets had become miscellaneous.

11
> You to whom love was peace, that now is rage,
> Who did the whole worlds soule contract, and drove
> Into the glasses of your eyes
> (So made such mirrors, and such spies,
> That they did all to you epitomize,)
> Countries, Townes, Courts. . . .
>
> (Donne, 'The Canonization', ll. 39–44)

The idea of lovers 'looking babies' – seeing each in miniature in the other's eyes – was a familiar love conceit. It is of course only in someone else's eye that one can see oneself; hence being contracted [in]to one's own eye would suggest a bizarre kind of self-regard.

12 See Anne Ferry, *The 'Inward' Language*, Chicago, Ill., 1983, ch. 4, 'Shakespeare

and Sidney', for a close analysis of the parallels between the two sonneteers.

13 Rosalie Colie, *Shakespeare's Living Art*, Princeton, NJ, 1974, p. 72.

14 After this, the lovers embark on a new quatrain, which no doubt we are to think would have developed into another sonnet, had the Nurse not interrupted. An early instance of Shakespeare's interest in paired sonnets?

15 Castiglione, *The Book of the Courtier* (1528), trans. Sir Thomas Hoby (1561), Everyman's Library, London, 1966, p. 130.

16 Denis Mitchell (1911–90) quoted by Sir Denis Forman, British Independent Television, Channel 4, 6 December 1990.

17 Shakespeare's metrics in the *Sonnets* are reviewed in Ramsey, op. cit., pp. 65–98.

18 Here Q's punctuation at 74.1 is suggestive: if there is no pause after 'But be contented', the lines mean 'But when I die, accept it equably; my life survives in this poetry'. If there is a pause, as many editors determine by putting a colon after 'But be contented', the phrase assumes a much more absolute sense – 'Content you' or 'Be contented' meant 'Calm down', 'Cool it!' The implication would then be that 73 describes, and 74 tries to counteract, the emotional agitation of the young man *now* as the speaker hypothesises it ('thou maist behold'). The whole twenty-eight lines become much more highly charged and immediate; without the pause, they are philosophical and elegiac.

19 Horace, *Odes*, Liber III. 'Carpe diem' is the tag taken from the poem 'Tu ne quaesieris' in Liber I.

20 Q's brackets at 'Tis thee (my selfe)' raise a problem: Q does not often bracket words or phrases, but it is clear that the brackets can indicate a suddenly inserted term of address, as at 89.4: 'Thou canst not (love) disgrace me halfe so ill'. But the same sonnet has them marking an appositive phrase: 'Lest I (too much prophane) should do it wronge'. The reader has a choice: is 'my selfe' a sudden interruption addressed to the beloved, or is it a word describing 'thee'? The effect is to riddle the pronouns in the final couplet, which Shakespeare is very prone to do.

10 THE SEVENTEENTH CENTURY: HERBERT, DRUMMOND AND MILTON

1 Just on the border between the sonnet sequence and the flourish of dedications is a strange *corona*-sequence by Joshua Sylvester (1563–1618) which appears as dedication poetry in his translation of Du Bartas' *Divine Weekes and Workes*, 1605. There are eleven sonnets, the first of which has an extra couplet; the remainder are linked in proper *corona* fashion. They are addressed to King James, and are remarkable – indeed unique – in being shaped sonnets, printed to resemble columns on the page. Herbert, it will be recalled, flirted with this fashion in 'Easter Wings' and other lyrics in *The Temple*; but no sonnets of his are so laid out. Sylvester's strange sequence was first noticed by J. L. Potter, 'Sylvester's shaped sonnets', *Notes and Queries*, September 1957, pp. 405–6.

2 The standard collection of madrigal and lute-song books is E. H. Fellowes (ed.), *English Madrigal Verse, 1588–1632*, Oxford, 1920. His division of the book into two sections, madrigalists and lute-song writers, each with its own contents and index, recognises the existence of two distinct musical forms, at the price of forcing the inquirer to look up everything twice; but those who published both kinds were naturally anxious for sales as wide as possible, and the

prefatory material often assures the purchaser that the musical contents can be handled by any conceivable grouping of voices or instruments.

3 Herbert's texts are taken from the excellent edition by F. E. Hutchinson: *The Works of George Herbert*, Oxford, 1941, reprinted 1978. The double sonnet, first printed in Izaak Walton's 'Life of Herbert' in *Lives of Donne, Herbert, Hooker and Sanderson*, 1670, is on p. 206.

4 *Works of Herbert*, ed. Hutchinson, p. xxii. Donne's 'La Corona' sequence probably dates from 1607; his 'Holy Sonnets' from after the death of his wife, in 1617; and they did not appear in print until the publication of *Poems by J.D., with Elegies on the Authors Death* in 1633. Even so, seven of the 'Holy Sonnets' (those now numbered I, III, V, VIII, XVII, XVIII and XIX) remained in manuscript.

5 The text is from the 1633 *Poems* – corrections as noted.

6 Forse vuol Dio tal di vertute amica
torre a la terra e 'n ciel farne una stella,
anzi un sole.

[Perhaps God wants to take so great a friend of virtue
away from earth and make her a star in heaven,
or rather, a sun.]

(*Rime* 254, ll. 7–9)

7 These three openings – many more could be found – are of sonnets by Milton, Wordsworth and John Addington Symonds (1840–93); this last, on the principle that what very minor poets do is more likely to be representative of taste than what geniuses do.

8 Herbert mixed his sonnets in with his other lyrics in *The Temple*, apart from the two sonnets to his mother (1670). In alphabetical order of title, with the page numbers in Hutchinson's edition, they are:

'Avarice' (77)
'Christmas' (80) (two poems, only the first of which is a sonnet)
'Holy Baptisme I' (43)
'Joseph's Coat' (159)
'Love I and II' (54) (two paired sonnets)
'Prayer' (51)
'Redemption' (40)
'Sinne' (45)
'The Answer' (169)
'The Holdfast' (143)
'The H. Scriptures' (58) (two sonnets, not obviously paired)
'The Sinner' (38)
'The Sonne' (167), and
Two sonnets sent to his mother, New Year 1609/10 (206)

9 *Works of Herbert*, ed. Hutchinson, p. 169.

10 Not all the sonnets of each: see n. 3 and n. 4 above.

11 John Hughes, who edited Spenser's *Works* in 1715, refers in his 'Remarks on the Shepherd's Calendar, etc.' to 'the *Sonnets*, a Species of Poetry so entirely disus'd, that it seems to be scarce known among us at this time'. '*Milton* hath writ some, both in *Italian* and *English*, and is, I think, the last who has given us any Example of them in our own Language.' Reprinted in R. M. Cummings (ed.), *Spenser: The Critical Heritage*, London, 1971, p. 276.

12 The standard edition of Drummond's poems is still the meticulous and very informative two-volume edition by L. E. Kastner: *The Poetical Works of William*

Drummond of Hawthornden, Manchester, 1913. Kastner researched the terrifyingly complicated bibliography of Drummond's works (he was given to making up preliminary issues of his books to pass to friends, and then changing his mind about the contents), and put all future scholars in his debt by turning up a very large number of the sources which Drummond drew upon – these are given in the notes. There is a very readable biography by David Masson, *Drummond of Hawthornden*, London, 1873, a heavily Romantic critical account by French Rowe Fogle, *A Critical Study of William Drummond of Hawthornden*, New York, 1952, and a useful setting of Drummond in the Scottish Italianate tradition in Ian Jack, *The Italian Influence on Scottish Literature*, Edinburgh, 1972, pp. 113–44. I have taken my quotations from Kastner's edition, cited as Kastner I.123.

13 He wrote two poems to her (Kastner II.271 and 277), and the second of these says that her

> spacious thoughts with choice inventions free,
> Show passiones power, affectiones severall straines. . . . (ll. 5–6)

'Spacious thoughts' might well refer to the prose romance *Urania* in Lady Mary's 1620 volume; 'choice inventions' sounds like a reference to poems. But we cannot be sure. Lady Mary's poems have been edited by Josephine A. Roberts, *The Poems of Lady Mary Wroth*, Baton Rouge, La, 1983. They were written in the second decade of the century, and are a close imitation of Sir Philip Sidney's sonnet sequence, in tone, conceits and approach. Like her uncle, she invents an *alter ego*, Pamphilia, who stands to her both in the prose romance and in the sonnet sequence much as Philisides to Sir Philip Sidney; but, despite the female voice, one notes what one notes in the sonnets of Gaspara Stampa and her female poet colleagues in Italy in the previous century: unless there is a specific marker of sex inserted, the Petrarchan mode is the mode of interior desire, and is not gender-specific. Her competence is at times low – she has no idea how to write a *corona*-sequence, for example – and she is addicted to enjambment, almost to the point of mannerism. But her voice moves rapidly, without involving elaborate conceits or metaphors in her sonnets, and at her best she can achieve the kind of decisive self-assured terseness that Herbert commands. A very short account, with a selection of her verse, is by Margaret Hannay in Katherina M. Wilson (ed.), *Women Writers of the Renaissance*, Athens, Ga, 1987, pp. 548–65; the same anthology also contains essays on and translated selections from Gaspara Stampa, Vittoria Colonna and Veronica Gambara. A longer essay on Lady Mary is by Elaine Beilin, *Redeeming Eve*, Princeton, NJ, 1987, pp. 208–43.

14 However, see my own suggestion (below, p. 196) that a line in Milton's 'Methought I saw my late espoused saint' echoes a line of Drummond's in the Second Part of his 1616 *Poems* (Kastner I.64)

15 'The Author's Life', in *The Works of William Drummond of Hawthornden*, ed. Thomas Ruddiman and John Sage, Edinburgh, 1711, p. v.

16 The remark is Gabriel Harvey's, quoted by Frank Whigham, *Ambition and Privilege*, Los Angeles, Calif., 1984, p. 26.

17 R. H. MacDonald, 'Drummond, Miss Euphemia Kyninghame and the poems', *Modern Language Review*, vol. 60, 1965, pp. 494–9.

18 Drummond was one of the very few sonneteers not to number his sonnets: the numbers are inserted by Kastner. See Kastner, I.22.

19 For a good account of Marino, see James V. Mirollo, *The Poet of the Marvelous*, New York, 1963.

20 Kastner II.214.

21 Milton is not in the least interested here in the self-expressive power of poetry, but in the learning of the decorums of poetry, as much through the study of poetics as through the writing of verse; so far from being a Romantic view of poetry, this section, with its complete neglect of vernacular verse, seems considerably more old-fashioned than Bembo's views of poetry in the previous century:

> And now, lastly, will be the time to read with them those organic arts, which enable men to discourse and write perspicuously, elegantly, and according to the fittest style, of lofty, mean or lowly. Logic, therefore, so much as is useful, is to be referred to this due place with all her well-couched heads and topics, until it be time to open her contracted palm into a graceful and ornate rhetoric, taught out of the rule of Plato, Aristotle, Phalereus, Cicero, Hermogenes, Longinus. To which poetry would be made subsequent, or indeed rather precedent, as being less subtile and fine, but more simple, sensuous and passionate. I mean not here the prosody of a verse, which they could not but have hit on before among the rudiments of grammar; but that sublime art which in Aristotle's poetics, in Horace, and the Italian commentaries of Castelvetro, Tasso, Mazzoni and others, teaches what the laws are of a true epic poem, what of a dramatic, what of a lyric, what decorum is, which is the grand masterpiece to observe.
> (*Prose Works of John Milton*, ed. J. A. St John, 5 vols, London, 1864, vol. 3, pp. 473–4)

22 'On the New Forcers of Conscience under the Long Parliament': this is a sonnet with two tails, rhyming ABBA ABBA CDE DECc$_6$FFf$_6$GG. It is a satirical sonnet, for which purpose the tailed form was often used by Italian poets.

23 The dating of the sonnets is reviewed by E. A. J. Honigmann, *Milton's Sonnets*, London and New York, 1966. For the most particular details, see the definitive biography of Milton: William Riley Parker's *Milton: A Biography*, 2 vols, Oxford, 1968.

24 The woody valley of the Reno, referred to in the sonnet (l. 2) is in the region of Italy known as Emilia, and the 'noble ford' may be either the ford of the Rubicon in that region or the point where the Via Aemilia crosses the Reno. The honour of discovering this concealed name belongs to J. S. Smart, *The Sonnets of Milton*, Glasgow, 1921.

25 The text of this and of all the sonnets quoted in this chapter is taken from *Milton's Poetical Works*, ed. Helen Darbishire, 3 vols, Oxford, 1955, vol. 2, pp. 146–57. Darbishire's text, with corrections, is taken from the sonnets as printed in the two editions of Milton's lifetime, his *Poems* of 1645, which contains ten sonnets, and his *Poems, etc. upon Several Occasions* of 1673, which adds ten more; four further sonnets were published in 1694, but badly, and Darbishire's text of these comes from the Trinity Manuscript of Milton's poems. The roman numbers following the sonnets quoted are hers, based on Milton's own numbering, which did not, however, extend to the four sonnets of 1694. On this topic, see Honigmann, op. cit., pp. 59–75.

26 Maurice Kelley, 'Milton's Dante–Della Casa–Varchi volume', *Bulletin of the New York Public Library*, vol. 66, 1962, pp. 499–504.

27 Daniele Ponchiroli and Guido Bonino (eds), *Lirici del Cinquecento*, Turin, 1958, revised 1968, p. 311.

28 The remark is Tasso's: 'Non v'è quasi verso che non passi l'uno nell'altro, il qual rompimento de' versi, come da tutti i maestri è insegnato, apporta grandissima gravità: e la ragione è che il rompimento de' versi ritiene il corso

pell' orazione ed è cagione di tardità, e la tardità è propria della gravità' (quoted in ibid., p. 311).

29 Ibid., p. 371.

30 See above, Ch. 2, p. 19.

31 The title is Milton's own, in his own handwriting in the Trinity Manuscript.

32 Entitled (by an amanuensis) in the Trinity Manuscript, 'To the Lord Generall Cromwell May 1652 On the proposalls of certaine ministers at the Committee for Propagation of the Gospell'.

33 Catherine or Katherine Woodcock died in February 1658. It has been suggested that the sonnet refers to his first wife, Mary Powell, who died in 1652; against that, as Helen Darbishire points out in *Milton's Poetical Works*, II.327, is the fact that it appears last of all the regular sonnets in the 1673 volume, immediately after a sonnet written in 1655, in an order which Milton intended to be chronological.

34 The sequence of ideas – a woman in the care of a superior power, her purification from taint, the transfer of love from earth to heaven, and the veiling/rejection of outward charms – occurs in both sonnets. But Drummond's limpid linearity seems merely pleasing alongside Milton's subtle and moving mimesis of sexual and familial longing:

> Sith it hath pleas'd that First and *onlie Faire*
> To take that Beautie to himselfe againe,
> Which in *this World of Sense* not to remaine,
> But to amaze, was sent, and home repaire,
> The Love which to that Beautie I did beare,
> (Made pure of mortall Spots which did it staine,
> And endlesse, which even *Death* cannot impaire)
> I place in him who will it not disdaine.
> No shining eyes, no Lockes of curling Gold,
> No blushing Roses on a Virgine Face,
> No outward Show, no, nor no inward Grace,
> Shall Force hereafter have my Thoughts to hold:
> Love heere on earth hudge Stormes of Care doe tosse,
> But plac'd above, exempted is from Losse.
>
> (Kastner, II.64)

BIBLIOGRAPHY

This selected bibliography includes the works referred to in the text indexed by surname of the author: Giacomo da Lentino, for example, is indexed under Lentino. Where possible I have drawn Italian examples from readily available anthologies; British examples are taken from modern critical texts. Some minor sonneteers have not had a modern reprint; I have used two useful collections: that of Holger Klein (*see under* Klein) which reproduces in facsimile; and the older collection by Sidney Lee (*see under* Lee) which though not produced to modern critical standards still makes available minor poets not otherwise printed. The major modern bibliography of the British sonnet (to 1982) is by Herbert S. Donow (*see under* Donow).

Ahern, John Joseph, 'The new life of the book: oral and written communication in the age of Dante', PhD thesis, Indiana University, 1976, Ann Arbor University Microfilms, Ann Arbor, Mich., 1979.

Alabaster, William, *The Sonnets of William Alabaster*, ed. G. M. Story and Helen Gardner, Oxford, 1959.

Alexander, Sir William, *Aurora*, 1604: *see* Klein, Holger M.

——, *The Poetical Works of Sir William Alexander, Earl of Stirling*, ed. L. E. Kastner and H. B. Charlton, 3 vols, Scottish Text Society, Edinburgh and London, 1929.

Alighieri, Dante, *De Vulgari Eloquentia*. *See* Purcell, Sally.

——, *Literary Criticism of Dante Alighieri*, ed. Robert S. Haller, Lincoln, Neb., 1973.

——, *Dante: Vita Nuova*, ed. Domenico de Robertis, Milan and Naples, 1980. *See also under* Musa, Mark.

——, *Dante Alighieri: Vita Nuova, Rime*, ed. F. Chapelli, Milan, 1965.

Angiolieri, Cecco, *Le rime di Cecco Angiolieri*, ed. G. Cavalli, Milan, 1959.

Arezzo, Guittone d', *Le rime di Guittone d'Arezzo*, ed. F. Egidi, Bari, 1940.

Ault, Norman (ed.), *A Treasury of Unfamiliar Lyrics*, London, 1938.

Baldi, Agnello, *Guittone d'Arezzo: fra impegno e poesia*, Salerno, 1975.

Barnefeilde, Richard, *Cynthia*, 1595. *See* Klein, Holger M.

Barnes, Barnabe, *Parthenophil and Parthenope*, ed. V. A. Doyno, Carbondale, Ill., 1971.

Beccadelli, Ludovico, *Vita del Petrarca*, 1569–71. *See* Frasso, G.

Beilin, Elaine, *Redeeming Eve*, Princeton, NJ, 1987.

Bellay, Joachim du, *Défense et illustration de la langue française*, 1549.

Bembo, Pietro, *Pietro Bembo: Prose della volgar lingua, Gli Asolani, rime*, ed. Carlo Dionisotti, Turin, 1989.

Biadene, Leandro, *Morfologia del Sonetto*, 1888, reprinted Florence, 1977.

Bishop, Morris, *Petrarch and His World*, Bloomington, Ind., 1963.
Boitani, Pietro (ed.), *Chaucer and the Italian Trecento*, Cambridge, 1983.
Boyde, Patrick, *Dante's Style in His Lyric Poetry*, Cambridge, 1971.
Bullock, Walter L., 'The genesis of the English sonnet form', *PMLA*, vol. 38, 1923, pp. 729–44.
Calvert, Hugh, *Shakespeare's Sonnets and Problems of Autobiography*, Devon, 1987.
Castiglione, Baldassare, *Il Cortegiano*, 1528, trans. Sir Thomas Hoby, *The Booke of the Courtier*, 1561.
Catenazzi, F., *L'influsso dei Provenzali sui temi e immagini della poesia Siculo-Toscana*, Brescia, 1977.
Ceva, Bianca, *Brunetto Latini*, Milan, 1955.
Chamberlin, E. R., *The World of the Italian Renaissance*, London, 1982.
Chapman, George, *Poems*, ed. Phyllis Bartlett, New York, 1941, reprinted 1962.
Clausen, Anna M., *Le origini della poesia lirica in Provenza e in Italia*, Copenhagen, 1976.
Colie, Rosalie, *The Resources of Kind*, Los Angeles, Calif., 1973.
——, *Shakespeare's Living Art*, Princeton, NJ, 1974.
Collinson, Patrick, *The Elizabethan Puritan Movement*, London, 1967.
Constable, Henry, *The Poems*, ed. Joan Grundy, Liverpool, 1960.
Crosland, T. W., *The English Sonnet*, New York, 1917.
Cummings, R. M. (ed.), *Spenser: The Critical Heritage*, London, 1971.
Daniel, Samuel, *Poems and A Defence of Ryme*, ed. A. C. Sprague, Chicago, Ill., 1930, reprinted 1965.
Darst, David H., *Juan Boscán*, Boston, Mass., 1978.
Davanzati, Chiaro, *Rime*, ed. A. Menichetti, Bologna, 1965.
Davies, Sir John, *The Poems of Sir John Davies*, ed. Robert Krueger, Oxford, 1975.
Davies of Hereford, John, *Wittes Pilgrimage* [1605?]: *see* Klein, Holger M.
Della Casa, Giovanni, *Rime*, ed. Adriano Seroni, Florence, 1944.
Donne, John, *The Divine Poems*, ed. Helen Gardner, Oxford, 1952, reprinted 1978.
Donow, Herbert S., *The Sonnet in England and America: A Bibliography of Criticism*, Westport, Conn., 1982.
Drayton, Michael, *Minor Poems of Michael Drayton*, ed. Cyril Brett, Oxford, 1907.
——, *The Works of Michael Drayton*, ed. J. W. Hebel, K. Tillotson and B. H. Newdigate, 5 vols, Oxford, 1931–41.
Dronke, Peter, *Mediaeval Latin and the Rise of the European Love Lyric*, 2 vols, Oxford, 1968.
Drummond of Hawthornden, William, *Poems by That Most Famous Wit, William Drummond of Hawthornden*, ed. Edward Phillips, London, 1656.
——, *The Poetical Works of William Drummond of Hawthornden*, ed. L. E. Kastner, 2 vols, Manchester, 1913.
——, *The Works of William Drummond of Hawthornden*, ed. Thomas Ruddiman and John Sage, Edinburgh, 1711.
Dubrow, Heather, *Shakespeare's Captive Victors*, New York, 1987.
Ducrot, O. and Todorov, T., *Encyclopedic Dictionary of the Sciences of Language*, Oxford, 1981.
E.C., *Emaricdulfe*, 1595. *See* Klein, Holger M.
Elbaz, Robert, *The Changing Nature of the Self*, London, 1988.
Fellowes, E. H. (ed.), *English Madrigal Verse, 1588–1632*, Oxford, 1920.
Felperin, Howard, *Beyond Deconstruction*, Oxford, 1985.
Ferry, Anne, *The 'Inward' Language*, Chicago, Ill., 1983.
Fineman, Joel, *Shakespeare's Perjured Eye*, Los Angeles, Calif., 1986.
Fletcher, Giles (the elder), *The English Works of Giles Fletcher*, ed. L. E. Berry,

Madison, Wis., 1964.
Fogle, French Rowe, *A Critical Study of William Drummond of Hawthornden*, New York, 1952.
Forster, Leonard, *The Icy Fire*, Cambridge, 1969.
Foster, Kenelm, *Petrarch: Poet and Humanist*, Edinburgh, 1984.
Fowler, Alistair, *Kinds of Literature*, Oxford, 1982.
Fowler, William, *The Works of William Fowler*, ed. H. W. Meikle, 2 vols, Scottish Text Society, Edinburgh, 1914.
Frasso, G. (ed.), *Francesco Petrarca e Ludovico Beccadelli*, Studi sul Petrarca 13, Padua, 1983.
Fubini, Mario, *Metrica e poesia: del Duecento al Petrarca*, Milan, 1962.
Fucilla, Joseph, 'The present status of Petrarchan studies', in A. Scaglione (ed.), *Francis Petrarch, Six Centuries Later: A Symposium*, Chapel Hill, NC, 1975, pp. 48 ff.
Fuller, John, *The Sonnet*, London, 1972.
Getto, G. and Sanguinetti, E., *Il sonetto*, Milan, 1957.
Googe, Barnabe, *Eglogs, Epytaphes, and Sonettes*, 1563, ed. Edward Arber, English Reprints series, London, 1871.
Greenblatt, Stephen, *Renaissance Self-Fashioning*, Chicago, Ill., 1980.
Greene, Thomas M., *The Light in Troy: Imitation and Discovery in Renaissance Poetry*, New Haven, Conn., 1982.
Greville, Fulke, *Poems and Dramas of Fulke Greville*, ed. G. Bullough, 2 vols, Edinburgh, 1939, and New York, 1945.
Griffin, Bartholomew, *Fidessa, More Chaste than Kind*, 1596. *See* Lee, Sidney.
Guillen, Claudio, *Literature as System*, Princeton, NJ, 1971.
Habington, William, *Castara, 1634–1640*, ed. Edward Arber, English Reprints series, London, 1870.
Hager, Alan, 'The exemplary mirage', in Dennis Kay (ed.), *Sir Philip Sidney: An Anthology of Modern Criticism*, Oxford, 1987.
Harrier, Richard, *The Canon of Sir Thomas Wyatt's Poetry*, Cambridge, Mass., 1975.
Hathaway, Baxter, *The Age of Criticism: The Late Renaissance in Italy*, New York, 1962.
Herbert, George, *The Works of George Herbert*, ed. F. E. Hutchinson, Oxford, 1941, reprinted 1978.
Hill, R. T. and Bergin, T. G. (eds), *Anthology of the Provençal Troubadours*, 2nd edn, New Haven, Conn., 1973.
Honigmann, E. A. J., *Milton's Sonnets*, London and New York, 1966.
Houston, John, *The Rhetoric of Poetry in the Renaissance and Seventeenth Century*, Baton Rouge, La, 1983.
Jack, Ian, *The Italian Influence on Scottish Literature*, Edinburgh, 1972.
Jacoff, Rachel, 'The poetry of Guido Cavalcanti', PhD thesis, Yale University, 1977, Ann Arbor University Microfilms, Ann Arbor, Mich., 1980.
James VI (of Scotland), *The Essayes of a Prentise, in the Divine Art of Poesie*, 1585, ed. Edward Arber, English Reprints series, London, 1869.
——, *The Poems of James VI of Scotland*, ed. J. Craigie, 2 vols, Scottish Text Society, Edinburgh and London, 1955–8.
Javitch, Daniel, *Poetry and Courtliness in Renaissance England*, Princeton, NJ, 1978.
John, Lisle Cecil, *The Elizabethan Sonnet Sequences*, New York, 1938.
Kay, Dennis (ed.), *Sir Philip Sidney: An Anthology of Modern Criticism*, Oxford, 1987.
Kelley, Maurice, 'Milton's Dante–Della Casa–Varchi volume', *Bulletin of the New York Public Library*, vol. 66, 1962, pp. 499–504.
Kelso, Ruth, *The Doctrine of the English Gentleman in the Sixteenth Century*, Urbana,

Ill., 1926.
Kennedy, William J., *Rhetorical Norms in Renaissance Literature*, New Haven, Conn., 1978.
Klein, Holger M. (ed.), *English and Scottish Sonnet Sequences of the Renaissance*, 2 vols, Hildesheim, 1984.
Labé, Louise, *Oeuvres complètes*, ed. Enzo Giudici, Geneva, 1981.
Langley, Ernest, 'The extant repertory of the early Sicilian poets', *PMLA*, vol. 28, 1913, 454–520.
Larner, John, *Culture and Society in Italy, 1290–1420*, London, 1971.
Latini, Brunetto, *La rettorica Italiana*, ed. A. Maggini, Florence, 1915.
Lee, Sidney, *The French Renaissance in England*, Oxford, 1910.
—— (ed.), *Elizabethan Sonnets*, 2 vols, London, 1904.
Lentino, Giacomo da, 'A critical edition of the poetry of Giacomo da Lentino', ed. Stephen Popolizio, PhD thesis, 1975, Ann Arbor University Microfilms, Ann Arbor, Mich., 1980.
Levao, Ronald, *Renaissance Minds and Their Fictions*, Los Angeles, 1985.
Lever, J. W., *The Elizabethan Love Sonnet*, London, 1956, reprinted 1968.
Lewis, C. S., *The Allegory of Love*, Oxford, 1936.
Linche, Richard, *Diella: Certain Sonnets*, 1596. *See* Lee, Sidney.
Lock, Anne, 'A meditation of a penitent sinner', *Sermons of John Calvin, upon the Songe that Ezechias made*, London, 1560.
Lodge, Thomas, *Phillis*, 1593. *See* Lee, Sidney.
Lok, Henry, *Ecclesiastes . . . compendiously abridged . . . in English Poesie*, 1597, in *Miscellanies of the Fuller Worthies Library*, ed. A. Grosart, Blackburn, 1871.
Lytle, G. F. and Orgel, S. (eds), *Patronage in the Renaissance*, Princeton, NJ, 1981.
Macdonald, Hugh (ed.), *England's Helicon*, 1600, Muses' Library, London, 1949.
Macdonald, R. H., 'Drummond, Miss Euphemia Kyninghame and the poems', *Modern Language Review*, vol. 60, 1965, pp. 494–9.
Markland, Murray F., 'A note on Spenser and the Scottish sonneteers', *Studies in Scottish Literature*, vol. 1, 1963, pp. 136–40.
Marti, Mario, *Storia dello Stil Nuovo*, Lecce, 1972.
—— (ed.), *Poeti del Dolce Stil Nuovo*, Florence, 1969.
Masserà, A. F., *Sonetti burleschi e realistici dei primi due Secoli*, 2 vols, Bari, 1920.
Masson, David, *Drummond of Hawthornden*, London, 1873.
Mazzaro, Jerome, *The Figure of Dante: An Essay on the 'Vita nuova'*, Princeton, NJ, 1981.
Menzini, Benedetto, *Poetica e satire*, Milan, 1808.
Milton, John, *Milton's Poetical Works*, ed. Helen Darbishire, 3 vols, Oxford, 1955.
——, *The Prose Works of John Milton*, ed. J. A. St John, 5 vols, London, 1864.
Minta, Stephen, *Petrarch and Petrarchanism*, Manchester, 1980.
Mirollo, James V., *The Poet of the Marvelous*, New York, 1963.
Moleta, Vincent, *The Early Poetry of Guittone d'Arezzo*, London, 1976.
Monch, W., *Das Sonett, Gestalt und Geschichte*, Heidelberg, 1955.
Monte, Alberto del, *La poesia popolare nel tempo di Dante*, Bari, 1949.
Montgomerie, Alexander, *The Poems of Alexander Montgomerie*, ed. James Cranstoun, Scottish Text Society, Edinburgh and London, 1887.
——, *Poems of Alexander Montgomerie . . . Supplementary Volume*, ed. George Stevenson, Scottish Text Society, Edinburgh and London, 1910.
Montrose, Louis A., 'Of gentlemen and shepherds: the politics of Elizabethan pastoral form', *English Literary History*, vol. 50, 1983, pp. 433–50.
Muir, Kenneth, *The Life and Letters of Sir Thomas Wyatt*, Liverpool, 1963.
Murray of Gorthy, Sir David, *Caelia*, 1611. *See* Klein, Holger M.
Musa, Mark (ed. and trans.), *Dante's 'Vita Nuova'*, Bloomington, Ind., 1973.

Muscetta, Carlo and Ponchiroli, Daniele, *Poesia del Quattrocento e del Cinquecento*, Turin, 1959.

Neale, J. E., *Queen Elizabeth I*, 1934, reprinted Harmondsworth, 1960.

Pagani, W., *Repertorio tematico della scuola poetica siciliana*, Bari, 1968.

Parker, William Riley, *Milton: A Biography*, 2 vols, Oxford, 1968.

Parks, G. B., 'The route of Chaucer's first journey to Italy', *English Literary History*, vol. 16, 1949, pp. 174–87.

Patterson, Warner F., *Three Centuries of French Poetic Theory*, 2 vols, Ann Arbor, Mich., 1935.

Percy, William, *Sonnets to the Fairest Coelia*, 1594. *See* Lee, Sidney.

Petrarch, Francis, *Petrarch's Lyric Poems*, ed. and trans. Robert Durling, Cambridge, Mass., 1976.

——, *Le rime di Francesco Petrarca*, ed. G. Carducci and S. Ferrari, Florence, 1899, reprinted Florence, 1965.

Picone, Michelangelo, 'Strutture poetiche e strutture prosastiche nella *Vita nuova*', *Modern Language Notes*, vol. 92, 1977, pp. 117–29.

Pomeroy, Elizabeth W., *The Elizabethan Miscellanies*, Los Angeles, Calif., 1973.

Ponchiroli, Daniele and Bonino, Guido (eds), *Lirici del Cinquecento*, Turin, 1958, revised 1968.

Potter, J. L., 'Sylvester's shaped sonnets', *Notes and Queries*, September 1957, pp. 405–6.

Purcell, Sally (trans.), *Dante: Literature in the Vernacular* (Dante's *De vulgari eloquentia*), Manchester, 1981.

Puttenham, George, *The Arte of English Poesie*, 1589, ed. G. D. Willcock and A. Walker, Cambridge, 1936.

Ralegh, Sir Walter, *The Poems of Sir Walter Ralegh*, ed. Agnes Latham, London, 1929.

Ramsey, Paul, *The Fickle Glass*, New York, 1979.

Robb, Nesca, *Neoplatonism of the Italian Renaissance*, London, 1935.

Roncaglia, A., 'Sul divorzio tra musica e poesia nel Duecento italiano', *L'Ars nova italiana del Trecento*, Certaldo, 1978, pp. 365–97.

Rossetti, D. G., *Dante and his Circle, 1100–1200–1300*, revised edn, London, 1874.

Rossi, Nicolo de', *Il canzoniere di Nicolo de' Rossi*, ed. F. Brugnolo, 2 vols, Padua, 1977.

Saiz, Prospero, *Persona and Poesis: The Poet in the Poem*, The Hague, 1976.

Salmari, C., *La poesia lirica del Duecento*, Turin, 1951.

San Gemignano, Folgore de, *Le rime di Folgore de San Gemignano*, ed. G. Navone, Bologna, 1880.

Sannazaro, Jacopo, *Opere volgari*, ed. A. Mauro, Bari, 1961.

Santagata, Mario, *Dal sonetto al canzoniere*, Padua, 1979.

Santangelo, Giorgio, *Il Petrarchismo del Bembo e di altri poeti del '500*, Rome and Palermo, 1967.

Santillana, Marqués de, *Los sonetos 'Al Italico Modo' de Ínigo López de Mendoza, Marqués de Santillana*, ed. Maxim Kerkhof and Dirk Tuin, Madison, Wis., 1985.

Scaglione, A. (ed.), *Francis Petrarch, Six Centuries Later: A Symposium*, Chapel Hill, NC, 1975.

Scheiner, Louise, 'Recent studies in poetry and music of the English Renaissance', *English Literary Renaissance*, vol. 16, 1986, pp. 253–86.

Scott, Janet, G., *Les Sonnets élisabéthains*, Paris, 1929.

Shakespeare, William, *Mr. William Shakespeares Comedies, Histories and Tragedies*, London, 1623, reprinted, ed. Helge Kökeritz, London and New Haven, Conn., 1955.

——, *A New Variorum Edition of Shakespeare: the Sonnets*, ed. H. E. Rollins, 2 vols, Philadelphia, Pa, 1944.
——, *Shakespeare's Sonnets*, ed. Stephen Booth, New Haven, Conn., 1977.
——, *Shakespeare's Sonnets*, ed. W. G. Ingram and T. Redpath, London, 1964, revised 1978.
——, *The Sonnets and A Lover's Complaint*, ed. John Kerrigan, Harmondsworth, 1986.
Sidney, Sir Philip, *The Old Arcadia*, ed. K. Duncan-Jones, World's Classics, Oxford, 1985.
——, *The Poems of Sir Philip Sidney*, ed. W. A. Ringler, Oxford, 1962.
Sidney, Robert, *The Poems of Robert Sidney*, ed. P. J. Croft, Oxford, 1984.
Smart, J. S., *The Sonnets of Milton*, Glasgow, 1921.
Smith, Barbara H., *On the Margins of Discourse*, Chicago, Ill., 1978.
Smith, G. Gregory (ed.), *Elizabethan Critical Essays*, 2 vols, Oxford, 1904.
Smith, William, *Chloris*, 1596. *See* Lee, Sidney.
Solimena, Adriana, *Repertorio metrico dello Stil Novo*, Rome, 1980.
Soowthern, John, *Pandora*, 1584. *See* Klein, Holger M.
Spagnoletti, G., *Il Petrarchismo*, Milan, 1959.
Spenser, Edmund, *Spenser's Minor Poems*, ed. E. de Selincourt, Oxford, 1910, reprinted 1966.
Stewart of Baldynneis, John, *Poems of John Stewart of Baldynneis*, ed. Thomas Crockett, Scottish Text Society, Edinburgh, 1913.
Stone, Donald, *Ronsard's Sonnet Cycles*, New Haven, Conn., 1966.
Stone, Lawrence, *The Crisis of the Aristocracy, 1588–1641*, Oxford, 1965.
Surrey, Henry Howard, Earl of, *Poems*, ed. Emrys Jones, Oxford, 1964.
Svensson, Lars-Hakan, *Silent Art: Rhetorical and Thematic Patterns in Samuel Daniel's 'Delia'*, Lund Studies in English 57, Lund, 1980.
Tatham, Edward, *Francesco Petrarca: His Life and Correspondence*, 2 vols, London, 1925.
Tempo, Antonio da, *Summa artis rithimici vulgaris*, ed. R. Andrews, Bologna, 1977.
Tennenhouse, Leonard, 'Sir Walter Ralegh and the literature of clientage', in G. F. Lytle and S. Orgel (eds), *Patronage in the Renaissance*, Princeton, NJ, 1981.
Thompson, D. and Nagel, F., *The Three Crowns of Florence*, New York and London, 1972.
Thomson, Patricia, 'The Canticus Troili: Chaucer and Petrarch', *Comparative Literature*, vol. 11, 1959, pp. 313–28.
——, *Sir Thomas Wyatt and His Background*, Stanford, Calif., 1964.
Tilley, Arthur, 'Wyatt and Sannazaro', *Modern Language Quarterly*, vol. 5, 1902, p. 149.
Tofte, Robert, *Laura, the Toyes of a Traveller*, 1597. *See* Lee, Sidney.
Tomlinson, Charles, *The Sonnet*, London, 1874.
Tottel, Thomas (ed.), *Tottel's Miscellany*, ed. Hyder Rollins, 2 vols, Cambridge, Mass., 1965.
Vaganay, Hugues, *Le Sonnet en Italie et en France au XVIème siècle*, Louvain, 1899, reprinted Geneva, 1966.
Varchi, Benedetto, *Opere di Benedetto Varchi*, ed. A. Racheli, 2 vols, Trieste, 1858–9.
Vianey, J., *Le Pétrarquisme en France au seizième siècle*, Montpellier, 1909.
Waller, Gary, *English Poetry of the Sixteenth Century*, London and New York, 1986.
Waller, Gary and Moore, Michael (eds), *Sir Philip Sidney and the Interpretation of Renaissance Culture*, London, 1984.
Waller, Marguerite, *Petrarch's Poetics and Literary History*, Amherst, Mass., 1980.
Warkentin, Germaine, 'The meeting of the Muses: Sidney and the mid-Tudor poets', in Gary Waller and Michael Moore (eds), *Sir Philip Sidney and the*

Interpretation of Renaissance Culture, London, 1984.
Watson, Thomas, *The Hekatompathia* [1582]. *See* Klein, Holger M.
—, *The Tears of Fancie*, 1593. *See* Lee, Sidney.
Weinberg, Bernard, *A History of Literary Criticism in the Italian Renaissance*, 2 vols, Chicago, Ill., 1961.
— (ed.), *Trattati di poetica e rettorica del Cinquecento*, 4 vols, Bari, 1970–4.
Weiser, David K., *Mind in Character: Shakespeare's Speaker in the Sonnets*, St Louis, Mo., 1987.
Whigham, Frank, *Ambition and Privilege*, Los Angeles, Calif., 1984.
Whythorne, Thomas, *The Autobiography of Thomas Whythorne*, ed. James M. Osborne, Oxford, 1961: modern spelling edition, Oxford, 1962.
Wilkins, E. H., 'A general survey of Renaissance Petrarchanism', *Comparative Literature*, vol. 2, 1950.
Wilkins, Ernest, 'Cantus Troili', *English Literary History*, vol. 16, 1949, pp. 167–73.
—, 'The invention of the sonnet', *Modern Philology*, vol. 13, 1915, pp. 463–94.
—, *The Making of the 'Canzoniere' and Other Petrarchan Studies*, Rome, 1951.
Wilson, K. M. (ed.), *Women Writers of the Renaissance*, Athens, Ga, 1987.
Wroth, Lady Mary, *The Poems of Lady Mary Wroth*, ed. Josephine A. Roberts, Baton Rouge, La, 1983.
Wyatt, Sir Thomas, *Collected Poems*, ed. Kenneth Muir, Muses' Library, London, 1960.
Zepheria (anonymous), 1594. *See* Lee, Sidney.

INDEX

Lightning Source UK Ltd.
Milton Keynes UK
UKOW021501081211

183417UK00003B/73/A